The Theatre of Praise

The Theatre of Praise

The Panegyric Tradition in Seventeenth-Century
English Drama

Joanne Altieri

Newark: University of Delaware Press
London and Toronto: Associated University Presses

Associated University Presses
440 Forsgate Drive
Cranbury, NJ 08512

Associated University Presses
25 Sicilian Avenue
London WC1A 2QH, England

Associated University Presses
2133 Royal Windsor Drive
Unit 1
Mississauga, Ontario
Canada L5J 1K5

The paper used in this publication meets the minimum requirements of the American National Standard for Permanence of Paper for Printed Library Materials Z39.48-1984.

Library of Congress Cataloging-in-Publication Data

Altieri, Joanne.
    The theatre of praise.

    Bibliography: p.
    Includes index.
    1. English drama—17th century—History and
criticism.   2. Praise in literature.   3. Opera—
England—17th century.   4. Music and literature—
England.   I. Title.
PR678.P66A48   1985   822′.4′09357   84-40479
ISBN 0-87413-275-4 (alk. paper)

Printed in the United States of America

Contents

Preface

This study began in an effort to understand why the operatic adaptation of Shakespeare in the later seventeenth century took what seemed to the author, when she began to work, such a strange route. From their inherited repertoires, the two Restoration companies chose to attempt no *Otello*, not even an *Amleto*, but instead to defuse the emotional element in *Macbeth* in fattened roles for the witches, who now literally flew about the stage. Despite the era's "she-tragedies" and intense interest in the passions, neither Purcell nor Betterton nor Dryden seemed to want to make of Shakespearean opera a home for the emotions, visceral or intellectual. I knew my expectations were not purely anachronistic; the Camerata and Monteverdi had, after all, hung up a banner for opera's realization of the emotions three-quarters of a century earlier. But the English seemed to have other ideas. I wanted to know what they were.

There was little help at this superficial level from the scholars. Edward Dent agreed that it was a strange and troubling situation. Our best critic of the opera, Joseph Kerman, wrote in *Opera as Drama* that "composers of the past left, not a series of immature experiments, but a number of solutions, each distinct, and each with the potentiality of artistic success within its own limitations"—surely the correct attitude. Yet when he came to speak of *Dido and Aeneas,* he eliminated "its own limitations," calling *Dido* "a unique work, innocent of any indigenous operatic tradition".[1] I knew from training in Renaissance literature that *Dido and Aeneas* was not innocent as charged, at least not in an operatic tradition that extends beyond music per se to the theatre and to literature. Too much of Purcell's masterpiece has visible roots in the Jacobean and Stuart masque, and too, Dryden, Purcell's coadjutor on

6

other occasions, had said that the opera was born in such courtly events and still served their purpose.

Having decided to trace more exactly the map implied in Dryden's remarks and Purcell's achievement, I began to work up from Shakespeare's theatre and back from Dryden's, meeting myself at William Davenant, where no student of literature really wants to find herself very long. Exposure to Davenant from this angle, though, convinced me that his stage accomplishment was both greater and more pervasive than I had realized looking at him, as we mainly do, from the perspective of his earlier twentieth-century critics. In the effort to analyze and articulate that accomplishment, I found myself in the midst of a number of the late seventeenth-century theatre's central issues: the place of the passions and how they can be represented, the problem of idealization and its connection to contemporary politics, the inclusion of the demotic in aristocratic forms.

All these issues extend well beyond the question I had initially set out to answer. I have tried in thinking and writing about where my question led to keep within manageable bounds, but the nature of the subject field has carried me necessarily into what I have just identified as "central issues." I do not regret the excursions; they attach my narrow subject to a context of far broader concerns and interests, and they do so from a heretofore insufficiently explored perspective. It is one that in partially solving the original problem, also casts new light on the problem's surroundings—on the masque and civic pageantry, on the heroic play, on Davenant and Dennis, and, I hope, on Shakespeare in a nonoperatic context as well.

I did not know of the recent collection of essays edited by David Lindley, *The Court Masque,* until my book was well into the production process. A number of the subjects I take up here, particularly the Orgel/Gordon view of the masques and Dryden's *King Arthur,* are broached from fresh perspectives, which I have not, because of the timing, tried to engage. I regret the omission.

The author wishes to express appreciation to *Philological Quarterly* and to *Studies in English Literature* for permission to reprint parts of two essays that appeared in different form in those journals: "Romance in *Henry V*" in *SEL* 21; "Baroque Hieroglyphics: Dryden's *King Arthur*" in *PQ* 61.

Part of the work for this book was carried out with the help of a fellowship from the Huntington Library.

The nature of the subject has also led me to reliance on libraries housing the infrequently published material on which my study depends. The staffs of the Huntington Library and Stanford's Bender Room, as well as of the Public Record Office in London and my home library, Suzzallo, have been unfailingly helpful. The Huntington has been my particular source, of texts and fellowship. For the latter I am also indebted to my colleagues Charles Frey and John Webster, who read and commented on parts of my text, and to my husband, Charles Altieri, to whom I dedicate it.

The Theatre of Praise

— 1 —

Introductory: Models and Their Representation

At the close of the seventeenth century and of his life, Dryden looked back in an interlude at the generations of praise the Stuarts had won from their poets. He pointedly called his piece *The Secular Masque* and reviewed succinctly there the central form of the tradition that this book takes as its subject:

> All, all of a piece throughout:
> Thy Chase had a Beast in View;
> Thy Wars brought nothing about;
> Thy Lovers were all untrue.
> 'Tis well an Old Age is out,
> And time to begin a New.[1]

In these lines Dryden encapsules both the Stuart century and the allegorical masque that expressed it, as part of the tradition bridging the gap between the pre– and post–Civil War theatres. A significant tradition, it has been neglected for reasons easy to specify. First, its practitioners are not always very good poets. Its pivotal figure is William Davenant, whose enduring talent is by no means obvious. Even more important than poetic lack, though, has been the failure to see that the masques and interludes and the works that developed from them were not simply alternatives to stage plays but rather stages in the development of an idea that reached its culmination not on the eighteenth-century dramatic stage but rather in the musical theatre. Approached as mimetic drama, much of what was accomplished

11

seems crude, artificial, and oversimplified, but as precursors to the musical productions, these plays and masques can be seen as experiments, way stations, extraordinary redirections of one artistic tradition into another. Within the Stuart century, writers like Davenant, Dryden, Shadwell, and Fleckno worked out a set of aesthetic principles quite different from, though not independent of, those of conventional stage plays. My object here is to define the tradition, to trace it through its changing manifestations and later developments, and to explore its connection to its wider cultural and theatrical context.

I

The line of mythological kings Dryden's stanza alludes to had its primary realizers in Ben Jonson, Davenant, and Dryden himself. All were active men of the theatre, whose work in all its varieties had wide consequences among their peers. Taken together, they outline the epideictic tradition that spans the century.[2] Townshend, Carew, and Davenant follow Jonson as creators of the court masque in which the tradition begins. Davenant goes on to elaborate from the masque the heroic play *(The Siege of Rhodes)* and semiopera (the Dryden/Davenant *Tempest*). In both of these he is followed by the majority of practicing dramatists, first of the sixties and seventies and the vogue of the heroic play, then through the end of the century in the musical offspring of *The Tempest*. Dryden had joined Davenant in making *The Tempest* musical and ultimately wrote the best of the semi-operas, *King Arthur.* That work returns to the heroic play's outline and dresses it in its proper operatic guise, leaving behind political argument and instead celebrating English governance, much as the original masques had done, though a great deal more has been changed than the expressed ideology.

This is, of course, far too simple a picture, particularly in grouping together as one the varied descendents of *The Tempest* and in implying that the heroic play is an equivalent of the masque. I shall try in the course of the book to expand and justify the outline. One would be foolish to claim that an array of Restoration plays as disparate as *The Empress of Morocco, Psyche, Circe,* and *The Prophetess* follow simply from masque beginnings or are even similarly intended. They record instead the breadth and variety of the manipulation of representational conventions that Davenant made viable on the stage. Only Dryden returned to the expressly, and narrowly, epideictic, first with *Albion and Albanius* (1685) and then, quite successfully, with *King Arthur*

(1691). His was an historically well-informed effort to use music and praise for what he was certain they could do: not, as he saw it, inarticulately to dramatize ineffable emotions, but to represent the power of English institutions in their manifest forms. He returned, then, to the first intentions of the masque, the effort to convince its audience to accede to the praise offered, to accept, and even revel in, the work's communal praise as expressive of the audience itself. The long stage life of *King Arthur* indicates the success of his effort. I take the work as normative of the essential tradition; normative, but in no sense exhaustive, as the list of plays near the head of this paragraph makes plain.

By the mid-seventies musical theatre, all of it indebted to the masque tradition, had become extremely varied[3] and all of its claims open to attack. What I am perhaps covertly assuming to be its virtues, the times themselves were far more ambivalent about. The stage thrived on music now and, for awhile at least, on Davenant's heroic models. Yet from the very beginning, long before the Restoration stage itself, there were dissident voices, early epitomized in Bacon's criticism of the masque, as later in Roger North's measured rejection of the semiopera. Critical history has by and large agreed with Bacon and North, or, from within the works themselves, with *Henry VIII*'s Buckingham and *Britannia Triumphans'* Imposture.

Once modern appreciative literary criticism begins, so do attacks on the tradition—with Addison, who wrote a parodic opera, and Dennis, who wrote a straight one. The attitude of literary men toward these works has been overwhelmingly negative, ranging from Bacon's dismissal of the masques as toys, to Dennis's xenophobia, which saw opera as a threat to British morals; from Addison's sense that the conventions of romance in which opera abounds are extreme, unrealistic, and absurd, to Pope's utter decimation of all public panegyric as hackwork, self-interested crowns of the kingdom of dulness. Settle and his City pageants become in *The Dunciad* the type of all that is disreputable, morally and aesthetically, in the literary scene.[4]

The few positive voices are Dryden's own, ambivalent toward the value of conjoining words and music but consistently willing through much of his career to try it within the narrow confines that will be explained in chapter 5. Dennis, who was later to attack so violently the hegemony of Italian opera, had at first, in the 1690s, felt that operatic composition was the perfect means of realizing the emotions and explained why in an essay that prefaces his *Rinaldo and Armida*.[5] By the time Scott edited Dryden, the question was academic, and he could treat *King Arthur* as a lovely fairy tale, made even more unreal by its lovely music. Its political and social overtones he presumed lost in its repeated revisions.

This presumption has been shared by the musicologists who have been the primary critics of the operas during the twentieth century. Where Dryden scholars usually hurry past his operatic works with pragmatic explanations of their existing at all, Purcellians love *King Arthur*—for its music alone. Typically, the most substantial work dealing with this tradition is a musicologist's—E. M. Dent's *Foundations of English Opera,* dating from 1928.[6] Dent discussed virtually all the pieces related to the epideictic tradition and, within the limits of an overwhelmingly romantic aesthetic, he treats them well. Yet for him *Albion and Albanius* is simply a "monument to stupidity." It is so, largely I believe, because Dent had only scorn for the masque tradition from which it springs. Now that Welsford and Gordon and Orgel have made the masque less "stupid," it should be possible to read the epideictic enterprise more nearly on its own terms, at least for what it was, if not for what it can any longer be. To do so, this book will pursue a historical argument derived primarily from the practitioners themselves, whose theoretical notions will be outlined shortly.

The book as a whole progresses from the masque to the opera in terms of what seem to me their most definitive connective means and ideas. I begin with Shakespeare, whose history plays are, among many other things, a dramatic reaction to the masque venture, replacing that with another kind of royal praise impossible to the function and therefore to the means of the masque. Shakespeare allows me to establish more explicitly the problems that the tradition will encounter at the same time that he illustrates early positive effects of the tradition in the theatre. Bacon, like Shakespeare, helps one to understand the contemporary sense of the masque's use and also of its aesthetic values. It is in terms of the first that I move on to the form's adaptation in civic pageantry and then to its development after Jonson in Carew and Davenant.

A caveat is in order at this point. While we will follow Stephen Orgel and D. J. Gordan rather closely on the masque, I have departed from them on significant points, which I shall explain in section 3 below.[7] Here I must acknowledge my desire to avoid their insistent stress on Platonized iconography and symbolic form because it seems to me that that stress has made it easy to minimize other classical influences—those that are less idealistic than otherwise persuasively rhetorical, less Platonic than Aristotelian.

The sudden transformation in which the masques abound is, after all, only a theatrical version of the *prius-nunc* topos basic in political epideixis; similarly, the praise of the hero through the magnification of his efforts for domestic peace and the promotion of national unity is a gift as much of epideictics (useful since Isocrates' *Panegyrikos*) as of James's Solomon identification or his desire to be valued for uniting the kingdoms.[8] Such praise in theatrical epideictics is directed as much by the effort to produce its effect, admiration, as by the desire to produce ideal worlds. Platonic idealization has become a means here to achieve Aristotelian demonstrative ends, perhaps a natural development in the theatre and one that will certainly control and empower the theatre throughout the century. When epideictics move out of the court itself onto the public stage, the rhetorical intention remains, while the Platonic intention survives only in conventions of presentation.

Further, the participatory aspect of the masque that Orgel has emphasized in the general dancing that closes a masque, could not survive the translation to the public stage for obvious practical reasons. It has its adulterated continuities in the banquets of civic pageantry, which had enacted selected masque features in a public setting all along, but at the theatres themselves one could no more feed the audience en masse than lead it in a general ballet.

There are, however, at least two senses in which as participatory an inclusiveness as a public theatre could create was instrumental throughout the century and beyond. Most simply, we have Dryden's notion and creation of opera as celebration, offering to the full audience the means and the occasion for feting themselves and their governance at "a time of general joy." More complex, and obliquely related to Dryden's celebratory function, the expressly emotional identification with the work itself, by means of poetic and musical affect, creates participation through metaphoric movement, literal enough to Hobbesian and Cartesian psychology. Admiration has led to new and complicated ends.

Whether the masque ever had a more meaningful participatory function than that is a subject I will raise in discussing Bacon's essay. The general dance as a form of social codification achieved through the vivifying of an exclusive iconography is perhaps a less self-confirming notion if we look at the actual breadth of the iconography's dispersal in the society. The City pageants, my chief example, are rife with it, perhaps (as Gordon thinks) only in order virtually to connect mercantile life with the courtly world,[9] but the shared language and the shared values are happily expressed year after year, with no sense of anomaly, less sense of disjunction than within the court forms themselves. If the merchants are aping their betters, they are successful largely because their adaptation reflects true facts of the real world and because within the allegorical mode the classical world and the Bible can be easily amalgamated. One can ape without losing one's own proper identity. The world of the triumph of virtue in explosive transformations and defeated mountebanks was as comfortable in Saint Paul's yard as in Whitehall. The group was infinitely expandable. *Everyone* watched and said it was fine.

Having recognized that, one is prepared to take more seriously the effort, if not the result, of Davenant's attempt to revivify those politically celebratory functions of the masque in the heroic play and his and Dryden's efforts to retain the theatre's social effectiveness through the communal appeal of ceremonial drama. The second element from the language of the masque—second in importance only to allegory—that Davenant called on to create that communal appeal was music. Dance, as we know from James's famous remark and will see in Bacon's essay, was that element of the masques that was most attended to and most enjoyed, going further than Jonson's ideal visions to create a sense of communal activity and identification among the participants. Ferrabosco and Lanier had extended the use of music, underscoring the basic moods and conflicts staged, to full composition, setting the entire masque at least once.[10]

Music's role, in both their practice and their theory, is affective and broadly mimetic, aimed both at expressing the ideas of the piece and affecting its viewers. This accords with traditional notions, music having been understood from Greek thought on as the source of the fabled *affetti*, mythified in Orpheus and Timotheus, sanctioned by the Church from Augustine to Luther, its negative potential called up by Calvin only to create his insistence that strict controls in its use be observed because it is so potent.[11] Amphion, Orpheus, and Arion are always prominent figures in both the courtly and the public epideictic forms, underscoring affective intentionality.

Affective and, through them, expressive theories of art achieve prominence in music years before they do in literature, and they arise first in the group context, in public worship. Hooker speaks of the uses of music in the fifth book of the *Ecclesiastical Polity:* music is as decent an accoutrement of weighty solemn actions as of private meditation because of

> an admirable facilitie which musique hath to express and represent to the mind more inwardly than any other sensible means the very standing, rising and falling, the very steps and inflections every

way, the turnes and all varieties of all passions whereunto the minde is subject.[12]

We shall hear a great deal of talk about literature in these terms late in the seventeenth century, yet it emerges around music as early as More. John Stevens adduces it in the *Utopia* as well as in Hooker, remarking the historical significance of the step taken there:

> It had scarcely escaped the notice of the Middle Ages that men are affected by what they hear. The novelty consists in making a logical connection between "expression" and "emotion." . . . The worshipper will be moved to exultation because the composer *expresses* exultation; to sadness because the composer *expresses* sadness.[13]

This is obviously the application to musical thought of an Horatian rhetorical principle: *si vis me flere dolendum est*—but in music at the turn of the sixteenth century, the subjective element was articulated firmly on the Continent and in England by such composers as Moteverdi and Morley. Although the rhetorical goal might remain constant, eye on the object, audience response, the subject conceived as the author's expression of his response to the subject of the work finds a new place.[14]

The shift in the position of the musician from mediator of preexistent harmonies to feeling creator of emotional realities, hardly universal or exclusive, yet frankly definitive for opera, parallels the equally broken shift from allegoresis to mimesis, from the audience's engagement in correspondences of wit to its participation in direct emotional experience. This is an issue of means and not of ends: neither change is exclusive in that allegorical procedures like even the extreme of mathematical musical paradigms, Prythagorean proportions, surface throughout the century: the text and quaint diagramming of Thomas Mace's *Musick's Monument* (1676) bear witness.[15] What is exclusive is the ideal basis on each side of the shift: on the one side a normative intellectual order to be translated into correspondences grasped by wit, and on the other prerationalized emotional life to be illusionistically replicated whole.

That emotional life strives to become a normative order throughout the century and, under the doctrine of imitation, to become taxonomized as determinately as the Pythagorean/Plotinian ratios and their political and psychological correspondences once were. We see that most baldly in the *affektenslehre,* specified more fully by the Germans than the English, and the theatrically parallel Betterton acting instructions, which Brewster Rogerson discussed at length as exemplary of this effort. Such taxonomies were of course attempts to reduce to order and practical application the implications of the new dispensation; the dispensation itself enhanced expressive and affective goals in a general elevation of the passions to primacy among objects of imitation.[16]

In Davenant we can see the first efforts to translate those concerns into stage practice. In fact, he turned to music for its affective power even before he brought it to the stage. In the Preface to *Gondibert*, he admits that his choice of a stanzaic form rather than the couplet for his epic, as well as its division into cantos was based upon his somewhat self-conscious hope that his poem would, like Homer's, "be sung at Village-feasts though [this is 1650] not to Monarchs after Victory, nor to Armies before battel."[17] This was a more practically attended and specific dream than the hope that his spirits, too, would, like Homer's, "long after his bodies rest, wander in musick about Greece." The stanza he chose was, he thought, well suited to composition and performance in *stilo recitativo,* a dream he fulfilled later, in palmier days, with *The Siege of Rhodes. Gondibert's* alternate rhyme would not be less heroic than the couplet because it is adapted to "a plain and stately composing of Musick; and the brevity of the *Stanza* renders it less subtle to the Composer and more easie to the Singer, which, in *stilo recitativo,* when the Story is long, is chiefly requisite" (p. 19).

While the idea of listening to *Gondibert* sung from start to finish may not strike us now as especially appealing (and was not striking enough for that secret singer, Hobbes, to comment on in his "Answer"), Davenant's theoretical notion is clear: musical performance made Homer's works an "inspiration to glory" to monarchs "and of valor" to their soldiers—model of and model for the monarchist cause. This sense of affect is a commonplace of the time, but being commonplace is no less meaningful to Davenant's intentions and their process of execution. Plain and stately music, along with a heroic tale in clear and definitive act/scene development would lead to the programmatic political affects on an audience to which it is understandable that a Royalist of Davenant's stamp would commit himself.[18] Of the various masque affects that Davenant carried over to the heroic play from the masque, full-scale musical performance was the shortest lived but perhaps the most significant—both for its simplification of language, action, and character and its passional stress.

That stress is abetted by the primary element of the masque's language, allegory, as Davenant treats it. The point is essential to the connection I would make between the two halves of the century's epideictic theatre stylistically and, through style, thematically. With Davenant, I move, in the second half of the study, to several musical productions of the Restoration that extend the masque function directly, as in *King Arthur* and *Albion and Albanius,* and indirectly, as in *Dido and Aeneas,* amplifying moral modeling in allegorical forms with a new intensity, foreign to the masque that is its source, escaping the psychological limits of its conventions through music and a remarkably fluid manipulation of the allegorical mode for which Davenant laid the groundwork. By maintaining the conventions, but enlarging their semantics, he gave to Dryden a tensile instrument with which to encounter the central problem posed by epideictic theatre and its offshoots in the last third of the century: how does a writer who wishes to praise the civic order adapt the magnification model to a world in which the applicability of that model to common life is in no way clear? How does the writer deal with the problem most convincingly raised in *Henry V,* the great man's relevance to the rest of us? One of the central questions left to the public stage by the great Jacobean dramatists, and one that must be answered if the stage is to remain truly public, is implied here: can one praise the heroic any longer; can one present positive versions of the civic order without heroic roles; what happens to courtly mythology in a culture increasingly demotic?

All these works trace their roots, as Dryden knew, to William Davenant. Because several of them were written by better artists than Davenant they significantly modify his ideas; yet on the whole they share his initial conception of a play and its uses, a subject I shall describe briefly here and in more detail when I turn to Davenant's own works later. One of the problems he addresses is the question I just posed. In looking at his plays, we stress usually the audacity, the unreality of his figures and underplay the efforts he made to fit his great men—and women—to commonalty: the domestication that Solyman undergoes in successive rewritings, the parodic viewpoint universally maintained among the semiarticulate nameless, and most important, the universalizing function of the passional stress. For Davenant added to a background of masque writing a Cartesian analysis of character that perceives humans as abstractable bundles of properties that, taken together, make up the soul. The Cartesian bundle is inherently analyzable in essentially the same terms as the masque abstractions. Each scene or situation discretely contains an element of the bundle that, placed before an audience one by one, can be recognized, since they are universal, and reassorted as the person dramatized. In fact, theoretically the audience ought to do the work of reassembly automatically, since this is what people in one's real experience also are, souls compact of passions and intellect, determinately analyzable into the parts that make up the whole. So Davenant could portray character quite as the masque had ideas, piece by abstracted piece. Thus the allegorical figures of Davenant's thirties masques become by 1656 Solyman and Roxolana, still the passions, but the passions in a human embodiment.

Davenant never wrote allegory of the Spenserian stamp that he condemned as "a continuance of extraordinary dreams," but instead his own dreams in the direct and clear typological allegory of later Jonson—Beauty and Britanocles, Cupid and Jealousy. When Love had become Ianthe and Jealousy Roxolana, the directness and clarity were unaffected, only their human result made more visible. Generic passions, and not the mere history of narrative fact, remain the proper business of the poet. He is followed in this practice by the heroic play generally, which presents analyzed character scene by scene in terms of those passions of which the particular soul is composed. Thus the action as a unified representation of a completed meaning is of little interest to Davenant, or his followers, but rather they conceive action as a collection of acts which, taken together, present life analyzed to its elements.

Davenant's is thus a fundamentally anti-illusionistic sense of theatre, as of literature more generally. He was taken to ask on precisely this point by Rymer, who objected to his authorial intrusions in *Gondibert:*

> But before he falls on any other business, he presents the reader with a description of each particular *Heroe*, not trusting their *actions* to speak for them, as former Poets had done. Their practice was fine and artificial; his (he tells us) is a *new way*.[19]

Rymer's essay overall is an argument against visible artifice, finding artfulness in unbroken illusionism, modally consistent and "reasonable" to itself and to "life." His guiding principle remains always probability, and our memory of what he did to *Othello* in its name should not blind us to his perspicacity in reading Davenant. Probability for Rymer does not, for instance, require the elimination of the miraculous (as it did for Davenant), only its consistent environing, which for Rymer means modal consistency. Consistency within that rubric satisfies Rymer because it assists in the presentation of a unified action, his final principle. Allegory he abhors because it crosses both his bases: it is a superstitious affectation of Spenser's age that destroys probability in the pursuit of "a mystical meaning," and it affronts the action by leading us "blindly rambling on marvellous Adventures" where all is "fanciful and chimerical."[20]

Davenant's stake in action was as slight as Rymer's was great, for he thinks of action as simply the agency of men, and of drama as passion ("For wise Poets think it more worthy to seek out truth in the Passions than to record the truth of Actions").[21] Though he, too, condemns Spenserian allegory, he does so on quite other grounds: its obfuscations lead to moral uselessness (pp. 6–7).

The emphasis throughout the preface to *Gondibert* on social utility, on moral usefulness conceived as a political duty of the poet, marks Davenant's essay as a far less sophisticated critical statement than Rymer's, whose interest, however narrowly applied, is firmly centered on the ontology of the literary work. Yet the central notions of the *Gondibert* preface are repeated often enough by other writers that we can see it as more fully expressing the conscious intentions of mid-century authors. Credibility, the passions, and social utility are the determinative criteria of poetry, a credibility more narrowly conceived than Rymer's probability and far more unabashedly didactic in its application. This probably explains what Rymer attacks so fiercely—both Davenant's and Cowley's unwillingness to let the action speak for itself, preferring as they do the safety and clarity of determinate interpretive possibilities.

Because for Davenant passion is the definitive quality of drama and the prime convention of representation is the highlighting of that passion through its presentation directly to the audience as states of consciousness—a convention born of masque abstraction wedded to Cartesian analytic procedures—action understood in even as Aristotelian a sense as Rymer's is out of the question. It is not up to *action* to create for the audience an experience leading to cathartic effect, historically the source of the passional stress; the representation of states of feeling will accomplish that. It is not a complete action that is imitated, but the feelings generated in the characters by the course of events, feelings that will be conveyed to the audience directly on the grounds of the universal cogito. Emotion thus is attached to the isolated sign rather than to whole situations that ramify and in their ramification convey their meaning.

Dryden's early commitment to the same notions is clear in the "Essay of Dramatic Poesy," whose emphasis on passion at the expense of action is well-known.[22] The most straightforward statement there is Neander's extension of Eugenius' definition of a play: in observing the characters, the audience watches "the movement of their minds as much as the changes of their fortunes," the former being the work of

the poet, the latter the historian. The fullest example in the essay is
the preference for the passions of Shakespearean drama over the
correctness of dispassionate Jonson. Dryden shares with Davenant as
well, and more concertedly, the willingness to exhibit artifice; in fact
in Dryden, that willingness has become not simply allowed but a positive source of the pleasures of fiction. *Ars celare artium* may remain an
often-cited principle of the period, yet for Dryden the recognition of
the artist's hand is a deep source of satisfaction. In defending the use
of rhymed verse, Neander makes an extended argument against
icastic mimesis, the line of thought that would demand of all plays
prose as the medium closest to actual speech. Ultimately Neander's
line of thought leads him to a defense of repartee and of Pegasus:

> But you tell us this supplying the last half of a verse, or adjoining a
> whole second to the former, looks more like the design of two than
> the answer of one. Suppose we acknowledge it: how comes this
> confederacy to be more displeasing to you than in a Dance which is
> well contrived? You see there the united design of many persons to
> make up one Figure: after they have separated themselves in many
> petty divisions, they rejoin one by one into a gross: the confederacy
> is plain amongst them; for chance could never produce any thing so
> beautiful. . . .[23]

Dryden amplified the point in "The Defense of an Essay," responding to Howard's claim that "a play was still supposed to be a composition of several persons speaking *ex tempore*": "If I am not deceived a
play is supposed to be the work of the poet, imitating or representing
the conversation." The rule of art transcends the rule of nature; it is
not surfaces we copy, it is their essence. Nor need the act of the copyist
hide itself away; it too is part of the meaning. From Jonson ("Others
aspire to Truth so much, as they are rather Lovers of likenesse, than
beauty")[24] through Dryden, the epideictic poets as poets of the ideal
are ultimate scorners of illusionism as a meaningless end, and a rather
simple-minded one.

The analogy to dance in Neander's defense of poetic "license" is a
further implicit defense of an audience's complex consciousness of
artifice, which a second metaphor only apparently retracts:

> 'Tis an Art which appears; but it appears onely like the shadowings
> of Painture, which being to cause the rounding of it, cannot be
> absent; but while that is consider'd they are lost: so while we attend
> to the other beauties of the matter, the care and labour of the
> Rhyme is carry'd from us, or at least drown'd in its own sweetness,
> as Bees are sometimes bury'd in their Honey.

Taken together the two attitudes anticipated in an audience perfectly describe the double awareness that any act of reading—or play going—should entail. *King Arthur* fulfills splendidly Dryden's sense of artifice, thematizing it to exemplify the place of reason in Dryden's scheme. I shall return to this much later; what I would note here is how fully the line of the heroic play commits itself to an art dependent on an audience both rationally apprehending the work and yet at the same time capable of that sense of "wonder," of "admiration" that ought to have been, by any non-Cartesian seventeenth-century analysis of wonder, contrary to such rational apprehension. On the basis of his belief in the double receptivity of the audience, its capacity to be fully involved in the fiction without being lost in the fiction, Dryden could accept and create a play of intense affectiveness without considering his act a commandeering of the audience's intellect, an obvious virtue in epideixis. With it, Dryden maintains the allegorical space of public theatre, a space that depends on an increasingly tenuous homology of mind and social order.

Yet there were limits. Irresponsible metaphor and music crossed them. Dryden's attack on Settle's *Empress of Morocco* makes clear that where poetic license becomes an appeal to irrationality through what he judges excess, he finds no comfort in dual apprehension or any other possible response. Looking at Settle's stage, he no longer can see music as the unalloyed potentiality Davenant saw in 1651. At the height of its early theatrical use, at that *Empress of Morroco* frequently seen now as expressing the latent power of music in the theatre, music and metaphor were yoked as media of irrationality.[25] Dryden is in no sense atypical in this regard. In addition to a series of attacks on theatrical music and the opera that echo him here, the public stage repeatedly uses music mimetically for the depiction of both irrational character and a chaotic world. It is never used to embody the heroic model, the ultimate rational man, however passionate.

John Dennis, the latest theoretically articulate writer I call on in this book, mirrors in the small compass of one career the course of Restoration theatrical music and the end of epideixis. Beginning in enthusiastic and intelligent experiment that recognizes the inherent difficulties of the enterprise, he ends finally by completely rejecting opera as it is and as he sees it in potential. It is particularly maddening to see this course in Dennis, whose theory made a home for precisely that passional stress one can easily imagine creating a workable rationale for opera. That no such thing happened can be laid at the door of patriotism and ideology and Dennis's conviction that theatrical music spells the death of a culture's poetry and therefore of a

nation. Music's affective power, its initial source of strength, had
finally killed it, and in the name of the same patriotic convictions that
led Davenant to it in the first place.

II

This, then, is the course of the century's own theoretical discussion,
the reasoning behind its evolving practices. I want now to explain
briefly my understanding of the achievement of meaning within the
tradition by describing more fully the definitive elements handed on
from the masque itself. In the process I will specify certain departures
from symbolic-form readings of the masque, departures that I believe
justify the direct link I have posited across the Interregnum. Despite
Dryden's efforts to convert royalist praise to a broader base in *King
Arthur,* the epideictic tradition is truncated; it is tied to the Stuarts as
Dryden himself implies in *The Secular Masque.* But the early tradition
brings into use a set of conventions that can be extended beyond the
expressly encomiastic and that shape many of the representational
means of the Restoration stage. Growing directly out of the earlier
masque, Blow's *Venus and Adonis* and Purcell's *Dido and Aeneas,* generally considered the two finest works of the line, show no closer connection to many masque conventions than an entirely different work,
Dennis's *Rinaldo and Armida* or even Charles Davenant's *Circe.* The
private stage, home of Blow and Purcell, and the public theatre, Dennis's and Davenant's staging place, are equally subject to courtly masquing. The nature of the inherited conventions determines in large
part the particular effects of the works. These conventions are my
subject now.

Aside from the Blow and Purcell, the musical conventions per se
prospered in England not in fully composed works (as they did, for
instance, in France, with Lully and Perrin), but in conjunction with
spoken plays. The bifurcation of the tradition into through-composed
(and works therefore potentially formally unified on a musical basis)
and mixed form (spoken text, intercalated music) was constant, however, from the beginning and not, as is often said or assumed, something pragmatically invented by the shameless entrepreneurs of the
Restoration theatre to keep nonsinging Betterton center stage. Jonson's part in the bifurcation is to have developed the spoken (comic)
text more and more fully at the same time that he collaborated in
Ferrabosco's and Lanier's introduction of contemporary Italian musical advances, which included full composition. Davenant's Interreg-

num experiments developed both halves of Jonson's practice into full drama, though only one was taken up vigorously by the public stage.

Whatever the form, what remains constant is the political intention. The epideictic tradition is first and foremost self-consciously expressive of officially sanctioned hierarchical cultural values. The writers are universally apologists for the powers they praise, though in many instances interestingly critical apologists. From the masque through Davenant's transmogrification of masque into opera to Dryden's attempt to create a heroic vision of the end of Stuart England, the epideictic theatre continually proposes idealized positive views of the institutions that currently govern and that control the theatre. To call them conservative works is a supreme understatement. Yet theirs is a conservatism of content. *Pace* Crocean aesthetics, it allows the intensive formal experiment through which the English will try to naturalize continental advances and to develop their own theatre. During the Stuart years, the same institutional point of view is expressed in a less innovative medium as well: the masque had its public parallel in the civic pageants, which spread the epideictic venture out to include a broader world than the court. It too has a continuing interrelation with the stage.

Both forms, masque and pageant, were traditional, conservative, and intrinsically comic in their overall movement—the defeat of disruptive forces by the powers of good—and in the particular realizations of the disruptive forces. They were also, given their general shape, intrinsically heroic. The conservatism of content allowed a concentrated attention on the nature of the heroic and of the comic, so that it is here that variety and development will take place. Heroism and comedy will be retained by Davenant as he elaborates more fully and more concretely the power and nature of the heroic center, conjoining stageable psychology to the abstractions of the masque in order to convert its ceremonial intentions to a dramatic presentation. The comic will continue to play its role, now necessarily a modifying one. Wherever the elements of masque become drama (compare *Henry V*), the comic follows this course. One of the recurrent subjects of this book will be the varieties of comic modulation among the works we shall encounter.

We know the masque as the clearest form of theatrical diversion that evolved from the necessity placed on and accepted by the poets of the late Renaissance to entertain the court by glorifying both it and its center, the sovereign. It was an outrageously expensive, majestically gorgeous expression of both courtly power and self-indulgence, whose monetary and aesthetic prodigality imposed a high degree of self-consciousness on far more observers than simply the poets. But certainly on the poets, too. Their primary rationalization for both the excesses and the beauties of the masque was the didactic function fulfilled. Though didacticism justified serious interest in all the arts, it had had its birth in literature, in rhetorical theory, teaching being the raison d'être wrung from Horace and the classical rhetoricians to articulate morally unobjectionable functions for more ambiguous activities.[26] It remains the byword throughout the century with the masque-related form—heroic play, opera, ambigue—even after a more complex psychology of response was available to theory.

Jonson raised the didactic justification to a high art, creating in the masque that "education in revels" Orgel has stressed in speaking of Jonson and Inigo Jones, whose influence remains after Jonson's departure. As soon as masque developed a significant text, that text spoke in terms of education and enlightenment. Its language was allegory. Because the business of the masque was to show the ruler and the court in their ideal manifestations, allegory was inherent to its logic. Similarly, its expression demanded intense formal artifice, the physical demonstration of the idealization proposed.[27]

Artifice, allegory, and didacticism create the chessboard and its rationale just as they create a chess-man of the hero who will play out the comedy. He will be, given the rationale, an ideal model, ideal modeling being as intrinsic to didactic literary theory as it is useful to authoritative power in search of a rationalizing myth. The presentation of the ideal model throughout the period 1600 to 1640, when these court theatrical activities passed through their zenith, was accompanied by his (and her) negative opposition, a virtual necessity of the desire to claim utility for the ideal and of the practical need to reelaborate the masque, which must recur every Christmas season. The negative figures—or in some few cases, plot lines—are given us as the force against which the model is measured, ironized, or cast in active combat. Through the defeat or control of the negative forces, the ideal model asserts the power of monarchical values in a transference of moral values to the political sphere. In Jonson, the wedding of classical and Christian values that allows this transference is expressed in figures that usually transcend the merely personal, successfully displacing James Stuart with Love or Wisdom without dropping us into mere vacuity. But that danger is omnipresent in the masques, and even Jonson does not always avoid it.

The allegorical process is thus synonymous with that of all romance. Speaking schematically, we can distinguish two broadly conceived kinds of Renaissance romance idealization. I shall label them, for the sake of convenience, by their greatest practitioners, the Ariostan and the Spenserian. In both, the strength of the negative force's portrayal elevates the value of the heroic oppostion, but only in the first does comparatively realistic common life appear as part of the heroic world's environment. Common life may or may not be part of the negative opposition insofar as the narrative is concerned, but symbolically it is always part of that negation. It "proves," at a level that involves our lives through its direct mimesis, the relevance of heroic value to mundane experience, the need for the extraordinary. And so the lesson of the power of power is learned, or at least proposed.

Jonsonian masques began as the ideal, self-enclosed allegory of Spenser: it is always the Truth Jonson seeks to image. But over time, Truth is more and more frequently brought into relation with sweating cooks and alchemists, taking on through stage comedy the Ariostan task. These are the works we still most admire, among Jonson's masques (*The Gipsies Metamorphosed* is a good example) as among the objects of a broader literary world. We do so partly, no doubt, because of our own social views as well as our taste for the irony that is always available in the Ariostan. For in the Ariostan the negative evolved into a full voice, a perspective on the idealization that apparently truly tests it, making the work bimodal. So works as diverse in others ways as *Orlando Furioso, Henry V,* and, among Jonson's other masques, *Neptune's Triumph* contain within the texts themselves and quite apart from issues of production and performance, their own potential negation. The stronger the possibility of negation, the more powerful the surviving praise. The evolution of such bimodal texts was probably inevitable, a logical extension of the initial form. Dale Randall's case for the especial production irony of *The Gipsies Metamorphosed* is a theatrical example that depends heavily on conditions of production;[28] Davenant's later *Siege of Rhodes* or, even more, *The History of Sir Francis Drake* will further involve the text in satiric commentary on the enacted heroics.

Without such expressed negation, the sense of the poet as mere puppet is unavoidable; he knew that well enough to make it a theme through the conscious elaboration of reflexivity. The intense self-consciousness that marks the drama of the time finds a voice in the masque around the structured process of idealization and, by implication, the poet's part in that process. With negation expressed, the poet can propose the most outrageously glowing of ideal portraits while acknowledging the limits and limited acceptability of the idealization:

he knows where it fits in the real world and what the realistic objections to it are. Naturally, public forms went furthest in this regard—Davenant's works after the Restoration, *Henry V* and *Henry VIII*, or Middleton's *World Tost at Tennis*, to name an interesting example; but the Caroline masque followed suit as far as its function allowed. Among them, Carew's single masque is again the finest example. Because the poet acknowledges with the negative voice not simply the sentiments against his model, but also those against the literary processes of idealization, we could expect that the acknowledgment will grow with awareness of the sentiments that implicate him. Jonson expresses it as early as *Love Restored* (1612). It becomes more emphatic in his later masques, and Townshend, Carew, and Davenant, writing masques during the troubled thirties, are even more sensitive to the point. Though *Coelum Britannicum* makes the best use of the subject, I take Davenant's *Britannia Triumphans* to mark its apex and will discuss the masque, when speaking of Davenant in chapter 4, as both typical of the problems of masques in the thirties and ingenious in its treatment of reflexive idealization. Like all the rest, he records the opposing sentiments and handles them rather better than his reputation would lead us to expect.

Not so well, of course, as the norms—as Ariosto with his ironic parallel tales in the *Orlando* or Shakespeare's even greater ambivalence in the assortment of voices ranged against Henry V's epic grandeur or Jonson's comic recognition but full absorption of the Cook's analogy in *Neptune's Triumph,* a perhaps failed instance of "an education for the concluding revels," but a marvelously witty acknowledgment of the limits of making.[29]

This bimodality may be perceived as an aristocratic mode—romance idealization—in collision with a common mode—relative realism, where the common in some sense survives the encounter, an outcome we in the twentieth century always look forward to and that the seventeenth perhaps used only as salt, not an ultimate—at least in the masque, which is designed for court consumption. But with Jonson, the antimasque principle spills over into dramatic comedy, the home of the bourgeois, the common, to such an extent that Orgel frequently does not distinguish between comedy and the antimasque. In terms of symbolic function, little distinction need be made. Yet the distinction now often collapsed was rarely lost during the period, which thought of its masques less broadly symbolically than we have come to do and is more than likely to maintain modal unity by allegorizing the antimasque as fully as the masque itself, as obvious forces of incivility and disorder, *not* to survive the encounter. Comedy on the other hand becomes its own intrusive body, functioning as masque quite by itself in several instances (for example, *Christmas His Masque*, Captain Cook's monologue), so that the equation of comedy and antimasque misses the point.

It is through the development of comedy—by Jonson, who is followed here by Carew and Davenant—that masque includes popular drama, the common voice entering the masque theatre without entering the masque world until it loses its own identity. If we follow Orgel the Ariostan comedy is itself subsumed within the Spenserian self-enclosure. In this way, Orgel can claim, "What he achieved at his best was a synthesis of the world he wrote for and the world he created," Orgel being quite willing to admit that "at his best" is a narrow rubric.[30] If we read "the world he wrote for" from the masques themselves, we recognize that the synthesis relies on as high a degree of idealization on one side—that world, the court—as on the other—the masque world, its representation; Jonson prods "the world he wrote for" to learn to see itself as a best self we rarely recognize from other sources—Bacon's essay on the masque, Carleton's famous letter, Harrington's description of a Jacobean court fete in *Nugae Antiquae*. That is, Jonson's masques are an idealized representation of a world already ideal. As such, they must be expressly divorced from the particularity of his public stage comedy and present a figural typology that extends to their negations of ideal order and even to the masque comedy itself. As a result, the double mode of the work as a whole strives for resolution on the plane of ideality, independent of the incongruences raised by the collision of modes and perspectives.

The masque always retained such disjunction, easily containing within its broken sets, its separate entries, its allegorical pattern an alternation back and forth between the modes. The drama, on the other hand, cannot ignore such incongruences but must try to synthesize them. And it must do so through no participatory *ludus* such as concludes the masque, but in a vicarious reenactment of unified life. It does not always succeed. To a great extent the complexities of *Henry V* and, perhaps more obviously, *Henry VIII*, result from Shakespeare's bringing the two modes into conflict within the same world—the Porter's man set against the public fete of Elizabeth's baptism, we being asked to engage in both. Jonson's masques instead treat comedy ultimately as idealistically as they treat the court: to become part of the revels, the comic figure must become part of the figure that the masque makes, not only symbolically, but stylistically. Pistol needn't do that, but his displacer, Fluellen, can and does.

I shall argue that Fluellen does so because *Henry V*, though decisively drama, is epideictic theatre, the theatre of praise, focused on the nation in its dramatic embodiment and primarily communal in its orientation and desired effects. Epideictic theatre moves from masque through ceremonial play on to opera in terms of its communal function. I follow Herbert Lindenberger in designating *Henry V* and the heroic plays "ceremonial plays." This means taking their function to be far broader than Eugene Waith did when, basing himself in Orgel's Platonic paradigm, he interpreted Dryden's *King Arthur* as model advice directed at William of Orange. In the course of the century, the definition of the nation changes from the values and abstractions that can be embodied in a Jonsonian masque to a new set of abstractions, epitomized in Dryden's *King Arthur.* That work's regal embodiment, like *Henry V,* owes a great deal to the masque tradition, as Waith perceived, but also has undergone a radical enough realignment to allow for Dryden's far more ironic, far more critical attitude toward court and country.[31]

In proposing that the transition from masque to heroic play to opera is based on those forms' shared function of offering model political centers to a community, I could obviously not intend to suggest simple continuous formal development, though one can see specific formal connections. Nor do I mean to preclude any differentiation among the quite varied efforts individual poets make in coming to terms with their task. Each of them approaches the problem of praise differently as befits their diverse characters and talents and as befits intense differences in conditions of production: heroic plays do not have as their center a revel, an invitation to the audience to join the performers in dance, nor masques a dramatic representation of life. The masque is in essence allegorical—a representation of ideas; the heroic play is mimetic—a representation of the human. Yet both are highly idealized forms. Because of the degree of idealization in the heroic play, its mode borders always on the allegorical. Yet the fact of direct mimetic intention moves the heroic play away from allegorical expression, so that by the second state of *The Siege of Rhodes* (Q 2) we are involved less with personified Magnanimity and Jealousy than with Solyman and Roxolana, less with abstractions than with people.

Throughout the century, the discrepancy between allegorical and mimetic modes continues to affect heavily the masque-dependent forms. When Orgel notes that the dramatic and panegyric often work in opposite directions in the Jonsonian masque, he is remarking the same point in a more generically, less stylistically oriented language.[32] The discrepancy remains effectual in the masque throughout its production and in the heroic play, as in the early operas and Dryden's efforts to celebrate England's honor on stage in *Albion and Albanius* and *King Arthur.* Theatrical panegyric always remains closely tied to allegorical expression, even as cultural pressures are moving literary expression generally further and further away from such conscious artifice.

In the case of the heroic play, the quasi-allegorical mode is invasive enough to conflict (painfully) with the mimetically realized themes, disorienting a work like Tate's *Brutus of Alba* to the extent that Purcell, in his operatic setting of the play as *Dido and Aeneas,* only partially resolves the conflict, leaving the hero in a world stylistically separated from that of his now doubly lost lover. Aeneas stands for; Dido is.[33] Artificial ideational drama was not, of course, to survive, yet while it did, the pull exerted by the one mode on the other (an analytic oversimplification) created tensions that can be perceived as a form of strength that I hope to show is of the essence of these works. That *Dido and Aeneas* remains the most accessible of them for us is due, doubtless, to the fact of its musical medium. This is so not simply because Purcell's music is great, though it is, but because music bridges the modes by making the conceptual directly apprehensible. Blow's *Venus and Adonis* will show us this far more simply than *Dido,* just as Dennis's *Rinaldo and Armida* will illustrate a failure to absorb the conceptual. All three come late enough in the century to be concerned primarily with psychological concepts, and all three try to utilize both allegorical and mimetic means to dramatize them, without breaking the drama in two.

In these late-century operas we have the culminating appearance of the masque conventions, that form's figures of disorder having become the malign psychological powers of *Dido's* witches and Dennis's Phaenissa. The heroic model—Rinaldo, Aeneas, even more, Constantius in Granville's *British Enchanters*—is by implication more than by action the *theios aner,* "the divine man of . . . destiny whose mission is to defeat impious furor":[34] his stage representation springs so directly from Britanocles and James's various masque avatars that no means of realization exists for his action. The comic still exists, even shorn of its narrative rationale in Purcell, in sailors and prankster cupids who continue to measure the hero and satirize the mundane world as they always have done. But the comic shape of the action as a whole has been lost in more cases than *Dido and Aeneas.* The Platonic transformation that created the *volte-face* in the masque has become the excuse for magical moments, sorcerer-induced, on the Restoration stage. Because the allegorical implications of such magical intervention were fully recognized—Dennis's preface is quite clear about that—as often as not, ultimate power could not reside there. Solving the problem of the Christian supernatural is always a more conscious difficulty than dealing with the allegorical/mimetic split in terms of which it is usually handled.

III

One of the virtues of Orgel's remarkable restitution of the Jononian masque to aesthetic and intellectual respectability is its capacity to absorb all such junctures as the one I have been worrying. Because he reads the masques as symbolic forms, breaks in surface and texture are always ultimately containable within the larger structures. As so frequently occurs in symbolic interpretation, those specifics that are less than vital to the symbol, no matter how prominent to our response, tend to disappear or be interpreted solely in relation to the proposed symbolic form. Thus Jonson's many references to the poet as educator become additional counters in the construction of the ideal world of the mind of the poet, leading the audience to compliance in his vision, rather than the protests of Jonson against the perceived frivolity of the whole enterprise—which they surely to some extent are.

Once the subject of the work has become the mind of the writer, the work can absorb anything as the mind dreams on its visions, rather like Jonson watching the Turks and Tartars fight it out on his great toe. The two forms of Form—ideal vision of idealized world—in Jonson's masques make up a closed circle, self-contained and self-generating, equated by Orgel with the dual audience who both see and are the masque: the spectators, who merge with the masquers in the concluding revel "in effect transforming the courtly audience into the idealized world of the poet's vision," and the king, the primary audience, who throughout is the central act as well. It is *his* mind that the poet expresses, paradoxically enough, the "is" and the "ought" having quite changed places. Jonson is the director in this solipsistic dream, moving everything toward an ideal vision of the court that the court itself makes up in dance and that makes up the king's mind.[35]

The works record thus an ideal vision that obviates any need to ask questions of a more practical nature. The equation of the mind of the poet and the mind of the king does away with the problem of flattery or the poet's self-awareness. The poet is not, after all, serving the king's ego or his propaganda needs: he is creating a perfection that mirrors not reality but the king's own ideals. Such charmed closed

circles also bypass questions about reception, accepting the poet's vision of the work's intended reception as something actual. We have
much evidence that it was in fact quite negative all along, but that is
irrelevant to the ideal audience imagined here. The practical negative
(the recorded distaste and dissatisfaction with the masque) becomes a
breathtaking positive (the audience is still learning the lessons of illusionism that Jones and Jonson are annually teaching them). The
"education in revels" need be relevant only to Jonson's Platonic theory
of the masque and its textual enactment. We must not expect it to be
reflected in actual experience. The entire masque is, after all, in the
subjunctive mood.

The closed world of symbolic forms is perhaps the most useful
approach to Jonson's literary achievement, work by work, yet it is not
so fruitful for understanding either the Caroline masque as a whole
or the works that follow from it, because it avoids as self-evident the
fact of panegyric and the poet's relation to panegyric as well as the
relation of Jonson's vision to the world for—and from—which he
generated the vision. It is not enough to say "Let us beware of calling
this flattery: its name is convention," a category shift that begs the
question.[36] Why did it become a convention, and how? What are the
nature of the interests served by such conventions? What toll did it
take of the artists to comply with them? What problems does it cause
Jonson or Davenant et al. to conceal the answer to these questions by
idealizing themselves, too, as educators, poets of the *utile dulci* in its
expressly political form? Flattery has many names, only one of which
is convention. Nor is it only the shortsighted democratic imagination
that mistakenly calls it by its clearer name, as Orgel has at times
suggested. Beaumont and Fletcher have Strato define a masque in *The
Maid's Tragedy:*

> they must commend their King, and speake in praise
> Of the assembly, blesse the Bride and Bridegroome,
> In person of some god, there tied to rules
> Of flatterie.[37]

Jonson himself blustered to Drummond of another role than masque
writer before the Stuart kings:

> he heth a minde to be a churchman, & so he might have favour to
> make one sermon to the King, he careth not what yr after sould
> befall him, for he would not flatter though he saw Death.[38]

The poet who extends the masque by elaborating its other—whether
we conceive that as the antimasque proper, which grows and grows

throughout the twenties and thirties, or as the comedy, which asks an unenthusiastic court to sit through mere vicarious drama before it gets to the dance—that poet is suggesting something more to the king than that this is the perfected inside of his own idealizing mind. What he is suggesting has a great deal to do with the comedy's non-Platonic ironic suggestions. All ideal literature (the literature of what I called the Spenserian line of romance is a good example) makes up the closed circle of the two forms of Form, and if, as Orgel notes, the dramatic and the panegyric move in opposite directions in the case of Jonson's idealism, that is probably because the dramatic has moved outside the circle.

It is indubitable that the dramatist who praises his king, like any other panegyrist, recognizes the degree of idealization such acts require. That he will cast himself in the role of moral mentor is traditional (back to Pliny or, if we confine ourselves to modern times, to Erasmus). But it is hardly necessary or even useful to our questions that we assume he was successful in creating his Platonic effects—least of all the central one, on the king himself. Given James's refusal to enjoy the text of the masque, his preference for the dancing and such broad comedy as *The Gipsies Metamorphosed* provided, reflecting ambivalent glory on the favorite, Buckingham, we recognize that there are in symbolic readings no answers to our questions since they tell us at best what the poet hoped for. The questions themselves are vulgar in an idealistic context; yet avoiding the appeal of the ambivalence that Buckingham as gypsy entails is perhaps too Platonic a stance finally to maintain toward an object itself a monument to vulgarity, as Jonson in the end felt.

Seeing from outside the expressed symbolism of epideictic works, seeing them, that is, less intrinsically, may help to preserve their relation to their real contexts, to place them in history and to recover them in less intentional terms. I have tried to do that in my reading of *Coelum Britannicum*, a thoroughly Platonic masque but one far less interesting for its conventional Platonism than for Carew's political concerns and his more or less conscious self-representation. In addition, another group of symbolic readers, whose frame of reference is, because ahistorical, far broader than the Warburgian's, can also be useful without making it necessary to deny anything of the latter's recoveries.

Anthropology has long pursued an interest in ritualistic forms, including the masque, as part of an enterprise that reverses the interests of literary studies: where we try to understand individual works as emergent from a culture, they try to understand the culture expressed in the forms and functions of the works.[39] In the terms of anthropology, the masque is understandable along lines commensurate with those of Orgel and of Gordon, yet less Platonistic and more universal and therefore more continuously applicable to the products that appear once one has emerged from the Platonic confines of the Stuart masque. There is no conflict here with what we have learned from the Warburgians about the masque, but we obtain a point of view that makes it possible for us to see the masque as one answer to an ongoing cultural need, a functional necessity that does not disappear with the last court revel.

In Gordon's view and, less absolutely, Orgel's as well, the masque is "secular ritual," effective ceremony.[40] It loses its ritual character during the Caroline years when nonparticipatory theatre, vicarious entertainment, encroaches on the masque through comedy and antimasque proliferation as well as mechanical elaboration, emptying the form of its earlier participatory function. By the time the masque returns, at the close of the Commonwealth, it has become effectively nonparticipatory, on the stage to stay, receding behind the proscenium. Among the anthropologists, Victor Turner would not allow us the term *secular ritual,* preferring *ceremony* on the grounds that *ritual* always implies a "transformative self-immolation of order as presently constituted" through which a true reconstitution, an "authentic reordering," comes about.[41] Transformations abound in the Stuart masque, but no one has claimed that this reordering springs from even a theatrical self-immolation.

Turner would presumably disallow the notion that such repetitive, virtually liturgical ceremonies as the court masque serve a true ritual function at all. The transformations of the Jonsonian masque, whether experienced by the audience as finally included players or by the king as sole and signal player/audience, remain merely "the impressive institutionalized performance of . . . normatively structured social reality," the limit of whose effectiveness is statement. Yet the statement is allowed a broad, paradigmatic function as both "model of" and "model for" social states and statuses: "model for" in the sense that it "can anticipate, even generate, change"; "model of" in that "it may inscribe order in the minds, hearts, and wills of the participants." These are the claims that Orgel and Gordon have made, in far more elegant language, for Jonson's intention in the masque, disallowing mimetic magic (that is, for Orgel, talisman, for Gordon, exorcism) as one of the functions of the form and thereby disallowing it true ritual status.[42]

Instead, the two audiences are presented with normative models of moral excellence and social order whose appeal is essentially, Orgel insists, to the audiences' mind. They are presented not with some magic propitiatory display directed at the gods, as Frances Yates had claimed, seeing in the masques something of that power Turner would limit to true ritual; instead they see "models of" for the general audience, "models for" the audience of One, the king, if the didactic functions of epideixis are to be taken seriously.[43]

Both Gordon and Orgel are careful to separate Jonson's literary achievement in the masque from its ritualistic repetitive social self-enactment. Gordon insists that Jonson's manipulation of his classical figures is governed "not by magical or allegorical reasons but by historical ones . . . The classical world, that most prized of ancient cultures, has to be got right because it is real and recoverable." Like Rubens, Jonson handles the classical figures expressively, consciously, unconventionally:

> They are not signs. They are figures that embody, as much through their accuracy as through their grace and grandeur, the power of that true, historical, ideal domain—the power of *sancrosancta vetustas,* holy antiquity. Crowning his home with them, Rubens asserts his role, and thereby his identity. This is not an act of allegory or magic. It is a declaration, a substantiation, the creation of a self.[44]

By the same token Orgel would interpret the development in Jonson's masque productions as a movement away from emblem and into drama, away from the magical acts of allegorical transformation as the masque abruptly overcomes the antimasque to rational acts of conversion whereby the vital energy of the satyr world is redirected toward the same end served by the glories of the masque proper in a quasi-dialectical movement toward a known end. In both cases the exorcistic is brought under the control of the intellectual through the sheer force of Jonson's (and, as Orgel stresses, Jones's) artistic power. Yet Orgel never really forgets that the revel, the closing general dance, remains not only the goal, but the primary interest of contemporary audiences and participants. And once a poet of Jonson's distinction is gone, all that remains is this husk of ceremonial appeal. Of *Salmacida Spolia* Gordon writes,

> 'A kind of exorcism' that last masque has been called: if this is so, it is a singularly ineffectual kind. Imagery and style work together to sustain only a group's image of itself, in effect to point to and sustain its frightening isolation. Outside Whitehall a far different vocabulary was formulating and directing throught and act.[45]

But I will insist that this is not a change. The later poets of the masque are inferior to Jonson as poets and elaborate their self-creation less finely; but they are not inconsequential masque devisors, least of all when we consider them, as Gordon does here, in relation to the world outside the doors.

If we stand outside Jonson's own Platonic claims, we can see that the effect of the masque was always "singularly ineffectual" as anything but sustenance for a "group's image of itself." Even the makeup of the group is highly questionable. The Caroline masques, including *Salmacida Spolia,* record a full awareness of the irrelevance of the court's vocabulary to the world outside Whitehall. Their effort to neutralize that other by defeating it in representation is no more thoughtless and blind than Jonson's own, only less poetically accomplished. All were engaged, in Turner's anthropological terms, in these efforts at redress to stabilize—ineffectively, as it turned out—the social conflict, in this case by telling themselves they speak for a larger constituency than they do. That is a fairly ageless move of epideictic rhetoric, as is its invitation to the audience to imagine itself a part of the constituency.

The same drama will be played out a generation later as the Stuarts again watch themselves enacted in heroic guise while the revolution simmers, more civilly, about them. The masque will have lost a good part of its participatory quality, conceived as the active involvement of the audience, for the movement into vicarious entertainment that Jonson himself had instituted. As Buckingham played his role in *The Gipsies Metamorphosed* and Charles and Henrietta Maria theirs in many later masques, so the Princess Mary will play the chaste nymph in *Calisto,* a regal mistress and her daughter Venus and Cupid in *Venus and Adonis*—the court still playing itself to the court, the public still pleased to know who at court played what roles, participating only vicariously in its games. We can see an example of that continuing interest in the printed texts that include the noble actors in the dramatis personae.

Political allegory, however much resisted in its more arcane manifestations, is identified as the theatrical language of the court throughout the Jacobean years, a mode of speech of the established order, representative of the sense of hierarchy that sustains it. When Middleton turns to courtly satire—in *A Game At Chess* or *A Courtly Masque: A World Tost at Tennis*—he does so by turning his realistic stage into a chessboard, the actors his carved pieces and "starches" to be moved about as counters in an artificial game.[46] He played it as skillfully as he played the realistic mimetic one we still easily respond to in *The Changeling;* but that was for him not the courtly mode. Obviously the power of allegorical representation on the seventeenth-century stage was not born of monarchist politics but reaches back, like all allegory, to Philo and Augustine. But what began in moral ideas had its longest stage life in politics. Allegory's usefulness to monarchist ideology and therefore to any attack on that ideology kept it vital there in its least adulterated forms—and also its least transcendental. Pure typological allegory shades off into the merely topical in court productions throughout the century (as witness *Venus and Adonis*) in England as in France, always able to become a vehicle for court gossip wherein the figural is of far less importance than the doings of the day. Benserade, whose duple significances were celebrated tours de force in mid-century France, was only the cleverest of the group. But in the hands of a good writer, a Dryden or a Quinault, the figural can reassert its power even till the end of the century. By that time, it is a moribund language, shortly to expire in the "truths" of human psychology more directly represented. The expiration is what Dryden recorded in *The Secular Masque.*

— 2 —

Shakespeare and the Imperial Myth

*T*he next two chapters will try to establish the extent of the spread of the epideictic techniques that had their zenith in the courtly masques, the complexity of the response to such techniques, and the relation of them to the heroic modeling that is the central abiding feature of the endeavor. Throughout the period of their development, both those who used them and those who simply watched were highly self-conscious about these techniques. The writers (my prime examples are Shakespeare and Carew) examined carefully both the implications of the enterprise and their own involvement in it, and the articulate viewers—I instance Bacon and later Pepys and Evelyn—remained highly critical, unimpressed by the quality and validity that could be attributed to, first, regal and, after it, civic mythologizing. What the writers intended and what they achieved were apparently quite different, as Orgel has sometimes too ingenuously chronicled in his work on Jonson. What they achieved was a new hero, detached and distanced, and a remarkable portrait of his relation to the world. It is a portrait that discovers the apparent incompatibility of heroic grandeur and common life and that tries to find grounds for reconnecting the severed halves of a culture. In the effort to ratify the figure of the highest cultural values, to propose his praise as vital and valid, the writers uncover disjunctures they cannot heal.

Shakespeare, the first great commentator on theatrical epideictics, unfortunately for my purposes made his comments as always, indirectly. His career-long reaction to the masque and its ideology is the subject of this chapter. I want to show not how *Timon* implements the genre nor how *The Tempest* enriches its themes through masque theatrics, but rather how Shakespeare turned the problems implicit in heroic modeling into drama—that is, away from masque—by examining the promulgation and effects both on the men and on the nation of Renaissance monarchist self-representation. The subject is a complex one since the Lancastrian tetralogy involves many issues other than the one I am concerned with—the question of the nature and validity of political mythologizing. I shall, I know, be neglecting the other issues in order to make clear the connection of mythologizing to the philosophically grander theme, the relation of signs to reality. Henry V's meaning is ultimately derived from a measuring of the man against his myth. Much later, *Henry VIII*, a play written when the court masque had achieved its full development and influence, returns to the central issue, showing us in a new Henry an even more absolute sovereign, whose myth is both simple and opaque, whose reign itself a virtual masque insisting on emblematic interpretation.

That Shakespeare was not averse to the regal compliment that is the raison d'être of the masque and central to so much courtly literature is clear in *A Midsummer Night's Dream*, where the occasion to celebrate Queen Elizabeth is created quite gratuitously, independent of any dramatic need. He introduces into the play a piece of the mythologizing iconography that the masque was to elaborate seemingly eternally, and he handles that in a fashion that assures us he can master such classical givens as the Astraea myth with the aplomb of a Jonson. And this he can do at roughly the same time that he is dramatizing the greatest dramatic victim of such compliments, Richard II. The primary exponent of political iconography in Shakespeare, Frances Yates, has showed us to what extent the imbedded Astraea myth enriches Oberon's plan for a recalcitrant Titania and how deeply based in classical literature this expression of ideology is.[1]

> *Tit.* The fairy land buys not the child of me.
> His mother was a vot'ress of my order,
> And in the spiced Indian air, by night,
> Full often hath she gossip'd by my side,
> And sat with me on Neptune's yellow sands,
> Marking th'embarked traders on the flood;
> When we have laugh'd to see the sails conceive
> And grow big-bellied with the wanton wind;
> Which she, with pretty and with swimming gait,
> Following (her womb then rich with my young squire)
> Would imitate and sail upon the land
> To fetch me trifles and return again,

As from a voyage, rich with merchandise.
But she, being mortal, of that boy did die,
And for her sake do I rear up her boy;
And for her sake I will not part with him.
Obe. How long within this wood intend you stay?
Tit. Perchance till after Theseus' wedding-day.
If you will patiently dance in our round,
And see our moonlight revels, go with us;
If not, shun me, and I will spare your haunts.
Obe. Give me that boy, and I will go with thee.
Tit. Not for thy fairy kingdom. Fairies, away!
We shall chide downright, if I longer stay.
                              Exeunt [*Titania and her train*].
Obe. Well, go thy way. Thou shalt not from this grove
Till I torment thee for this injury.
My gentle Puck, come hither. Thou rememb'rest
Once I sat upon a promontory,
And heard a mermaid on a dolphin's back
Uttering such dulcet and harmonious breath
That the rude sea grew civil at her song;
And certain stars shot madly from their spheres,
To hear the sea-maids music?
Puck.   I remember.
Obe. That very time I saw (but thou couldst not),
Flying between the cold moon and the earth,
Cupid all arm'd. A certain aim he took
At a fair vestal throned by [the] west,
And loos'd his love shaft smartly from his bow,
As it should pierce a hundred thousand hearts;
But I might see young Cupid's fiery shaft
Quench'd in the chaste beams of the wat'ry moon,
And the imperial vot'ress passed on
In maiden meditation fancy-free.
Yet marked I where the bolt of Cupid fell.
It fell upon a little western flower,
Before milk-white, now purple with love's wound,
And maiden's call it love-in-idleness.
Fetch me that flow'r; the herb I showed thee once.
The juice of it on sleeping eyelids laid
Will make or man or woman madly dote
Upon the next live creature that it sees.
Fetch me this herb, and be thou here again
Ere the leviathan can swim a league.
Puck. I'll put a girdle round the earth
In forty minutes.[2]

                                        (2. 1. 122–74)

The appeal of the myth for sheer beauty and transformative power is
thus expressed in a context where its unreality is an asset, another

version of the shaping power of imagination in a play devoted to giving life to that theme. I cite the compliment to Elizabeth in its complete immediate context, because the metaphoric context gives the compliment its power, just as the full context, the play, taking her flower as the playful source of the dream action, confers on the flower the capacity to stand for the feat of imagination that the play as a whole embodies. Beginning from its own displacement of the hyacinth myth, the flower sends out successive ripples that spread here to include the facts of British history within its transforming prisms. Oberon's "imperial vot'ress" is amalgamated by verbal association with Titania's "vot'ress of my order" and in the amalgamation redeems her.

Titania's vot'ress, by the power of metaphoric displacement, herself subsumes the "embarked traders on the flood" in the "rich" womb that imitates the sails, "big-bellied with the wanton wind," ships that also "return again," their wombs "rich with merchandise"—the nautical vot'ress conferring on the ships a life-enhancing amplitude as changeling and merchandise coalesce in our minds. The richness of a culture girdling the earth now faster than leviathan and bringing back its wonders has its source in a woman's womb, which imitates the sails, which, by metaphoric simultaneity, imitate her.

If this were allegory we would be compelled by its logic to continue in a linear fashion and see the death of the vot'ress portending the outcome of those voyages. But it is not; no such extension is required or even suggested, Shakespeare instead moving us away from ruminating on the death of the vot'ress by returning us immediately to the vivid dramatic context. He modulates through mortality, revels, and a quiescent argument to a new and stabler key in Oberon's voice.[3] The key is established in a new immortality at "My gentle Puck, come hither," the mermaid singing on the dolphin's back "dulcet and harmonious," civilizing the "rude sea," accompanying the passage from Greek to British myth, the passage of the vestal through Cupid's threat to her emergence in the status of "imperial vot'ress," displacing in chaste perfection the original maternal vot'ress.

None of this is real, of course. It is all as "invisible" as Oberon, outside the realm of sense perception and beyond the realm on sense. Like most of what happens in the play, it is a "musical confusion" that "grows to something of great constancy" against the role of logic, the rule of allegory. The vivifying and justificatory myths of English imperialism can be thus deftly incorporated into the evolving themes of the play—the combined classical-native world of goddesses and fairies, hyacinths and pansies, which the imagination produces out of airy nothing and a text or two, earlier airy nothings whose levels of reality need never be tested against the reality we "know." The mortal may in fact die in childbirth, but that need not stop us here: Elizabeth is a vestal, her womb, barren in fact, in poetry fructifies in the virtues and power that establish and sustain her culture.

A Midsummer Night's Dream sustains itself in comic consistency where bushes can become bears, bears, bushes, answerable ultimately only to its own self-enclosed logic, the limits of dream, but the history plays take on the burden of reality and in doing so subject the imperial myth to its most searching literary examination. Elizabeth herself recognized that, seeing in Richard II a type of her leadership. "I am Richard II. Know ye not that?" she asked, without paranoia, considering Essex's activities. No believer, like Richard, in the magical power of names, she understood the difference between the literal sign and its figurative power and acquiesced in the admonition attendant on the revival of that play. Perhaps this is the key to her being "the most legendary and most successful of all exponents of the royal progress," a ruler who loved the masque and adulation but did not mistake their meaning and provenance.[4]

Bolingbroke, that tremendous spokesman for reality, holds an illegal trial of Richard's henchmen when he has returned from France in *Richard II*. He condemns Richard by proxy, recounting the crimes that were enacted against him absent by the now absent king, sign against sign:

> [I have] stoop'd my neck under your injuries
> And signed my English breath in foreign clouds,
> Eating the bitter bread of banishment,
> Whilst you have fed upon my signories,
> Dispark'd my parks and fell'd my forest woods,
> From my own windows torn my household coat,
> Raz'd out my imprese, leaving me no sign,
> Save men's opinions and my living blood,
> To show the world I am a gentleman.
>
> (3.1.19–27)

It is momentarily surprising to hear the man who places so little value on the imagination's power to impinge on reality (cf. 1, 2, 294ff.) spend two lines on his property to four on his heraldic device. But reading signs, saving oneself from the misinterpretations that Richard is eternally subject to, is not for Henry an act of imagination, an effort to "cloy the hungry edge of appetite by bare imagination of a feast." For Bolingbroke *res et verba* are always separate and distinct, so he can come back Lancaster as he was banished Hereford with none of the questions of continuity of self and of the reality of being that create Richard's more splendid poetry and exquisite theatre in his failed efforts to disentangle *res* from *verba* from the third through the fifth acts. For Henry a sign is just that, valid "to show the world" a meaning; for Richard it is everything: "Is not the king's name twenty thousand names? / Arm, arm my name! A puny subject strikes / At thy great glory" (3.2.85–87). And so the apex of the drama is—predictably, it seems in hindsight—Bolingbroke's lesson to Richard in how to read signs: dashing to the ground the mirror in which he read his brittle glory, Richard moralizes,

> For there it is, crack'd in an hundred shivers.
> Mark, silent king, the moral of this sport,
> How soon my sorrow hath destroy'd my face.

and Bolingbroke quietly replies:

> The shadow of your sorrow hath destroy'd
> The shadow of your face.
>
> (4.1.289–93)

Though his succeeding *explication de texte* is faultless in all its nervous pathos, its efforts to recoup control, Richard cannot accept its lesson now, but ends the play, weaving out dreams in prison where, having been "unking'd by Bullingbrook," I "straight am nothing."

The lyricism of Richard's protracted end is the modal equivalent of his choice, faced with the necessity to separate the "I" from the "we." His drama measures how much greater the burden of the sign is for kings than for common men, even gentlemen. The "I" lost with the "we" is monodically reasserted over and over again as if to give it a substance that Richard himself no longer believes in.[5] Metaphor, disengaged from the real, cannot figure the *mind's* transformations in a mental world that sees "the word itself" set against "the word." And all language becomes a self-referential toy, having lost its basis in the destruction of those systematic correspondences on which Richard's identity was founded; his christological assumptions, whereby the Logos that defined him as regal logos, are now recognized as untenable:

> I have been studying how I may compare
> This prison where I live unto the world:
> And for because the world is populous,
> And here is not a creature but myself,
> I cannot do it; yet I'll hammer it out.

> My brain I'll prove the female to my soul;
> My soul the father, and these two beget
> A generation of still breeding thoughts;
> And these same thoughts people this little world,
> In humors like the people of this world;
> For no thought is contented. The better sort,
> As thoughts of things divine, are intermix'd
> With scruples and do set the word itself
> Against the word. . . .
> . . . .
> Thoughts tending to ambition, they do plot
> Unlikely wonders: how these vain weak nails
> May tear a passage through the flinty ribs
> Of this hard world, my ragged prison walls;
> And for they cannot, die in their own pride.
>
> (5.1.1–14, 18–22)

Shakespeare acknowledges the difficulty of the regal burden again in the adjustment of the descriptions of Henry's desire to journey to Jerusalem from the close of *Richard II* to the opening of *1 Henry IV.* What had been an essentially private act of conscience becomes a public venture:

> I'll make a voyage to the Holy Land,
> To wash this blood off from my guilty hand.
>
> (5.6.49–50)

Actively involved in maintaining his throne, Henry speaks of the same venture in new terms in *1 Henry IV:*

> Those opposed eyes,
> Which like the meteors of a troubled heaven,
> All of one nature, of one substance bred,
> Did lately meet in the intestine shock
> And furious close of civil butchery,
> Shall now, in mutual well-beseeming ranks
> March all one way and be no more oppos'd
> Against acquaintance, kindred, and allies.
> The edge of war, like an ill-sheathed knife,
> No more shall cut the master. Therefore, friends,
> As far as to the sepulchre of Christ—
> Whose soldier now, under whose blessed cross
> We are impressed and engaged to fight—
> Forthwith a power of English shall we levy.
>
> (1.1.9–22)

The personal guilt for Richard's death, which will be recalled throughout the Henry plays, has quite disappeared here behind the practical concerns of kingship. We think of Henry's advice to Hal,

drawn from his years of warring rule, "Be it thy course to busy giddy
minds / With foreign quarrels" (*2 Henry IV* 4.5.213–14), and of Hal's
taking his father's recommendation up, in *Henry V*. In both the advice
and the enactment of it, Shakespeare presents the maneuver in the
mythic dress devised for it by the emperor Charles V, whose resurrection of the Crusades can be seen as part of the medieval chivalric
coloration with which princes of the sixteenth century mystified their
aims.[6] Shakespeare's awareness of the maneuver as ideological
manipulation is unquestionable; that he rejected it wholesale is less so,
though ironic readings and performances of *Henry V* have taken that
rejection more and more as a necessary concomitant of the awareness.
I believe that that is not the case, that Shakespeare is not in *Henry V*
involved in simply exposing Machiavellian political manipulation, but
rather environing the imperial hero in a relatively realistic world that
tests the possibility of our accepting heroes at all. In passing the test,
Henry brings together the "I" and the "we" in a reassertion of unified
identity that includes the body politic within the body natural on
grounds less fragile than Richard's.

From one point of view, the problem that faced the Lancasters was
always, as Shakespeare presents it, a purely ideological one. Shakespeare reiterated throughout the history plays the same slippery
point: Henry V, having inherited the throne from his father, would
hold it more justly in the minds of the people and therefore more
firmly than Henry IV ever did or could. Richard himself abrogated
the rule of primogeniture, a point that through York, Shakespeare
makes the efficient cause of Richard's demise; thus Henry V is left
with the task of reinstituting it bodily. But the problem of primogeniture that figures so strongly in the legal ambiguities of *Richard II* and
on which Holinshed bases his own condemnations of Henry IV has all
but disappeared from view in *Henry V*, Henry's right to the throne
being treated as a given. What will come of that right is the remaining
question. For Henry to figure as a great king requires his establishing
a myth that will win and hold the imagination of the people on whom
his rule depends in the way that Richard's held Gaunt and held York
until his own actions destroyed it. Without that myth, that appeal
beyond mere fact, Bolingbroke's world becomes Machiavelli's, the
world of constant struggle of force against force (*1 Henry IV*) or fox
against fox (*2 Henry IV*). This is the struggle over which Hal rises by
never leaving the ground—nor even going to the Holy Land, but
dramatically redefining the quest in new terms—terms as potentially
idealistic as those of Charles V's fete, but expressed in a language at
once native and common and proved against reality to such an extent

that it can hold the popular imagination with a success that vehicles in the courtly mode never enjoyed. In *Henry V,* Shakespeare rewrites the imperial dream in the language of the common man, but it remains at root the imperial dream and must base itself, therefore, in romance.

To function adequately among believably representative men, the romance had to be translated into a theatrical language that dramatizes *their* imagination, not merely the court's. It must move out of the world of ceremony into an acceptable popular variant of that world, in a unified stage version of Ariosto's shuttlings back and forth among the modes of narrative poetry. An instance of the same movement occurs in *Richard II* when the formal, stylized ceremonial of Richard's self-enactment in the confrontation of Mowbray and Bolingbroke in act 1, scenes 1 and 3, the rigorously hierarchical displays of role and power, becomes the popular theatre of Bolingbroke's parallel confrontation with Aumerle in "the Beggar and the King" of act 5. Both are self-consciously theatrical events, both are comic in their implied shapes, but only the second works. Bolingbroke's nameless ambiguity necessitates the flexibility he displays here, the ability to play the monarchical role extempore, as the situation dictates. Henry V must incorporate that ability, and by the time he becomes king, he has had plenty of practice.

In a splendid essay on *Coriolanus,* D. J. Gordon develops several themes dependent from the question of the status of names. One of them is central to my point: naming is an act of language that is understood in Shakespearean politics to be an act of community that reaches far further than to stained glass imprese.[7] Mowbray's response to banishment early in *Richard II* is a long lament equating the loss of his language community with death:

> The language I have learnt these forty years,
> My native English, now I must forgo,
> And now my tongue's use is to me no more
> Than an unstringed viol or a harp,
> Or like a cunning instrument cas'd up
> Or being open, put into his hands
> That knows no touch to tune the harmony.
> Within my mouth you have enjail'd my tongue,
> Doubly portcullis'd with my teeth and lips,
> And dull unfeeling barren ignorance
> Is made my jailor to attend on me.
> I am too old to fawn upon a nurse,
> Too far in years to be a pupil now.
> What is thy sentence [then] but speechless death,
> Which robs my tongue from breathing native breath?
>
> (1.3.159–73)

Mowbray's understanding of the power of language to grant life by granting access to community, to disenjail us by its harmonious touch, is echoed and reechoed throughout the history plays, duplicated in the actions of the Lancastrian kings, and developed most fully in the story of Hal's maturation. It is an ideal of language that the plays themselves embody in their form of enactment. The Lancasters know that to depart the language of one's community is to die and that no amount of imaginative lyricism will lessen the "deal of world / I wander from the jewels that I love." They also know that "Honour" is neither "air" nor an object to be plucked from the "pale-faced moon," but a communal dispensation, which must be earned in action, but also must be conferred—and enacted to win that conferral—in the language of the community. Mastering the disparate languages of his community allows Hal both to drink with any tinker and to convince his father that he too is an honor-worthy son. Dramatically "Hal" becomes "Henry" not by following Falstaff's "reality," but by assimilating to that reality Hotspur's "romance," leading the audience through the merely real to a valorization of what in chivalric notions the play itself proves valuable. Shakespeare's extended portrayal of Hal follows the same route, rejecting the Falstaffian milieu for the Renaissance romance of monarchy, while assimilating that milieu to the extent that it can. If Falstaff in the end refuses to be displaced, his loss redeemed by his displacers in the way of Titania's vot'ress, it is because the audience rejects the displacers as insufficient recompense.

The history of the reception of *Henry V* suggests that that is the case. The distaste for Henry goes back at least to Hazlitt, the insufficiency of the new cohorts to make us forget Falstaff, Pistol, Bardolph, and Poins at least to Johnson. During the last thirty years the play has become, first among critics, then among producers, its own ironic subversion, the old invitation to communal celebration finally an antiwar play, plain and simple. The play is, of course, anything but plain and simple, though perhaps only producers ever see it that way, giving us Henries who laconically recite the act 3 speeches tongue-in-cheek to assure us of their awareness of the speeches' absurdity. In a review of a straight, heroic production a few years ago, Stephen Booth identified the fatal error of such procedures: they do not trust the text. "The production," he reports,

> moved straight ahead with the vigor and confidence promised by the Chorus and persistently sabotaged by the scenes and characters Shakespeare provided. . . . [It] set out to make Shakespeare's Henry V appear before the audience as "the mirror of all Christian kings"—unclouded, sans crack or flaw. That, of course, cannot be

done, but—precisely *because* it cannot be done—that is exactly the right thing to try to do. A production that seeks to augment or even acknowledge the play's self-sabotage (tries to substitute a clean, clear negative for the play's imperfect and difficult positive), disengages the play's rhetorical motor.[8]

I tried to argue convincingly for a romantic heroic reading of the play several years ago, with little success.[9] The heroic reading seems determinate, and determinate meanings have now become signs of that shortsighted and narrowly conceived overdetermination that relegates literary works to the scrap heap of antiquarianism. Yet the peculiar indeterminateness proposed for *Henry V,* an indeterminateness that turns genre against itself, is based upon an elevation of the play's negative, subversive scenes and characters to a consistent and single-plane opposition to Henry's heroism that they do not in fact constitute.

We begin in the ironic and refuse, having allowed that viewpoint a foothold, to admit the possibility that the ironic can be sublated. Once it is there, it reigns to become a new, and I believe equally determinate, meaning, but one with which we agree.[10] Yet in both the later Henry plays—*Henry V* and *Henry VIII*—Shakespeare gives us ironic perspectives on the hero and *does* supersede them, for a "difficult positive." In both cases the supersession includes the ironic perspective within a comparative modality that rejects the extremes of irony and the romance I too singlemindedly argued for and tries to carve out a median perspective that the audience will accept as synthetic. The model is, of course, Hal's relation to Falstaff and to Hotspur, its means of development the same paradigm of character deployment, though more extreme in its enactment as its results must be more extreme.

The extremity begins with the Chorus through whom Shakespeare presents not so much the "conclusions dictated by popular history" as their *reductio* or, from a less ironic perspective, their ultimate magnification—a view of Henry that elevates his actions well above what the popular histories presented, giving us their logical extreme. The play itself, through both the scenes and characters the Chorus ignores and its specific enactment of the scenes the Chorus does promise us, proves by comparison "real." And yet that reality is idealized far beyond what Shakespeare's sources gave him.[11]

An example will clarify the point. Goddard, in his early, thoroughgoing ironic reading of the play claimed that Shakespeare's choice of scenes for the battle of Agincourt could not have been better had he intended to deglorify the battle and the king. In Goddard's redaction, that appears true. He looks at the battle with Falstaff's eyes, seeing around the play's rhetoric, refusing all heroic parallels, and assuming the references to God are hypocrisy. But, if Shakespeare had wanted to deglorify Agincourt, he should have stayed even closer to Holinshed than he does. Two facts about Holinshed's rendition of the battle are relevant to what Shakespeare did want to do: in the first place Holinshed retains from earlier histories a heavy emphasis on the providential explanation of the English victory, an explanation consonant with the paternal advice repetitively attributed to Henry IV: "Thou shalt attribute and ascribe to him all things wherein thou seest thyself to be well fortunate, be it victory of thine enemies, love of thy friends. . . ."[12] In the second, Holinshed is much troubled by the slaying of the French prisoners. For him it is Henry's one act in France that requires explanation, and he can find none. Nonetheless, he reports the incident itself far more unblinkingly than Shakespeare cares to reiterate:

It is said, that as he heard one of the host utter his wish to another thus: I would to God there were with us now so manie good soldiers as at this houre within England! The king answered: I would not wish a man more here than I have, we are indeed in comparison to the enimies but a few, but if God of his clemencie doo favour us, and our just cause (as I trust he will) we shall speed well inough. But let no man ascribe victorie to our owne strength and might, but onelie to Gods assistance, to whome I have no doubt we shall worth- ilie have cause to give thanks therefore. And if so be that for our offenses sakes we shall be delivered into the hands of our enimies, the lesse number we be, the lesse damage shall the realme of En- gland susteine: but if we should fight in trust of multitude of men, and so get the victorie (our minds being prone to pride) we should thereupon peradventure ascribe the victorie not so much to the gift of God, as to our owne puissance, and thereby provoke his high indignation and displeasure against us. . . .

But when the outcrie of the lackies and boies, which ran awaie for feare of the Frenchmen thus spoiling the campe, came to the kings eares, he doubting least his enimies should gather togither againe, and begin a new field; and mistrusting further that the prisoners would be an aid to his enimies, or the verie enimies to their takers in deed if they were suffered to live, contrarie to his accustomed gen- tlenes, commanded by sound of trumpet, that everie man (upon paine of death) should incontinentlie slaie his prisoner. When this dolorous decree, and pitifull proclamation was pronounced, pitie it was to see how some Frenchmen were suddenlie sticked with dag- gers, some were brained with pollaxes, some slaine with malls, others had their throats cut, and some their bellies panched, so that in effect, having respect to the great number, few prisoners were saved.

When this lamentable slaughter was ended, the Englishmen disposed themselves in order of battell, readie to abide a new field.[13]

The confluence of this graphic description and the environing providentialism has precisely that irony, that debunking potential, that in
the modern world makes Machiavellis of us all. But Shakespeare has
not used it. He retains Henry's providentialism and eliminates the
pole-axing. The only French prisoner we have seen has already
bought his way out, his captor having been, happily for him, the *miles
gloriosus*, Pistol, and his scene given over affectively to the Boy whose
"murder" becomes motivation for the order.

If it does. Though Shakespeare handles the order to kill the prisoners quite differently than Holinshed, the incident caused him considerable trouble, too. Even if we can devise textual hypotheses that
will convincingly explain one of them away, two passages that present
Henry's motivation for the killing remain extant in the Folio and in
conflict. First, at act 4, scene 6, line 37, he is reacting to French rein-
forcements coming on the field; shortly, at act 4, scene 7, line 60, he is
reacting to the death of the boys and the plundering of his tent, in a
classically heroic outburst: "I was not angry since I came to France /
Until this instant. Take a trumpet, herald, / Ride thou unto the horse-
men on yond hill," and challenge them to combat. If they don't fight,
then we'll cut the throats of the prisoners (ll. 55–65). The process of
scenes 6 and 7 is an interesting example of the process of composition
in the play. The initial passage follows Holinshed closely and presents
his version of the tactically understandable though morally deplorable order. In the quarto, Pistol is on stage throughout the scene and
is given its closing line, the equally deplorable "Couple gorge." But in
the Folio, the vicarious bloodsucker has disappeared from the scene,
and we move instead directly to the more amenable response of Fluellen, Pistol's displacer in the play at large.[14] It is Fluellen who tells us
about the death of the boys and whose reaction mirrors, at a lower
level, Henry's own. The "arrant piece of knavery" justifies for both
Fluellen and Gower the "gallant king." It leads them also into an
extended comparison of Henry to Alexander in respect of rage and
furies, wrath and cholers, and destroying friends. Henry's final
speech about the prisoners, with its ambiguous time scheme, then cuts
off their conversation.

The entire Holinshed passage on the incident describes a series of
events Shakespeare could easily telescope and transpose into the
scene 7 treatment, though that treatment remains inconsistent with 6:
after a description of the plundering of the English tents, which included killing any servants who made resistance, Holinshed continues

with the outcry of the boys and lackeys and the order to kill the prisoners. The outcry of the lackeys and the boys had only to become the death of the lackeys and the boys, and Henry had far less humanly reprehensible motivation. Add the view from the eyes of Fluellen, once Pistol is dispensed with, and you have not Machiavelli, but Alexander the Great. In Holinshed, Henry's second threat against the prisoners (Shakespeare's 7. 55–56) is addressed to the French soldiers who would make the effort to rescue their fellows whose throats are being slit. In Shakespeare, it is instead defusing the sense that Henry acts from sheer expedience. While it is too much to say that Shakespeare gives us in Fluellen's view a definitive perspective, he has certainly obscured Holinshed toward heroic justification.

He does it again in front of Harfleur. Holinshed tells us that at the conclusion of the siege, which comes about, as Shakespeare is quite willing to recall, because the Dauphin finds the time not "convenient" for bringing aid,

> The soldiers were ransomed and the town sacked, to the great gain of the Englishmen. Some writing of this yielding up of Harfleur do in like sort make mention of the distress whereto the people, then expelled out of their habitations, were driven; insomuch as parents with their children, young maids, and old folk went out of the town gates with heavie heartes (God wot), as put to their present shifts to seek them a new abode. . . .[15]

At Shakespeare's siege, of course, all piteous results, all shrill-shrieking daughters, "reverend heads dash'd to the walls," "infants spitted upon pikes" are confined to—and by—Henry's splendid oratory. No word is spent on the sack, though many on the later order to discipline thieving English soldiers. Both choices in the text have proved difficult if not downright negative for modern audiences, or at least for modern critics, who are as apt to take Henry's rhetorical skill as proof of his Machiavellian political stance as to see the discipline enacted against Nym and Bardolph as more of the same heartlessness. Moving toward a Henrician whitewash, Shakespeare has unleashed the antirhetorical, democratic reactions of Hazlitt and his followers.

The implicit insistence in such attacks as Goddard's that in order to display a heroic battle, one must not taint it with the reality of blood, one must instead ignore the fact of the dangers to the men who do the fighting, is a covert insistence that battlefield heroism can only be played successfully as the French view it in this drama—sun gilding armor, a "fair show" that shall by mere appearance "suck away" the "souls" of the adversary ("Let us but blow on them. . . ."): the vision of Richard II in the language of Pistol ("To suck, to suck, the very blood to suck.")—or not played at all.

But Shakespeare's war is, comparatively, real. Only a real war can give rise to a model of heroism that has reference to anything beyond the silly posturing of the Dauphin, can extract from the chivalric its effective power. The fortunes of the Boy, who sits in for Falstaff, having all that is left in the play of Falstaff's verbal ingenuity and extemporizing power, illustrate the procedure. His scene begins the Agincourt sequence. He is in the scene because Pistol needs an interpreter in order to speak to le Fer. Goddard and the ironists naturally see the episode as undercutting the heroic enterprise itself whereas for me the parallel ransoms, Pistol's and Henry's, undercut what is left of the Falstaffian world, which has changed its shape and meaning through three plays. What of it Pistol epitomizes has no value, intrinsic or extrinsic. The Boy knew already, in act 2, scene 2 that he "must seek some better service," away from the mendacious thievery of a walking parody who is speechless but for rather funny lies. The Boy is our representative of those whose deaths are called on to mitigate the slaughter of the prisoners, his wit and self-possession typifying the enforced gallantries of the war. He is our constant reminder that they *are* enforced and, through his standing next to Pistol, that they still express one's being, the notion Henry relies on when he tells Williams that "every subject's soul is his own." One of the forms of heroism in the play is the frightened Boy's staying with the luggage. It would, of course, be better if he weren't in France at all. The cost of war is epitomized in the reality of the Boy's death.

What is not real in the play is what the French must become in order that Henry's heroism may survive its qualification by such actualities. They enter *in absentia* in act 1 to defuse that act's political ambiguity by giving Henry a Hotspurian occasion, making of him a composite figure who brings together his father's political capacity (the business with Canterbury and Ely) and Hotspur's chivalric ardor—hardly the Ariostan figure the Chorus has announced ("warlike Henry" assuming "The port of Mars"), but one instead in danger of becoming mere Machiavel until the Dauphin's tennis balls arrive. They supply the son of Bolingbroke with precisely the situation in which the absorber of Hotspur can ring out—and does. As careful as his father for the real threats of the situation (the concern for leaving sufficient arms against the Scot), he takes on the colors of Hotspur in vigorous zeal for the battle—a zeal grounded like Hotspur's on the defense of honor (the tennis balls made it personal) and, like Bolingbroke's, on the desire for political gains. Sheer romance would, of course, drop the second motive, making it easy to cheer; Shakespeare grounds Henry more firmly.

The French return, in the flesh, after the complicating action's two threats have been introduced and, from the point of view of Henry's character, settled in textbook fashion, the condemnation of Scroop, Grey, and Cambridge as unsentimentally and as decisively as the rejection of Falstaff a play ago. He is acting the way kings are supposed to act, though the Falstaff world will not go away (it is there in the Boy as well as the tennis balls and Mistress Quickly's report, however comic), and the Cambridge sorts may recur as constantly as they did during his father's reign. The French then enter not only as the proper antagonistic force of the play, but as an additional threat. They are reasonable and reasonably nonplussed leaders, not knowing quite how to respond to Henry's unorthodox requests—unorthodox and apparently ridiculous. They approach the problem he presents thoughtfully, carefully, taken aback by his arrival, regal (Shakespeare is not involved in parodying hierarchy in this play), and cautious.

The seriousness with which Shakespeare presents the French here underscores the reality of the threat of Scroop and company. It also makes us wonder if the Dauphin's tennis balls are at all typical of French political action—if Henry hasn't leaped into more than he expects—if the youthful game of honor baiting and honor seeking was not a hasty enterprise after all. It sets up the stage, in other words, for Henry's most monumentally heroic moment, his entry into Franch with "Once more unto the breach . . . ," and the stage it sets is full of doubt and questions. They are only intensified by the staged response to his stirring rhetoric, Bardolph ready to run up to the breach, Nym calling him to his senses: "Pray thee, corporal, stay. The knocks are too hot; and for mine own part, I have not a case of lives" (3. 2. 35).

Though the doubt and questions are never resolved, they are staved off in two ways: by the emergence of displacers for Nym et al. and by alterations in the treatment of the French. The Dauphin becomes their primary figure, weaving verbal garlands for his palfrey, taking the attitude that informed the tennis ball gift toward the English presence as a whole. The conversations among the French lords, replete with shiny armor, fiery horses, and smutty jokes, are played off against the honest doubts, the fears, and, ultimately, the commitment of the English soldiers: Williams may question the whole enterprise, but he fights as a true Englishman. As Henry gains dramatic strength and power, the French recede into that simplicity that underscores his force: they cease to assess him accurately, they undervalue

his will and determination (made all too palpable for us by his response to the hanging of Bardolph), they behave like the silly adoles-
cents the tennis balls claimed Henry to be. They play at dice for the
English, while the English, "like sacrifices, by their watchful fires sit
patiently and inly ruminate / The morning's dangers" (4. Chorus. 23–
25). These lines come from the Chorus, so one may be tempted to
ignore them as another of his simplicities, but they describe pretty
accurately what Shakespeare depicts as the eve of Agincourt.[16] While
the comparison of the English and French courts reveals nothing
discrepant—one is very much like the other, the king of France even
has the same difficulties controlling his son that Henry IV has with
Hal—the comparison of the two armies is a piece of romance.
(Specifically, it is the *paragone* of court and country, artificiality versus
naturalness, plumes against leeks.) and the romance extends beyond
the self-projection of the French, extends as far as the miracle of
Agincourt proper, which could not, in the natural order of things,
have happened according to *any* perspective in the play.

When Charles V organized progresses through his widespread and
culturally disparate empire, he tried symbolically to turn what was in
fact one of the great debilities of his reign into a virtue by making the
progresses deliberate demonstrations of multinationality.[17] Like so
many of Charles's ceremonial displays, these efforts to create in
nationalism a secular locus of valorizing self-definition were replicated throughout the European monarchies. Such devices enabled
the propounders of the imperial myth to transcend sectarianism and
regional self-interest. Shakespeare adopts it wholesale in Henry's
army, though he restages it in dramatic dress, disengaging it from the
emblematics of the progress, but not, certainly, from their immediate
intention. Though the Scot and the Irishman have minimal parts,
their presence is necessary to make the essentially symbolic point that
Henry unifies a disparate nation, a projection that Shakespeare seems
as interested in as in the final unity—with France.

Both points, drawn from romance, the one political and the other
literary, have been centers of difficulty in the play. They are not real,
they are not believable, the marriage to Katherine as love match is as
unacceptable as the jolly captains.[18] Yet the united nation of Fluellen,
Gower, MacMorris, and Jamy is not without its internecine warfare
through which romance encounters the level of reality that substantiates its ideality, so well that, like Henry's oration before Harfleur, the
squabbling among the captains is now offered as proof of the ironic
intentions of the play as a whole. The audience that cannot see the
captains as incipient trouble is yet apt to follow Johnson in finding

them insufficient recompense for the Boar's Head group whom they replace. Though Fluellen catches some imagination, the group as a whole has seemed an unfortunate idealization of the regal cohorts. Whether or not they are unfortunate, they are—*pace* the ironists—an idealization, as all essentially Utopian pictures are. The sense of fellowship that Henry and his new associates embody lacks the wit and intensity of Falstaff's, yet it is more honest to the actual constraints of the kingly role—to the "we" of the "I-we" of the King's two bodies. If we blanch when Fluellen, recalling Falstaff as Henry's "turn'd away" companion, cannot remember Sir John's name, we recognize that Fluellen is a fitter associate for the warrior king. The loss is his more than ours, a loss that he willingly sustains for the good of all.

Through the transference, never fully accepted by any audience, I suspect—Shakespeare made certain of that by recalling Falstaff in act 2—we register the personal loss and measure it against the national gain, a process Henry himself never goes through. He accepts from the beginning the submergence of the "I" in the "we," accepts, that is, the necessity of his hieratic role. He is more than willing to play the part imagined for him by the theoretics of monarchy responsible for the Chorus' attitudes. Because of Henry's acceptance, the Chorus' outline of his reign is never repudiated. Its fanciful avoidance of reality—the failure to recognize the existence of Williams's questions about just wars and regal responsibility for individual deaths—is recorded silently, but its assurance that England fulfilled a destiny with Henry is let stand. Because the hieratic figure is environed in the real, because flesh is hacked, blook sucked, and Williams asks his questions, the figure participates in that reality but refuses to seek out the "I" whose torment accompanied Richard's destruction.

Had he not, the play could be that "implicit tragedy" modern criticism so often finds it. Henry could recognize or enact a split in his single state of man; he could worry about his becoming nothing. But he doesn't. The play is implicitly tragic on one of two grounds: there are the repressed historical facts that stand behind Northrop Frye's initial use of that label as behind Norman Rabkin's "hope that society can solve our problems with our knowledge that society has never done so."[19] And there is the loss of the person in the role. Una Ellis-Fermor discerned it first, sensing a recoil in Shakespeare from the perfect king once constructed. Alvin Kernan, Anne Barton, and others have followed her in the recognition of Henry's human hollowness, the loss of the I in the we. Based upon that loss and *Henry V*'s position in the canon, they have vigorously argued for his portrait as an initial step in the line leading through *Julius Caesar* on to Octavius in *Antony and Cleopatra* and its opposition between personal and public values. The tragedies do follow *Henry V,* and that opposition is one of their constant themes, but we bring it to this play extrinsically, either from the tragedies or from *2 Henry IV.* Shakespeare's daring is to bring Falstaff back, though not in the flesh, and prove that Henry is clear of the Boar's Head, to disallow the Boar's Head as Henry's sole access to selfhood. Act 2 is devoted to that proof, in Falstaff and in Scroop, old friends seen now as traitors. We would on the whole prefer a Mark Antony, who would not give up the past, but the play does not and subverts tragedy in French wars, heroic occasions wherein the realization of the self is a public project, an undertaking perhaps too externalized for us to believe in except as ironic. It is, after all, largely because of later Shakespeare we can expect this in drama, can expect in so externalizing a form so thoroughly internalized a character as we want to find here. The alternative to that will be the death of serious drama eventually, or at least its submergence for a pair of centuries.

The always simplistic Chorus must himself recognize the repressed historical facts, the social reality our ideal hopes for society are posited against, and in the recognition he comes to terms with the distance between Henry conceived as historical personage and Henry as hieratic model. After the play is finished, he steps forward with an epilogue reminding us that what we have seen is a construct placed upon history, and that history was not so kind as "our bending author." Just as the poet hopes to suggest "the full course of their glory," even having confined his heros "in little room," so Henry's greatness was confined in "small time," yet in that time "the world's best garden he achieved." The reference to the garden may remind us only of France in Burgundy's act 5 speech, which the Chorus echoes, or it may push us back further to the far more extensive gardening imagery of *Richard II,* which Burgundy echoed, or, since the garden is the "best," it may push us back to the Edenic analogue. However far we go, the quatrains paralleling the small space of the stage and the small time of Henry place the value of "this star of England" outside of space and time, in the realm of the imagination. Like the stage, Henry is supposed to be something outside the merely real, a "true thing." While the turn of the sestet must admit that history destroyed it, the garden was "achieved," and that is the point the play itself ends on. Consistently, then, with the aesthetic that informs his running commentary on the play—not on the history enacted, but on the theatrical means of enactment, the Chorus at the end sees the Henry of the play as a figural ideal. His commentary has depended on a theory of the imagination that sounds very much like Sidney's. As if he were aware of Sidney's injunctions against breaking the unities, he develops part of his position directly from denials of their importance, taking a stance more logical than Sidney's and more radical: if the play's reality depends from the first on an audience's ability to "piece out our imperfections with your thoughts," then the same thoughts can "carry them here and there, jumping o'er time (Prologue. 23, 29) and "well digest / Th'abuse of distance" (2. 32) because the only boundary is the imagination (3. 1–3) reined in by the truth of the reality imaged: "Yet sit and see, / Minding true things by what their mock'ries be" (4. 52–53). From the Chorus's point of view, the play presents the world of history on the ideal plane of perfected principles, Henry the imaginative fulfillment of perfected leadership.

It is in all essential points the same theory that justified a Jonsonian masque, where figural idealization had its apotheosis on the stage. But of course if Shakespeare's treatment of Henry's history includes far more than the Chorus cares to deal with, includes Bardolph, Pistol, and Williams's questions, then his play has gone beyond the figural, has presented us with both a leader whom we must complete in our minds and a leader about whom we know things contradictory to neat imaginative completions. The play tries to limit those things we know by its choices from Holinshed, by its treatment of the French, by its offering of Boar's Head displacers—by all those authorial acts that heroize Henry emphatically, but it lets in too much life to become a masque. Henry himself attempts to cordon it off in the way of a masque writer, making Bardolph and Pistol a contained antimasque, viewing his own victory at Agincourt as the masque *éclat;* and in a sense, it is. But Pistol escapes. He returns to England in the same frame of mind as he entered France, "to suck, to suck, the very blood to suck." Henry has done as much as a king can do, more than any other Shakespearean king has done, but his power remains human, and as always in Shakespearean comedy that implies limits, though not such limits as divorce us from heroism, only from the masque.

The more that Henry has done includes translating language into action, becoming in his own person the embodiment of justified kingship. It may be true that the "band of brothers" is mere wish fulfillment coming from a man who knows he cannot be anyone's brother, being a king. But the "band of brothers" is proved in the play like the speech at Harfleur. It is proved in its effect, which is, I believe, the final proof of rhetoric conceived as positively as the Renaissance conceived it. Pistol's role throughout the play is to parody heroic rhetoric, to present for rhetoric what the French soldiers present for chivalry, to clear a space in which Henry's rhetoric, like Henry's chivalry, may stand apart as "true." Its truth is posited on action: "Sword is an oath," Pistol tells us in act 2, scene 1, "and oaths must have their course," and while the course of Pistol's oaths is inevitably downward, for he "hath a killing tongue and a quiet sword," breaking words to keep weapons whole, Henry's all are kept. Pistol parallels the talkative Dauphin, just as his theatrical self-projection as Tamburlaine mirrors at the level of the popular stage the Dauphin's courtly knight. Both grant Henry a reality he could not have without such comparatives.[20] The lower is as necessary as the higher if Henry is to emerge as a valid representation of the monarch on a stage that by 1599 had seen enough of Tamburlaines to find their version of heroism ludicrous, their implicit politics oversimplified. If Pistol and company were not there, Henry would be in danger of moving in that direction himself. Yet the Dauphin protects him, too, from moving in the direction of the courtly aesthetic, from being identified as a figure in a progress pageant, the paper tiger of the time.

Sidney spoke out of the practical basis of that aesthetic when he insisted that one of the sins of the English stage was its failure of decorum in bringing together kings and clowns. It was the sin of that aesthetic—well after Sidney—not to recognize, in its very midst, that the multivalence of the popular stage relied upon precisely such transgressions, of which Shakespeare's are simply the most fluid. There is no better example of the hold that social commitments exercise over aesthetic thought than the identification of artistic unity with the social hierarchizing of the *Stiltrennung*. If it develops out of the stylistic levels recognized by the rhetorical tradition, yet it finds its logical manifestation on the stage in a strict social hierarchizing that followed to the letter, locked truly courtly art into that narrow aestheticism against which Spenser was to inveigh, softly, in book 6 of the *Fairie Queene*, recognizing its enforced distance from life.[21]

The tortuous role-playing games that are courtly arts' essential escape from its own unreality lead to lovely poems and a parade of palinodes. The theatre of *Henry V* escapes such necessities by embracing not a demotic antimonarchism, but a demotic stage language. That language implicitly rejects not kings, but kings who cannot "drink with any tinker in his own language during my life." Henry loses the possibility of the drinking bouts, but not of the multeity of language, and having retained that, he has a claim to his place, his power. Sidney would probably have been uncomfortable with Shakespeare's means of dramatizing that, for both political and aesthetic reasons. But he would not have been uncomfortable with Shakespeare's enterprise—with the effort to create in drama the center of national unity that offers in Henry's success a powerful model heroism, consonant after all with the idealizing intentions of the masque makers, but surrendering not a jot of drama's task of representation, appealing not to opaque mysteries and dancing revels but to the imaginative participation the Chorus asks for the completion in the mind of this ceremonial play. If we look on its heroic model "askaunce and strangely," it is only partially because of the changes in presuppositions caused by the passage of time. We do so also because Shakespeare gave us the means. But as in sonnet 110, the model finally remains, at least theoretically strengthened by "these blenches" and "worse essays," the means whose acknowledged threat to the ideal is so carefully controlled by the series of authorial choices we have looked at—the treatment of the French at Agincourt, the selective use of Holinshed, the deployment of defining characters, and so on.

When Shakespeare returned to the history play and the Imperial theme fourteen years later, he created a play far more mysterious, far more ambivalent than *Henry V. Henry VIII* has its ambiguity in part because it embraces so much more fully the opaque masque and its devices, acknowledging their current dominance on the stage by working through the masque's political theatrics. As *Henry V* included, in the Chorus' running commentary, its own version of the text over which Shakespeare's text was written, a commentary submitted by the play to a theatrical exegesis, so *Henry VIII* includes in its means of representation the text over which this text is written.[22] That the intertext here is not a primarily verbal one explains the enigmatic effect of the play, a palimpsest whose varying levels of interpretation do not stand out as they do in *Henry V*, as determinately definable perspectives on a clear object. That is, the question in *Henry V*—what perspective can we adopt?—becomes here in *Henry VIII*, what object are we looking at? There is no longer an appeal to audience completion in the imagination, to understanding the literal Henry in his reassessed figural value; here the figural is primary and the appeal is to identification and emotional participation in the lives that surround the kaleidoscopic king, an appeal that is apparently transmuted in the play's final scene into a direct masquing political fete that would include the audience in contemporaneous celebration, duplicating the stage celebration.

Whether we take him as Machiavellian or Platonic model, the last scene seems to require that we somehow see Henry VIII as the source of England's current greatness, the progenitor of the monarchical line that climaxes in James I, and therefore as the creator of a now-realized future. It does so so effectively that one can imagine the play as that wedding production Frances Yates so fondly hoped it was, stretching R. A. Foakes's earlier, simpler hypothesis out of all recognition.[23] When Foakes first suggested a connection between the play's pageantry and concluding fete and the wedding of the Princess Elizabeth to the Elector Palatine, he did so with great modesty, positing the likelihood of its performance there, but stressing the palpable relations in theme and pageantry between the attested wedding entertainments and the play. One could still surmise, more concretely than previously—possibly too concretely—an effort on Shakespeare's part to make use of what was currently popular and imaginatively powerful—not for the court, but for the popular theatre. After twenty years of Warburgian work on the masques, it was probably inevitable that Yates would turn such recognizable theatrical procedures into courtly elitism: "Last Plays" become now the encoded rites of a Rosicrucian Shakespeare, a figure formulated largely on the strength of the hypothetical wedding production.

While few would follow Yates in her particular search for hermeticism in Shakespeare's romances, more critically sophisticated versions of response, as much to Orgel's Jonsonian extension of the Warburg studies as to the plays themselves, have begun now to proliferate, suggesting that the play, while not a masque itself, *serves the function* of masque, projecting an ideal before the court in Henry as Platonic exemplar. But if he is, he is the strangest Platonic exemplar we have been asked to recognize—this man who puts away his wife, so idealized in the play, in order to marry a woman portrayed with great, if sympathetic, ambiguity; who enacts justice by placing himself above the law, in the Cranmer trial, after the play has stressed, in the Buckingham trial, the primacy of the law; who, if he is a figure of peace, achieves internationally what he loses at home. For the play does not provide the general atmosphere of peace and harmony frequently enough discerned in it, unless we can see two political deaths, one by execution, a divorce, a weavers' rebellion, and a final death as the stuff of peace and harmony. Shakespeare's late romances have the capacity to incorporate and justify a great deal of preliminary misery, it is true, but this seems rather more than usual. The test comes, of course, in the treatment of the miseries, the perspective taken on them and their resolutions.[24]

From Knight on, the fact that all three deaths are preceded by acts of forgiveness for Henry has been emphasized in his exoneration and in the creation of a sense of harmony in the play world. Yet the acts of forgiveness focus us on the forgivers, figure the states of mind of the dying and not the state of being of the forgiven. They are all acts that "render unto Caesar . . ." and in doing so as much achieve a separation of the court from heaven as create an air of harmony for that court.[25]

Similarly, Henry's position above the law, like his primarily peaceful reign have been aligned with James's preferred identifications, so frequently utilized in the masques—the "little god" of *Basilicon Doron*'s version of divine right, the Solomon typology he encouraged. James presumably could have identified happily with Henry VIII as Shakespeare portrays him.

It *is* the case that *Henry VIII* incorporates the masque devices and iconography, its emphasis on the emblematic and pageantic, its direct appeal to audience involvement in a final revelry (though vicarious), but it does so in the context of popular drama, a drama that had always contained the emblematic (Shylock with his scale and knife) but turned those emblems to its own uses. Henry may be a picture, he is also a contextually speaking picture and exemplifies for us what happens when an absolute monarch is dramatized rather than simply emblematized, though the emblems in which he is manifested have masque roots. As such he is heroic only in role, not in deed, insufficient in his actions to mediate the values that would justify his significance. If Shakespeare had intended to create a Platonic Henry, he cast the endeavor not in the language of masque but, once again, in the language of the popular theatre—realistic mimesis, *de casibus* falls, low characters who interact with high, idealization arising out of the mimesis. In being treated thus, the nature of the object changes, and Platonic Henry becomes the vicar of a *deus absconditus*, a notion more suited to the popular theatre than to any platonized mysterium, and probably just as acceptable to James.

Lutheranism has been identified as separating absolutely the spiritual life from political life, the spiritual congregation from the imperium, the realm of Christ from the realm of Caesar.[26] It is the point Henry V stood on in his argument with Williams and it is a point stressed again and again in this play. In displaying Henry as the bringer of Lutheranism to England, the play shows us not only the defeat of Rome—concretely in the fall of Wolsey—but also the final privatizing of the spiritual life (most obviously in Katherine's death masque, though it is apparent in all the death speeches) that renders unto Caesar the things that are Caesar's to render unto God those that are God's.

One need not propose an ironic intention on Shakespeare's part in suggesting that the play itself modifies significantly its own final scene.

He gives us a portrait of Henry's court in the structural format of the late romances, climaxing in the familiar masque *éclat,* which may well have been composed with an eye to James as Solomon, James as Jupiter, James as defender of the faith and dynastic cedar. But the life of the court that surrounds Henry must affect quite differently than the programatically controlled abstractions of the chess game of a masque per se. The direction of modification is controlled in part by the perspectival emphases Lee Bliss has explored so tellingly in a reading that masque claims must counter, and cannot. For my own purposes I will in effect restate some of Bliss's contentions in terms of the question of signs and language that seem to me central to Shakespeare's use of the imperial theme and its iconography. It is a question pursued as consciously here as in *Richard II* and justifies the Prologue's characterization of the play as tragic, by stressing the ironies to which those who live in Henry's world are subject.

The world is ironic not because Shakespeare is undercutting this Henry but because the dramatic world itself supports contradictory interpretations, not only by us, but by those who inhabit the center of its stage. What had been a subsidiary possibility in *Henry V*—a realistic or antiheroic view of Henry's acts raised at the play's edges and seams, there in the play's presence, but confined there by Shakespeare's manipulation of the facts of history and the overwhelming rhetorical solidity of Henry—becomes here both the center of the action and the metier, where act has become pageant and heroic activity has left the battlefield, retreating to closed council chambers, public heroism eschewing the public display of its enactment in favor of pageantic celebrations of its result. The metier is created, as Foakes remarked, by the "numerous scenes of walking lords and gentlemen" (p. lii) "who indicate the popular view" (p. liv) in conjunction with the continual comments within the action of one character on another, displaying a "variety of bias on the King, Katherine, Anne, Wolsey, Cranmer, and their relationships" (p. liv). Everyone tries to interpret the acts of everyone else, and the interpretations, based as they are upon personal motives, conflict. To us, the final viewers in the series of viewers the play proposes, the range of possibilities is as kaleidoscopic as the world they report.

Kaleidoscopic and private—in fact, kaleidoscopic because private. Whispering Henry, who engages in that form of speech more than any other Shakespearean hero, surmounts a hierarchy wherein whispering is as normal a medium of discourse as oratory is for Henry V, who holds back nothing, verbally either, of his magnificent energy. The privatizing of discourse in *Henry VIII* is the verso of its pageantry, the fact of that verso calling the pageantry into question. The word seems insufficient for this world where, we are told again and again, you had to be there, you had to see it; "the tract of everything / Would by a good discourser lose some life, / Which action's self was tongue to" (1. 1. 40–42). Not words but deeds speak us truly, for in the manipulability of language lies its untrustworthiness. So the weaver's rebellion has as its source a taxation and "the pretense for this / Is nam'd your wars in France" (1. 2. 59–60), and Buckingham falls before the report of his surveyor, whose self-interested motives are impugned by the Queen, who herself goes down before the legalistic manipulations of the "false professors," one of them Wolsey, who ultimately too, is the victim of "this paper," all of them made nothing by the treachery of words. But action throughout the play is acting as at the Field of Cloth of Gold, making the act, too, an ambivalent guide to meaning.

Through it all, the unnamed gentlemen, an old lady, a porter and his man press close to see, to hear, to prattle of what great ones do or, more often in this play, suffer. Those who hold power seem always aware of this potential audience: Henry appears first in an emblem, leaning on the shoulder of the Cardinal who sits then "under the King's feet on his right side." Henry appears next masked as an Arcadian shepherd, whose true identity Wolsey immediately discerns, disambiguated of the mistaken attribution Holinshed reports (to point the real identity shining through all masks, or to point Wolsey's capacity as player of such games?); Wolsey himself, the most constant whisperer, trying first to privatize the Queen's case, then to speak it in Latin till she catches him up, interpreting his maneuver for us:

> I am not such a truant since my coming
> As not to know the language I have liv'd in.
> A strange tongue makes my cause more strange, suspicious;
> Pray speak in English.
>
> (3. 1. 43–46)

Having watched the verbal manipulations for half a play, one wants to cheer her at this point, to honor her recognition of Mowbray's and the Lancaster's commitment to the communality of language.

It is a communality that has been destroyed by the privatizing powers of absolutism. Even the gentlemen, whoever they are, must protect themselves:

> 2. Gent. I think you have hit the mark; but is't not cruel
> That she should feel the smart of this? The Cardinal

Will have his will, and she must fall.
1. Gent.   'Tis woeful.
We are too open here to argue this;
Let's think in private more.

(2. 1. 165–69)

Or later, watching Anne's coronation:

1. Gent. . . . all the rest are countesses.
2. Gent. Their coronets say so. These are stars indeed.
1. Gent. And sometimes falling ones.
2. Gent.   No more of that.

(4. 1. 53–55)

Anne, too, in this world of secrets, must guard her words and, having become Machioness of Pembroke, would protect Katherine from that knowledge: "Pray do not deliver / What y'ave heard to her." To which the Old Lady replies, "What do you think of me?" (2. 3. 106–8).

To decide what one thinks of the Old Lady is not easy except that she certainly knows the use of words at Henry's court: when she announces to him the birth of Elizabeth as the arrival of "a lovely boy" *in posse* "as like you / As cherry is to cherry" (5. 1. 164ff.), Henry gives her a hundred marks. Hardly enough.

An hundred marks? By this light I'll ha' more.
An ordinary groom is for such payment.
I will have more or scold it out of him.
Said I for this, the girl was like to him?
I'll have more, or else unsay't; and now,
While 'tis hot, I'll put it to the issue.

(5. 1. 171–76)

This is not the only time in the play it is left to the lowlife to posture in heroic parody, but it is as close as we get to heroic self-projection until the Porter's man arrives. She runs out with Lovell, that arras-hugging wraith, to wheedle her reward out of Henry.

The only major character in the play whose motives are clear and irreproachable is Katherine and her idiom is resultantly straightforward: "I do believe / (Induc'd by potent circumstances) that / You are mine enemy," she tells Wolsey in act 2, scene 4, and further "Y'are meek and humble-mouthed, / You sign your place and calling in full seeming, / With meekness and humility; but your heart / Is cram'd with arrogancy, spleen, and pride." Earlier, before her case was called, allowed a pun: "No, my lord? / You know no more than others? But you frame / Things that are known alike, which are not wholesome /

To those which would not know them" (1. 2. 43–46). It is she who
enters the play as a spokesperson for the powerless, defending the
weavers in their suit against taxation (1. 2. 19ff.), and she who points
out the possible ulterior motive of the surveyor that strengthens our
sense of Buckingham's victimization (1. 2. 171–76). Throughout she
sees behind the masks to motive, revealing others as she does herself,
to lucidity. Putting her aside, Henry puts aside the play's only powerful character—dramatically and morally, certainly not politically—
leaving us after the clarity of her death masque in the glittering
ambiguity of act 5. But it should be noted that clarity in this play is
identified with powerlessness and not, as in *Henry V,* with power.
Katherine, the Old Lady, Buckingham and Wolsey after they have
been condemned and have nothing more to hide, all are clear. The
splendid series of last words, virtual gallows speeches, structure the
play in impotence, Henry V's high rhetoric finding a place in death
watches.

The great heroic achievements of Henry V are gone, replaced by a
series of political maneuvers, equally masterful as it turns out, but far
away from the arena of public glory, off in the council chambers
among men who know alternative truths and fall when theirs do not
coincide with Henry's, whose motives, because he never loses power,
are never allowed clarification.

The moment when this state is dramatically crystallized with shock-
ing force is the moment of England's culminating turn to Protestantism (Cranmer has been called to audience for causes unknown to
him). Lovell, the Mercury of the tale, stops to spy on the fate of
Cranmer, and Henry, its Jupiter, catches him out:

> King. Avoid the gallery. *(Lovell seems to stay.)* Ha?
> I have said. Be gone.
> What?   *Exeunt Lovell and Denny.*
> Cranmer. [*Aside*] I am fearful; wherefore frowns he thus?
> 'Tis his aspect of terror. All's not well.
> King. How now, my lord? You do desire to know
> Wherefore I sent for you.
>
> (5. 1. 86–90)

And we recognize that we are as fully in the dark and as fearful as
Cranmer, waiting for fortune's wheel to be turned again by this all-
powerful figure whose frown has meant disaster again and again,
whose frowns and smiles have been the linchpins on which the lives of
the play have turned. Cranmer's fear strikes us to the bone.

Knowing the "language I have lived in" no longer helps when I live among powers whose "words / (Domestics to you) serve your will as't please / Yourself pronounce their office" (Katherine to Wolsey, 2. 4. 113–15) and I am constrained to reading faces (as Buckingham is Wolsey's, 1. 1; Suffolk the King's, 2. 2; Norfolk Wolsey's, 3. 2; Wolsey the King's, 3. 2. etc.) and memorizing protocols (messages to the audience again and again: stage directions of 1. 2; 1. 4; 2. 1; 2. 4; 4. 1; 5. 2, where the empty chair is an emblem for the unresolved state of Cranmer's fate; 5. 3). The characters are thrown back on visual signs just as we are, repeatedly. When "words cannot carry / Authority so weighty" as to commit Wolsey to house arrest, the Great Seal is called for. When Cranmer moves to save himself from the Tower, he produces the King's ring. Yet visual signs are no more lucid than verbal. Whether verbal or material, the signs depend for their meaning on the King's will: it can alter them all. They are domestics to him in his private control of meaning. So, in the meeting that is to determine Cranmer's fate, the meeting that began in fear before his frown, Henry pronounces all those threats he had stressed with Buckingham, softens them by telling the kneeling Cranmer to rise—as he told Katherine—and ends it all, our review of his past decisions, by assuring the cleric he need not fear his coming trial, for "they shall no more prevail than we give way to." Would that Buckingham could have heard as much. The law, too, serves Henry, a Stuart king perhaps, but not John of Gaunt's or the Duke of York's model.

The preponderance of masque-related material in the play helps to create the sense of language gone awry, all signs dependent on the unknowable will, the secular *deus absconditus,* for their meaning. The most elaborate protocol in the play, the opening Field of Cloth of Gold, is expressly interpreted for us as having at least two meanings. In the first place, there is the intentional political message, the magnificence of two suns exchanging orbits before the audience, till "Twas said they saw but one, and no discerner / Durst wag his tongue in censure" (1. 1. 32–33), the perfect emblem of amity and the shared space of Henry and Francis, where individuation dissolves, and monarchy itself is celebrated. The pattern of the celebration is·clear to Norfolk: it realizes romance through performance (jousting so effective "that Bevis was believed") in royal order (2. 42–44). He reads it as Gordon and Yates would have us read a masque. But Buckingham wants to go behind the action to the puppet master for a second meaning:

> Who did guide—
> I mean, who set the body and the limbs
> Of this great sport together, as you guess?

Norfolk does not guess; he knows: Wolsey.

> Surely, sir,
> There's in him stuff that puts him to these ends;
> For being not propp'd by ancestry, whose grace
> Chalks successors their way, nor call'd upon
> For high feats done to the crown, neither allied
> To eminent assistants, but spider-like
> Out of his self-drawing web, ['a] gives us note
> The force of his own merit makes his way—
> A gift that heaven gives for him, which buys
> A place next to the King.

(1. 1. 45ff., 57–66)

That he bought it not with his own, but with an impressed nobility's money is the burden of the second meaning wherein the hollowness of the Field of Cloth of Gold is quickly revealed: "For France hath flaw'd the league" already. It is these two facts, Wolsey's exercise of self-aggrandizement and the actual political situation, that interest the lords, for which they read the fete as at best a pretty cover, at worst a costly vanity. Of course, none of their opinions is disinterested, since all are enemies of Wolsey. Yet it reminds us at the very opening of the play of the essentially political nature of the masque language and of its transparency as emblem. Perhaps of its ineffectuality as well.

Second-guessing masque meanings is not limited to Wolsey-inspired grumblings. When Henry appears at Wolsey's banquet, he has chosen a masquing entrance that is preliminary—the Arcadian lover—to his infatuation with Anne Bolyne's beauty. Preceding as it does all mention of the divorce, this royal manifestation lends credence to Suffolk's interpretation two scenes later of Henry's attack of conscience: "[*Aside.*] No, his conscience / Has crept too near another lady." We are, though, never to know whether Henry's attachment to Anne and to Protestantism is the cause Suffolk cynically makes it. We only know the irony of Wolsey's role in bringing England and the Reformation together, an action as fortuitous as his own downfall, brought on by the clumsily misfiled paper.

Masques *can* be lucid. They are so here in exactly the same situation in which verbal language becomes lucid—out of relation to Henry and to power. Katherine's dream vision, the simplest, and I suspect now most embarrassing, piece of pageantry in the play is the single event that has, pointedly, no audience, an emblem of the privacy of the soul. Katherine asks Griffith, but no, he has not seen "the blessed troop." In a play where everything is theatre, everyone viewed as Cranmer is viewed by Henry in act 5, scene 2—from behind a curtain, from the balcony, it is somehow reassuring that Katherine's dream *is* a dream and that the appearance of the masquing angels, golden-vizarded, crowned in bays, are the externalization of Katherine's mind and not part of a larger design whose unity is "dependent on a coherent scheme of abstraction" as was the case in the court masques.[27]

Conceivably these objectifications of Katherine's chaste and ecstatic faith have roots in Ripa, and conceivably knowing the precise significance of the golden vizards, the crowns of bays, the paired consecutive references might enrich the experience by specifying its cultural base, but, unlike the masques' case, here such knowledge would not make legible an otherwise arcane meeting. We still know, as indubitably as the original audience did, that Katherine has had a vision of Heaven, of harmony and peace, and of her own salvation. Like all supernatural events in Shakespeare, it is not explicable in terms of received notions of ghosts and angels (though it may coincide with those) nor of iconological handbooks (though it may coincide with those, too) but of the state of mind of the character it expresses. As such, the vision of Katherine—like the expressly masque-devolved appearances of Henry—is diametrically opposed to the sort of maque that we know *was* performed at Princess Elizabeth's wedding.

Chapman's preface to the *Memorable Masque* defines the form by its parameters: "All these courtly and honouring inventions . . . should expressively arise out of places and persons for and by whom they are presented"—not out of an independent action, not out of character, but out of the event, or as Stephen Orgel sees it, out of the idealization of the mind of the King.[28]

There is a sense in which the play's structure expresses the mind of the king here; however, it is the play's king, Henry, and not James whose mind directs the action's development. The serial nature of the play's structure can be referred back to chronicle history or over to the masque, both forms obviously effecting *Henry VIII;* but in each case, we would be referring to forms Shakespeare denied—the one he helped turn into well-organized drama and the other avoided altogether except as it was useful to the drama in which it was embedded. Both the masque and the chronicle history tend to be providential forms, resting their view of human history in God, in the case of the masque, through his earthy representative, however mythological his dress. In the case of chronicle history, serialism was replaced by the development of strong central characters whose will bestowed a legible teleology on the action. In *Henry VIII* that sense of purpose is gone until the close when Cranmer's prophecy throws back on the play precisely that teleology that the play itself has seemed to reject in the consecutively more fortuitous involvements of Henry in the lives of the others: the examination of the Duke of Buckingham's self-interested surveyor succeeded by Henry's infatuation with Anne, followed by the accidental inclusion of Wolsey's accounts in the state papers sent to Henry. Because Henry's will remains opaque, the action must take the form of serial progression, lightly concatenated *de casibus* falls rather than a firmly evolving, implicitly purposive climactic structure, such structure as the individual agons of the repetitive falls have one by one as they pass before us in masquelike review.

The providentialism that returns at the conclusion here can, of course, be ignored, for it is presented like so much else in the play, as political theatre, its audience the common folk, the people for whom Katherine spoke and who are represented in the play by the pragmatic, shrewd Old Lady, if we assume she is not too literally a "lady." They are all perfectly happy with the conclusion, the collective group untouched by the individual falls that prepared the way for this baptismal celebration. They have come like the "tide" to Moorfields, to Parrish Garden, "as if we kept a fair here," the Porter's Man says, reporting the most heroic action of the play: he stood successfully, though "not Sampson, nor Sir Guy, nor Colbrand," against a giant Bardolph redivivus, a haberdasher's wife, and some forty truncheoners of the nascent middle class. To them the King's blessing of Elizabeth and Cranmer's prophecy of England's greatness is played. And while the play as a whole has made us suspicious of such shows and their motives, we can assume that it is aimed at us as audience, too, that Shakespeare's dramatization of the baptism, besides giving us a picture of the political use of affairs of state, offers as graceful a compliment to the other Elizabeth as *A Midsummer Night's Dream* had to the original one, breaking the theatrical illusion to do so.

If the play transmutes thus from drama to masque, honoring the crown and inviting us to join the activity, it does so largely because the character of Henry is indefinite enough to move from the dramatic, wherein he acts as antagonist in the successive *de casibus* falls, to the hieratic wherein he stands for the idea of monarchy. Though I have stressed the first, both roles are explicit throughout the play; the second is kept so primarily on the strength of Norfolk's faith in Henry and hierarchy and of such statements as reach their culminations in the death speeches of the three tragic characters. The tension that exists throughout between the hieratic model and the enigmatic man is endemic not to masque, where the model alone is at home, but to the play that writes its drama over the masque certitudes, calling the model into question. In *Henry V*, I have argued, the question is resolved by the nature and actions of Henry himself, who as carefully articulated active hero could be offered as a believable imaginative projection of the values the model entails. In *Henry VIII*, the loss of heroic action or an adequately articulated substitute (in, for instance, the council chambers) means the creation of a vacuum where the hero once stood. That vacuum may be called the Platonic secret wisdom encoded in the king or, as I have preferred to see it, the *deus absconditus*, which I think accords better with the apparent irrationality and chance of the action and the predominant image of the veiled, whispering king. In either case, it is the vacuum that was called on often enough to justify absolutism. Shakespeare's treatment of the double-layered signification of language, legible public intention/true motive, from the Field of Cloth of Gold to Cranmer's trial, indicates that he recognized this as surely as we do now, with our more cynical political consciousness.

The drama of the popular theatre writes over the masque an indissoluble reassessment of Henry. As man, Henry can never become clear in the terms of the play, because his motives are never clarified; he must remain purely figural. The gap that the play dramatizes between legible intention and true motive is, though, never erased. The transition from courtly pageantry, the Field of Cloth of Gold, to civic pageantry, the baptism of Elizabeth, retains it. Henry's worth is not proposed in action; it is not demonstrated in an inspiring model; it is proved by the pragmatics of history, by the fulfilled prophecy of Cranmer. "Who set the body and the limbs / Of this great sport together?" Buckingham asked after the play's first pageant, and the answer was Wolsey. If we ask the same question after the last, the answer is the City. Henry has won the population and its leaders by no clearly discernible willed action but by having chosen, for no clearly discernible motive, Cranmer over Wolsey, Anne over Katherine, and produced thereby the Church of England and Elizabeth. This is what the crowd celebrates, not so much Henry as its own future. Henry has regained communality of language by making it all public, by succeeding in—momentarily, at least—subsuming the question of motive Miranda-like in "wonders." That is what Shakespeare leaves us with. We see thereby the means by which the courtly world regains its unifying power, means little less bloody than Henry V's though perhaps more modern in leaving heroism to Porter's men.

We can take the final act, then, as Shakespeare's own awareness of the awkward discrepency between Stuart claims and Stuart reality and preserve thereby Shakespeare's universal, ahistorical intelligence, a difficult but attractive position, or we can take it as a necessity of Stuart forms faced with the plenitude of contingent life Shakespeare's stage entails, a far more readily conceivable situation. A masque environed in a Shakespearean world almost automatically reveals its hollowness, the political iconology of the masque, its propagandistic ends. The play can thus be seen as an example of that series of alterations in meaning that results from our recognition that literary meaning "is a function not of 'the poem itself' but of the poem's historical relations with its readers and interpreters."[29]

The Shakespearean text is no freer of history than the Coleridgean text from which Jerome McGann develops his argument for a properly historical critical vantage superseding the closed circle of hermeneutics, from which we read ourselves in the text rather than recognizing its alterity. *Henry VIII* and *Henry V* are texts that "transcend their particular cultural circumstances not because they contain unchanging human truths but rather because their particular truthfulness has been so thoroughly—so materially—specified."[30] If in the case of both Henry plays that specification runs counter to the interpretive framework within which it is cast, the tension between framework and material truthfulness is part of the play's meaning— not simply an ironic subversion, but a dramatization of the labor of imaginative structuring, of the viable human ordering of recalcitrant life. When the form of order ceases to be viable, the particular truthfulness, "so materially specified" remains, to be reinterpreted within a new framework.

Henry VIII comes to us in the Folio, so that aside from a few comments, its "processive history," in McGann's terms, is its later stage production and critical history. *Henry V,* on the other hand, has a series of quartos that take the history of its audience relation back into Shakespeare's own lifetime. If we knew the relation of quartos to Folio, we could engage in an exercise like McGann's tracing of the evolution of "The Ancient Mariner." As it is, no such clarity exists. Gary Taylor has made a strong case for the Folio's authority and precedence over a memorially reconstructed quarto (Q1). Yet his is a two- and three-stage hypothetical case that does not pretend to know even if the Lord Chamberlain's Men, let alone Shakespeare, exercised a veto over the changes made in the conjectural reduced provincial company text recorded in Q1. What he has proved is that two quite different texts have claims to some degree of authority and that, if we think in terms of the argument I have been making, they represent a consistent movement away from (or toward, if Taylor is right in his conviction that Q comes later) an ironization of the heroic reading of Henry for which I have contended. In the Folio, Pistol's stage presence is diminished, the Dauphin's increased (as contrasting figure to Henry: in Q he is not on stage in 3.4 or 5.5); act 5, scene 2 is added entirely to make more explicit the contrast between the vaunting French and the thoughtful Englishmen with whom Henry has just talked; perhaps most significantly in this regard, the virtually speechless Jamy and Macmorris are added to give us on stage that united nation that is in Henry's figural status his *raison*. The Chorus is not there in Q, and the Epilogue itself, which interprets that status for us, concludes the text for the first time in print. All of these changes would seem most consistently explicable as an effort to minimize what we now find subverting Henry and to weight the (ideologically) positive reading.[31] Whichever text comes first, and whether or not Shakespeare or his company had control of the revision process, the existence of the two proves, I think, more than the practice of cut touring versions. They illustrate a conscious appeal to disparate audiences. Quite possibly the more ironic vision of martial heroics *was* played in Taylor's provinces, unusual as that would seem. Just as possibly it existed for the London audience itself, capable of taking more than one attitude toward Henry, neither of them Hazlitt's postmonarchist ire.

To go on would be to repeat in a new context what I trust I have made plain already: that both Henry plays consciously subject the forms of a courtly ideology to a broader, but not universally negative perspective; that aspects of the ideology that survived the initial confrontation have themselves fallen to further historical changes; and that what continues to survive—to be weighted as determinately meaningful—is what accords with our ideological horizon. We make as great a mistake in equating Shakespeare's point of view with our own as in assuming that because masque qualities and devices are functional in the plays, the plays and masques are ultimately functional equivalents, expressive of a shared political attitude. *Henry V* does criticize the basis of that idealism that shall become the ground of Jonson's masques, but it does so only to make clear what the act of idealization entails, not to throw out the act. *Henry VIII* emphasizes the usefulness of the enterprise to a community that, if it is a mob, is also a nation, where, as Henry V knew, "every subject's soul is his own."

3

Reception and Dissemination

*I*n this chapter I will look more closely at some of the ephemeral
products of epideixis in the context of the best contemporary statement of their ephemerality, Bacon's essay "Of Masques and
Triumphs." I shall discuss briefly Bacon's reactions to the Jacobean
masque and through the example of Carew's *Coelum Britannicum,*
move on to the Caroline masque and then to the masque's City
brother, the civic pageant. My intention is to show how the conventions of the masque spread beyond the Banqueting Hall at Whitehall
to become part of the literature—or furniture—of praise and how, in
part, that literature survived the Interregnum. The City pageants
afford the simplest evidence of a continuity that the succeeding chapters will try to define and analyze in its more complex literary forms.
In the light of Bacon's essay it seems legitimate to emphasize less the
Platonism that Stephen Orgel rightly sees as the masque's ideal
theoretical soul than practical connections to the real life of the
time—both the writers' and the culture's at large.

Several issues are at stake, involving audience, effect, and intention.
Angus Fletcher raised some of them in reviewing Orgel's *Illusion of
Power:*

> "Philosophically [Orgel tells us, the masque] is both Platonic and
> Machiavellian; Platonic because it presents images of the good to
> which the participants aspire and may ascend; Machiavellian be-
> cause its idealizations are designed to justify the power they cele-
> brate." Orgel takes "the democratic imagination" to task for failing
> to understand the higher aims of the "triumph." Yet it may well be
> asked how effective the court masques were, in their seeking "to

persuade, transform, preserve" the best of the royal wisdom, yet little seems to have rubbed off on King Charles.

That may be a narrowly pragmatic test of the works, but it seems to me still a necessary one if the Platonic function of the masque is to remain along with the Machiavellian, which is safe all along. While it is clear that the hypothetical Platonic justification warranted the artists, it is not clear that this is anything more than a comforting self-justification, useful to our understanding of Jonson's aesthetic intentions, but misleading in suggesting that those intentions were fulfilled other than as theoretical self-justification.

I labor the point because it seems to me that Orgel, and Gordon before him, try to claim a great deal more for the Jonsonian masques than can justly be claimed, try in fact to separate them from the tradition of panegyric of which they are a part in order to bestow upon them a degree of intellectual respectability rarely extended to their brothers. By doing so they distort the masque in three ways: creating a stronger break between the Jonsonian masque and its successors than is warranted, they minimize the purely aesthetic satisfactions the Jacobeans saw in the masque and also the extent to which Jonson's hegemony in the field is the result of his lyric power. There is no "Breake, Phant'sie," no "So beautie on the waters stood" in all the non-Jonsonian masques. The Warburg group has been, understandably, more interested in what is the less immediately apprehensible and has, I think, given a great enough emphasis to Jonson's serious scholarly pursuits in the masques to lead us to forget that these pieces of smooth and lovely epideixis were primarily structured occasions for the dance. Orgel has done so in the name of Platonism, Gordon on the grounds of a contemporary legibility that allows him further to posit a group identification, a self-selected exclusivity that led to a sociology of the court that the facts do not support.

Gordon's line of thought implies a monolithic court group that identifies itself *with* the king and universally *against* the forces of disruption that threaten him. We know from Lawrence Stone's *Crisis of the Aristocracy* that this view is more than inadequate. It makes of epideixis an exercise in group whistling in the dark; it disallows the persuasive rhetorical end by dissolving its possible audience, those who need to be convinced. But the court had many more than one opinion on the issues of the 1630s; the diversity will perhaps be reflected in even encomiastic literature.[2] We have seen in the last chapter what at least one writer enjoyed at court made from the masque; I will look now at what one writer much closer to the court than Jonson or Shakespeare made of the masque and of its imperial propaganda. I speak, of course, of Bacon, whose essay on the masque is always mentioned by Jonsonians and usually pushed quickly aside in favor of sight lines and iconography.

Gordon and Orgel have been willing to admit that Jonson's intentions in the masque were less than transparent for the audience of the day—including the king himself, whose mind the masques theoretically dramatize. While the picture Orgel has constructed over the years, out of text and sight lines, of a Platonic, dramatically educative ludus centered on and directed toward James in an ultimate reflexivity is seductively complete and self-verifying, the problem of its contemporary legibility remains—and therefore of its cultural status. Did anyone but Jonson and Jones know what their masques imported, or is the Gordon/Orgel picture itself an ideal anthropological study, reading the text of the past for what it unconsciously reveals of the time's political mythology? Gordon and Orgel want something a great deal more conscious than that, and so the question of communication can justly be raised along with Fletcher's broader question, of effect. Can one build a case for reading an audience response if there is no indication that the response existed?

Gordon expressed his own doubt early, at the close of "The Imagery of Ben Jonson's *Masques of Blacknesse and Beautie*," his first iconographical study in Jonson: "What one would of course really like to know is just how far the 'remov'd mysteries' of these two masques were appreciated by the spectators."[3] The two contemporary references he cites are on the one hand "ribald" and on the other "sadly" inaccurate. Gordon allays his own doubt by noting that Jonson cared as little about courtiers as about theatre customers and wrote his "masques as well as his plays . . . for the judicious. . . . No doubt the significances of *The Masque of Beautie* declared themselves to the sharp and learned amoung the audience at Whitehall—while the multitude gazed, said it was fine, and were satisfied. Jonson would have rested content with this" (p. 156). This may seem a more Miltonic stance than we really expect of Jonson, or indeed of anyone who spent his life writing for the theatre, but he did say something like it more than once about his plays, and the two audiences of mere gaping spectators and the judicious was a notion dear to the Renaissance theoretician, at least. If practicing dramatists were more forgiving, more prone to take their real audiences into consideration, they always had the notion to fall back on while they licked their wounds after a failure. Still, it is supremely difficult to imagine anyone more sharp and learned amoung the audience at Whitehall than Francis Bacon, who, already

King's Counsel at the time of *The Masque of Blacknesse,* could have been expected to see it.

When Bacon came to write of masques, he showed no interest in icons or any of the intellectual content Gordon traces so carefully. He speaks of the masques generically and would not, therefore, explicate any particular masque, an enterprise the *Sapientia Veterum* shows him quite capable of undertaking. But here, where dances that turn into figures are a "childish curiosity," one has the clear impression that such an endeavor would seem foolish.[4] That he wrote about them at all indicates his awareness of their importance at court. What he wrote about them, though, accords with Jonson's own later and far more negative views. He warns against undue expense, a useful admonition in 1625, and addresses himself primarily to their sensuosity, which is appreciated, not condemned. He speaks of the masque as a spectator, not a participant, though he regards them chiefly as vehicles for music and dancing. He begins with vocal music, expressing a preference for dialogue in the bass and tenor, no treble, for acting in music ought to be "strong and manly," "high and tragical." Dancing without acting in the masque proper he takes to be a "mean and vulgar thing." Bacon implies, then, an appreciation for the affective drama within the masque, for its lyric potentiality.

His attention is directed, as in the equally sensory aesthetics of the essay on gardens, toward primary sensory satisfactions, giving consideration to the specific appeals one by one: first the ear, in music, then the eye, in color and light ("The colours that show best by candlelight are white, carnation, and a kind of sea-water green," he says caressingly). Then the nose: "some sweet odors suddenly come forth, without any drops falling are, in such a company as there is steam and heat, things of great pleasure and refreshment." But olfactory satisfactions remain quite tertiary here to sound and sight whose controlled obfuscation is one of the pleasures of the event:

> Let the masquers, or any other that are to come down from the scene, have some motions upon the scene itself before their coming down; for it draws the eye strangely, and makes it with great pleasure to desire to see that it cannot perfectly discern. (P. 468)

Valuing the masques only as beautiful appeals to the senses, elegant and graceful, Bacon predictably wants the antimasque short.

We could psychologize Bacon's response, read it as a perfect expression of the ruling class's unconscious preferences in these things that are such as "princes will have"—pleasure before ordered beauty, delight in a somewhat soporific expression of that elegant grace that images their ideal world, impatience with the disorder that disrupts it but that also can be made to appeal, if only its antics and beasts are made interesting (*recreative* is Bacon's word) by the accompaniment of music "with some strange changes"—interesting, but resolvable, all dissonances closed. But it is not possible to see him having confined himself to the senses and unconsciously or diffidently left out the reading of figures that may have seemed worthy of comment in another setting: "And generally let it be noted that those things which I here set down are such as do naturally take the sense, and not respect petty wonderments," a comment with which he dismisses the symbolic changes, things of "great beauty and pleasure," so they can be quiet, "without noise." Like Norfolk, he admires the show, but unlike Buckingham, he doesn't bother to interpret one for us on any level or to suggest that such an activity is worth attention, cutting the essay off quickly with "But enough of these toys." It is impossible also to believe that Bacon, at court during the bulk of Jonson's masque-writing years, wrote this essay without having seen—perhaps even participated in—the best of the masques, as impossible as to believe that any masque writer had a more sharp and learned spectator, a more judicious audience. To whom then were the "remov'd mysteries" addressed? Perhaps it is in this sense also that one can see James and then Charles as the primary audience, though that hardly seems to have been Jonson's intention when he rested his case in a plural "sharpe and learned," or James's reaction when he said, "Why don't they dance? What did you make me come here for? The devil take all of you, dance!"[5] The readings and researches of the iconographers have made indubitable the care and coherence with which Jonson worked up his allegories, but they have never settled Gordon's 1943 doubt.

And yet Jonson was participating in what we recognize now as an ubiquitous courtly practice. On the Continent no masque-equivalent was without its scholarly antiquarian to create the program that Bacon praised and Jonson blamed Inigo Jones for obscuring. The general outlines, which were clear and which account for the "unfortunate correspondent of the *Mercure de France*," to whom Gordon refers, "mistaking Entheus for Mercury and Prometheus for Jove," were apparently and understandably what all but perhaps the scholars gathered from the masque's iconography.[6] For the intricacies of the fetes were indeed a language spoken by precious few and as valuable as signs of exclusivity as in the more usual—and opposite—function of language, communication. The masques and fetes proclaimed, for Gordon, not merely the centrality of the ruler but the unity of the ruling class. But this was a more embattled unity than he admits, accepting its own ideal self-portrait. If the skills of academic classicists could contribute to the vision of refined exclusivity by their creation of a coterie language, they would be made use of, and they were, whether or not anyone knew quite what they were saying.

For Jonson, this was not an unwilling co-optation, since the other against which he defined himself and his endeavors was precisely the excised nonreader of the idealization, whom he identified for the masque as for his public plays with the money-grubbing merchant mentality to which he gleefully assigned Jones: "Pack with your ped-dling Poetry, to the Stage, / This is the Money-gett, Mechanick age!" Where the uses of the masque were more publicly exercised, as in Katherine's dream in *Henry VIII,* such exclusivity as Jonson's and Chapman's was either avoided altogether or overgone in a clear, more general communicative act. Jonson himself moved, as we know, con-tinually away from the "remov'd mysteries."

I

One of Jonson's successors at the court masque, Thomas Carew, moved even further. In *Coelum Britannicum* (1634), still dressing his figures out of Ripa and having chosen as arcane a source as Jonson, he manipulates source and figures less toward the expression of "re-mov'd mysteries" than toward the development of explicit topical political commentary.[7] Bruno's *Lo Spaccio della Bestia Trionfante* gave him an already Platonized allegory through which to structure his masque, and it also gave him the characters through whom he could question the implications of that structure. In doing so, he dramatized the double role accepted by the masque writer who is also an intelli-gent man, fully aware of the conflicting demands that epideixis puts on him: he will praise the king and he will also refuse to be an ostrich-headed fool whose praise is blind and therefore worthless. He will be both Mercury and Momus. In the double role he will face down as effectively as he can the charge of irrelevant idealization. He does so by having Momus bring to prose life, in relatively realistic guise, a number of current political and social issues, thereby clearing a space for Mercury's Platonic verse idealizations.

Carew's masque is too good for me to claim that it is typical. Henry Herbert thought it was the "noblest of my time," and it is difficult not to agree. Yet I should like to use it as a type of the genre because it *is* so good, proving that an ephemeral kind can include works that tran-scend their occasion. In addition, given its production date, it is more

closely linked to my evolving concerns and has received far less attention than Jonson's, which might seem more appropriate at this point
in my argument. But even Louis L. Martz, who values Carew as highly
as one should, talked of *Coelum Britannicum* as a perfect example of
Caroline self-delusion, beautiful and vacuous.[8]

Orgel was much more sympathetic four years later, helping us see
its part in the Platonic politics that always underlie "remov'd mysteries," but leaving its true value unexplored.[9] That value inheres not
in the songs and revels, which do, as Orgel shows, repeat the idealistic
politics that the Jonsonian masque had elaborated; it belongs rather
to the comic introduction that brilliantly turns Bruno's premise into a
masque occasion by adopting extreme versions of the same combination of stances toward ideal models we have seen in Shakespeare.
Mercury is the poet as seer, the idealist; Momus, the god of ridicule, is
the poet as knowing satirist. Between the two the business of the court
poet is set out and his encomiastics justified. Then, when Momus has
left the stage, the revels can occur.

The relation of Mercury and of Momus to Bruno's premise will
illustrate the point. Bruno's narrative, frame for an ethics independent of the anthropomorphic theology he argues against, begins in
Jove's recognition of the immorality of the old gods. He wants to cast
the constellations out of the heavens because they are misleading
models, memorializing what Jove now understands to be immoral
activities. A new ethical system needs to be articulated and new stars
found to figure forth its values. Jove's motive in Bruno is self-
preservation: the great year may have come round again and he be
subject, like Saturn, to another castration. Carew's Momus follows
Bruno's Saulino in this interpretation. But Carew's Mercury knows
better: Jove has seen Charles and Henrietta Maria and found in their
love a pattern that showed him "his loathsome staines." *Thus* his conversion occurs and causes him to pull the record of his old adulteries,
rapes, and incests from the sky and place Charles there as the new
polestar. Carew has been criticized for what, at the literal level, can
seem a flaming blasphemy, Charles elevated above Jove. But this is to
misunderstand both Carew and Bruno by taking the literal level of
the allegory as its meaning, precisely the position against which Bruno
argued. Both writers are instead involved in allegorizing aspects of
mind and the processes of cognition. Carew does not, though, pursue
the epistemological arguments through which Bruno clarifies the
meaning of Jove and derives his ethical postulates. Indeed, it is impossible to imagine a masque doing so. If Carew's masque has a flaw, it is
in the assumption that he could simply presuppose what Bruno teases

out at length. We will encounter the same assumption in Davenant later, for the writers of the Caroline masque used their medium to work out political positions rather than the epistemological basis of their means. They are always reflexive, but only as a subsidiary theme.

The narrative frame, then, makes the same claim that masques always made for the king and his consort. To put it as Carew did elsewhere, as figures in the masque, they

> came downe to guide
> Our steerlesse barkes in passions swelling tide
> By vertues Carde, and brought us from above
> A patterne of their owne celestiall love.[10]

Within the frame, however, stands Momus. Because he is a doubting Momus, he brings to the masque the same reflexive concerns that Townshend and Davenant also less artfully introduce into the Caroline masque. Though he has heard, rather vaguely, of the model virtues of Carlomaria, he cannot recognize the actual king sitting before him, let alone recognize his value as model. What Momus sees is the mundane human world stripped of its abstract pretences. His recognition and reminder to us of that world's shortcomings justifies Mercury's enterprise. His view, attached to the line of Rabelais and Aretino and an unspecified French montebank who "wants their fang-teeth, and Scorpions taile" (l. 170), presents mere reality to the audience in the immediately recognizable form of contemporary abuses and complaints done up in energetic, rolling appositions, strikingly homely images, colloquial sneers, and the lively timing of his period's comic prose.

This licensed railer consistently, throughout the denuding of heaven and the cross-examination of the new star-candidates that make up the body of the comedy, maintains the Rabelaisian viewpoint in the language games of the lawyers it is Carew's job to contradict. (*Coelum Britannicum* answers the Inns of Court production of Shirley's *Triumph of Peace* and its position on the prerogative.)[11] Carew brings together that political goal and his more universal moral subject by having Mercury and Momus in effect gloss one another's speeches. What Mercury delivers in ideal abstraction, Momus restates in concrete terms. So the question of Jove's motive, alluded to already, is in Mercury's opening statement couched in the polite abstractions of Christian contrition:

> When in the Chrystall myrrour of your reigne
> He view'd himselfe, he found his loathsome staines;

And now, to expiate the infectious guilt
Of those detested luxuries, he'll chase
Th'infamous lights from their usurped Spheare.

(84–88)

Momus's version is, as I have claimed, Bruno's:

love is grown old and fearefull, apprehends a subversion of his
Empire, and doubts lest Fate should introduce a legall succession in
the legitimate heire . . . and hence springs all this innovation.

(229–33)

Contrition in Momus's version is itself laughable: Jove has "taken an
oath on *Junos* Breviary, religiously kissing the two-leav'd booke, never
to stretch his limbs more betwixt adulterous sheets" (202–4).

The concretion and particularity that turn praise into parody are
part of the legalistic manipulation of language in which Momus engages, swinging a two-edged sword that cuts both ways. He parodies
along with the prerogative question (mere legal hermeneutics in his
rendition [ll. 149–52]) a series of legal issues that includes the usage of
the prerogative courts (ll. 125–46), the royal proclamations aimed at
social engineering through the management of business practices (ll.
236–62), the control of American emigration (ll. 384–91)—a virtual
catalogue of the vital political disputes of the thirties. The American
emigration is the most straightforward instance of the alternative perspectives I have defined. The idealist Mercury comments, "They cannot breath this pure and temperate Aire / Where virtue lives, but will
with hasty flight, / 'Mongst fogs and vapours, seeke unsound abodes"
(392–94). The satirist describes the New England plantations as having "purg'd more virulent humors from the politique body, then
Guacum and all the West-Indian druggs have from the naturall bodies
of this kingdome" (388–90).

In all the issues raised, Momus takes a strong position that, though
it favors Charles, one would be foolhardy to identify directly with "the
Court's" as if that abstraction were a monolithic entity. In the case of
the social engineering, for example, Carew travesties Attorney General Noy's reform measures in their anti-Rabelaisian, pragmatic
moralism through an adept respecification of Bruno's parody of celestial reform. He integrates specific topical issues with a virtual translation of Bruno's parody to achieve a remarkably funny version of
standard complaints against the reformer who supervised Shirley's
opposition masque, complaints that were certainly shared by some
members of the courtly audience.

Among Noy's services to Charles stands the most effective piece of legalistic manipulation of language managed in the effort to firm up Charles' finances in the thirties: the rewriting of patent and monopoly legislation to skirt the terms and thus the "facts." His effort enriched the Crown's pocketbook and led to the full string of abuses with which Momus enlarges upon his powers under the "patent" of poet (ll. 135ff.); in reality the patents led to strong resentments, cutting as they did across Common Law with powers of search and seizure that Momus minimizes laughingly in the lines on the "perdu page or chambermaid." Of course, he didn't have to mention them at all, and irony, as usual, cuts two ways. Throughout his part in the masque, Momus as licensed railer pushes the espousal of Divine Right faith to arm's length, being himself a creature of ridicule who cannot see "this Presence," a king who manifests not simply worldly power but to the eye that can see it, its heavenly warrant.

The worldly power is what Momus sees. Thus he is able to parody in succession the lawyer; the statesman; the regal in its most public effectual form, the proclamation—the verbal worlds in which un-idealized regal power exercises itself through clever spokesmen who can wrest "the old to any whatsoever interpretation" along with the best of them. He can describe Jove's new Star Chamber that "hath on his bedchamber dore, and seeling, fretted with starres and capitall letters, engraven the Inscription of CARLOMARIA," but is as unable to see the originals of the emblem sitting in front of him as to allow the likelihood of the reforms utterly converting the purified world of old habits: virtue alone can install one in heaven now,

> yet if there be a Lady not competently stock'd that way, she shall not on the instant utterly despaire, if shee carry a sufficient pawne of handsomenesse; for however the letter of the Law runnes, *Jupiter* notwithstanding his age and present austerity, will never refuse to stampe beauty, and make it currant with his owne Impression.
>
> (ll. 318–26)

When the heavens have been emptied of their constellations in a series of dramatically integrated antimasques that visualize in dance the vices expelled, Momus has his climactic occasion, arrogating to himself, the satirist, and to Mercury, the constructive ideal voice, the provision of succession. This is poetry's role. Momus will quit, like a good figure of discord, before the job is done, but first he becomes the crier of royal proclamation, his clever adoption of the style complete with its careful qualifications and rationales, its formulas and et-ceteras, its representative transference of power. "Whereas" and "whereas" are succeeded by an "it hath notwithstanding" that in forty-one lines delegates absolute power to poetry, to satire and ideal projection to create the new heavens. In the course of the proclamation's reasoning, Momus persists in his inversions, the self-celebrations of Renaissance princes becoming the model of Jove's actions, the Star Chamber itself the pattern, by "propheticall imitation," of the constellations in which Jove commemorated his own military adventures in "the Amourous Warfare." Claims to secret wisdom and omnipotency are held up to justify Jove's apparently unnatural actions now, his darkening of the sky: "after mature deliberation, and long debate, first in our owne inscrutable bosome, and afterwards communicated with Our Privy Counsell, seemed meet to Our Omnipotency, for cause to Our selfe best knowne. . . ."

Jove's standing on his inscrutable wisdom and his absolute power, in the person of the god of ridicule and the language of Charles, may not be precisely a parody of Charles's parallel claims, but it strongly suggests that at least one of his courtiers could look on such claims as the stuff of laughter from behind the safety of Momus's mask. Such laughter, of course, is as often posited on convictions felt to be so assured and unassailable, they may be safely chuckled over as on convictions that are expressly under attack. They are not, surely, under attack here, though excessive solemnity about them as certainly is. Carew suggests the prerogative battle, fought finally over the king's omniscience and his omnipotence, is fair game for satire in which the king's "right" is less defended than the battle itself, the in's and out's of legal interpretation, made the source of laughter, at least when looked at through Momus's eyes.

The delegation of authority to Mercury and Momus to choose among the appellants for the role of precedence among earthly motivating powers will, as I have said, finally be averted, but it creates the rationale for the appearance of a string of claimants through whom the masque's ethical center is poetically enacted. Plutus, Paenia, Fortune, and Pleasure come forward one by one to present their claims for preeminence, each to be dismissed by the gods after an antimasque has illustrated the vices attendant on their service. In each case, Mercury dismisses in idealistic terms, Momus in mock legal ones, through the exposure of the rhetorical and logical fallacies the claimant employs. The presentation of the pretenders, like the dispelled constellations, is physically traditional. The old constellations departed with allegorical self-expressive dances; the new pretenders enter in full Ripan allegorical regalia. Carew however will not, like the masque generally, leave it to the eye to assess them. Each of the pretenders is given a speech that in sinuous blank verse verbally expresses the claim entered. While all of them make strong cases, I will instance only the last, the non-Brunesque addition, Hedone, because it seems to me the most revealing. Pleasure, the Cavalier god Carew has prasied in poem after poem, makes her claim:

> [the other pretenders] for my sake, I for mine owne am priz'd.
> Beyond me nothing is, I am the Gole,
> The journeyes end, to which the sweating world,
> And wearied Nature travels.
>
> (771–74)

Because all men seek pleasure individually, civil felicity, the general good, must reside in me. Even at the highest levels, the highest prices have been paid:

> Tell me what rate my choycest pleasures beare,
> When for the short delight of a poore draught
> Of cheape cold water, great *Lysimachus*
> Rendred himselfe slave to the Scythians.
>
> (796–99)

Mercury alone, the voice of idealization, can answer her, clothing common moral repudiations in fiercely direct statement and simple, traditional metaphor:

> Thou thyselfe art Paine,
> Greedy, intense Desire, and the keene edge
> Of thy fierce Appetite, oft strangles thee,
> And cuts thy slender thread; but still the terror
> And apprehension of thy hasty end,
> Mingles with Gall thy most refined sweets.
>
> (818–23)

The course of the pretenders' excisions—from the revealed aggrandizement of Riches, the self-deception of Poverty, the victimage of Fortune, to the seductions of Pleasure—explains the need for Mercury and makes it clear that the eye of Momus *requires* the vision of Mercury to complete the task at hand. Only Mercury can make the argument against the decadence implicit in Hedone's appeal to the pleasures of court life, pleasures dangerously close to those of the masque Carew described in the Gustavus Adolphus poem:

> Come forth my subtle Organs of delight,
> With changing figures please the curious eye,
> And charme the eare with moving Harmonie.
>
> (ll. 805–7)

If we are to distinguish between the glories of the good court and the troop of Hedone, we must see with Mercury's eye. Momus is sufficient to see the world's real shortcomings, but his power is limited to negation. If we are not to run aground at zero, we must have the constructive idealist to provide a route out.

Stripped to this bare statement, Carew's position reveals its root resemblance to Hobbes: the need for the Court is a stop against the human nature Momus knows; the need for the Court conceived Platonically is a stop against mere aestheticism. Carew, of course, does not strip his position down so far, though it is clear enough to make the desperation that motivates it reasonably obvious. Carew instead gives us the revels without having educated Momus to them. His opening challenge, "let it if it can," is never met; he never learns to see Charles. He remains his own man and bids "no bodie farewell." The satirist never alters his negative view of the world he is dealing with, nor does Mercury ever see it without the ideals it can manifest. He learns under Momus's tutelage to recognize false human motives, and when the satirist bows out, assured only that he and Mercury have the same goal in mind, Mercury carries on to prove to less-jaded eyes—presumably ours—that the fact of being has justly won out over the legalism of the pretenders. As he told Paenia, overriding her false dilemma logic with a new definition of riches, poverty acts only by deprivation; it nurses "Pedantique virtue / In the cheape Sun-shine,"

> Tearing those humane passions from the mind,
> Vpon whose stockes faire blooming vertues flourish,
> Degradeth Nature, and benummeth sense,
> And Gorgon-like, turnes active men to stone.
>
> (648–51)

Riches rightly understood directly encounter poverty's "low abject brood" with excess and its freedoms,

> Brave bounteous Acts, Regall magnificence,
> All-seeing prudence, magnanimity
> That knowes no bound, and that Heroicke vertue
> For which Antiquity hath left no name,
> But patterns only.
>
> (661–65)

What these patterns are and what they mean will be clear through contemplation of the "new enlightned Spheare" that the revels soon create.

The notion of myth as the imaginative projection of value is duly explicated in the revels themselves, explicated and exemplified. When the "Kingdomes" want to know how the splendid "antient Heroes" who perform the first dance can be both in heaven and in England, the Genius answers first abstractly ("their Fame shall flye / From hence alone") and then with a mythic figure from Bruno—Eridanus. The second answer encapsules the claims of Mercury throughout the masque: the materialist question, "How can the shaft stay in the quiver, / Yet hit the mark?" meets a counterquestion:

> Did not the River
> *Eridanus*, the grace acquire
> In Heaven and Earth to flow,
> Above the streames of golden fire,
> In silver waves below?
>
> (997–1001)[12]

Eridanus thus becomes the perfect symbol of imaginative projections that must at the same time function in a worldly context. There is little surprise in the song's now turning to the "triple Vnion" and to concord, the "immortal spring" in which the genius of the kingdom will renew himself, and even less in the next movement of the masque being toward the Queene, England's Eridanus—as imaginative projection, "Bright Deity," as earthly reality, "great Queene." The figure of love, she will conquer the conquerors, displacing martial virtues with "your peacefull pledges of warme snowe."

This, then, is the Caroline masque. It is aware not simply of the need to be understood if its case is to be made, but conscious also of what its acts of idealization ultimately require of the poet: the dismissal of Momus, the abandonment of the satirical eye that sees and understands prosaically, for the idealizing verse of Mercury and his songs and revels. But Momus has been seen and he has spoken; he has expressed the prosaic view and encountered the arguments against Charles and masque practice by recognizing their limited literalness and laughing them out of existence, or at least trying to do so. Rabelais has entered the Banqueting Hall finally to leave it unchanged, but energized by the self-awareness that makes momentary belief in the Platonic oxymoron possible. The goal is "warme snow"— pure, soft, inviting, and impossible to any literal world.

II

Bacon entitled his essay "Of Masques and Triumphs," but he apparently tired of the subject before he had run through his catalogue of courtly fetes and never reached the more public displays suggested by "triumphs." He yoked them together no doubt because he saw them all as appeals to the ear and eye, toys, and probably because he saw them as equivalent expressions of princely self-gratification ("princes will have these things"), whether or not enriched and deepened by the classicism of a Jonson. When Jonson's money-getting merchants adapted the language he was so instrumental in formulating to its own uses, a move he would in all likelihood ironize as he did Jones's cardboard and the appeals of Bartholomew Fair, they did so with far less benefit of classicism and a far greater concern for legibility. Yet they borrowed their syntax and semantics from the seat of royalty, spreading the courtly forms well beyond their original audience. What began in royal entries was extended to Lord Mayor's installations, the bourgeois type of those events whereby Jonson's other imagined itself a part of the whole.[13]

While there were other civic pageants in London during the year, none was so regular or swelled so in presentation early in the century as the annual celebration of the man who represented both the independence of the city and its connections with the kingdom at large. The civic self-celebrations have a history parallel to courtly masquing from early and simple cloudy beginnings through Tudor-supported formalization, the mayor becoming Lord Mayor, the accoutrements of his installation cousins of Medicean fetes, as merchants evolved if not into princes, at least into merchant adventurers who both wrote themselves Sir and were represented as heroic travelers in a new knightly quest.[14] With the Stuarts, the formalization of the celebration was completed as repetitive ritual in which civic pride had its apotheosis every 29 October as on Twelfth Night, at Whitehall, monarchical pride had its own. The celebration began on the new mayor's trip back to the city from Westminster and investiture. Still in barges on the Thames, the entourage would see a show or two "by water." They debarked at Baynard's Castle to follow a variable route, usually to Saint Paul's, and then on to the Guildhall. Along the route were placed pageants—most commonly six—with their declamations and allegorial representations of the mayoral virtues, the institution's history, the national powers, the threats to order. The ending at the Guildhall was a profuse banquet that included the City music, which had accompanied some part of the earlier business. The soul of the celebration must have been the procession itself and the crowd's concerted response; the remnant is the quite probably prepublished pageant descriptions and declamations.

Understandably, these are far less Platonic than *The Masque of Black-*

ness, but no less morally allegorical and self-congratulatory. What is praised here is not the secret wisdom of divinity but the more mundane mysteries of commerce, emphasizing by direct statement and in the allegory the value to the country at large of the trades and mercantile ventures of the various guilds represented. Because the lord mayor was chosen annually from one of the guilds, which then paid for the show, the emphasis shifts each year to the specific guild at the financial and ceremonial center of the fete, though trade in general—the assembled guilds—is always praised. Overall the message is quite the same early on as that underlying consciously formulated mercantilism over a century later: trade not only brings to England the goods of the world, the world is enriched by the civilizing function of British merchants, the creators and spreaders of civilization. The merchant adventurers have "brought to us," Thomas Heywood writes in the 1633 show, "in an abundant measure" all those rarities that we enjoy "for profit or for pleasure."[15] We have brought to outposts like America the gifts of civilization in exchange for her raw opulence, Thomas Jordan will show, forty years later. International trade is the web of the good life, whose security in England must be assured by a strong navy's toughening the moat capacity of the surrounding sea, a theme as dear to the heart of the Stuarts as to the merchants.

Heywood's truncated couplet suggests how little of intrinsic poetic value we can find in the pageants, even when Peele and Webster write them. Both their ephemerality and their conditions of production militate against that: shouted speeches amidst a crowd outdoors have rarely been the home of subtle language. Simplicity and repetition are the rule. Refinements are saved for the printed versions, though these, working out from the performed text, usually succeed only in extending banality. Yet the shows are capable of revealing both the concerns of the citizenry and of the particular writers, reflecting both theatrical and political changes. With Thomas Jordan, for instance, the musicalizing of the London stage after the Restoration appears in the heavy emphasis he gives to the musical entertainments at the Guildhall after dinner, just as history wears out as a theme of the pageants after Munday and Webster as the pageants follow the masque in pure allegory. Politically, in the sixties and seventies, America and the Portuguese become formidable, and concern for the little man becomes part of the symbiotic mercantilism of a Jordan where it had earlier, with Middleton, found expression in the execration of the decline of civic commitment among the capitalists.[16] It is rare enough, though, that such negatives as Middleton raises are allowed to speak, and we are usually constrained to read through the subjects of the shows, as of the court masque, what mollified dissension could find expression on epideictic occasions. So, for example, in 1639, a year when we might expect some degree of fear or dissatisfaction with the way things are, Davenant presented *Salmacida Spolia* at court, Heywood *Londini Status Pacatus* on the streets. Both works acknowledge England's troubles, and the difference in their doing so typifies the difference between the attitudes surrounding court masque and city pageant.

Davenant begins with a figure of Furie in a storm whose string of antimasquers, "the horrid, sullen brood," are destroyers of the State through the hypocritical appeals of false religion to greed. The storm is stopped, as it usually is in court masques, "on a sudden" by a secret Wisdom that "will change all their malicious hope of these disorders into a sudden calme, which after their departure is prepared by a disperst Harmony of Musique."[17] The masque does not ignore the dissension outside Whitehall; indeed it paints a rather horrific picture of the hellish uproars of dissension, not for the first time in masque and not for the last on the musical stage, but particularly relevant to the court's view of itself now. The wishful thinking of masque is only the more apparent in the context: his Majesty reducing the "tempestuous and turbulent natures" to a "sweet calme of Civill concord" on the strength of his being.

Heywood is less sanguine and more suppliant. In *Londini Status Pacatus,* Janus is the speaker in the second show by land. The dispenser of justice is preceded by Heywood's appeal to men of honor "to be constant in all their courses, but especially in the establishing and maintenance of true religion" and to stand against those who "seeke to undermine and supplant the prosperity of a faire and flourishing Common-Weale." Peace is lauded in the third show as the source of plenty, increase, and all terrestrial blessings by Orpheus, emblematic of harmonious governance. Orpheus's picture stands in contrast to the sixth show, wherein the Genius of the City recites an affecting description of war in images and tones that remind us how frightened by its specter London was now. Conditions in Germany are held up as the negative exemplar, its "throwes" contrasted to our blessed peace.[18] Heywood's appeal may turn out finally as wishful as Davenant's, depending as it does on the intelligent self-interest of a people, their efforts to come to terms with one another out of their knowledge of Plenty's reliance on Peace. But in the directness of his terms and the historical specificity of their realization, Heywood's seems a stronger view, more willing to call up the real situation.

Different as the attitudes may be, my brief description should have also shown how dependent the city pageants were on precisely the system of allegory that supported the masques. The masque éclat, its sudden conversion, could be dispensed with, but surely not Orpheus and Janus: the Lord Mayor is clothed in the same fabric that dresses Charles. The long line of historically oriented pageants in the first quarter of the century had insisted on yoking, factually accurately on the whole, the mayoralty and the Crown, reiterating the part played by Richard II, Elizabeth, and others over and over again in the moral and typological allegories that subtended mere economic reality. The virtues and values of their roles are expressed in duplicate emblemata, the moralization underscoring the snug interrelations of Crown and mercantile world in a language that effectively valorizes them both.

When the history has dropped out, the moralizations continue and also, of course, the allegory, which now implies, with little need of yet again beginning at Richard II, a nurturant hierarchy of timeless standing. So Heywood can clothe the praise directed at the new mayors of 1632 and 1633, Nicholas Raynton and Ralph Freeman, in mercantilized gods, whose power is transferred to the mayor by virtue of his role, the truth of the type, just as Charles is the truth of Britanocles for Davenant. Tatham is still using the same devices and the same language in the 1660s, even after the procedure has become, for a viewer like Pepys, archaic and rather silly.[19]

But in Heywood's time, the height of the Stuart masque production, devices that Pepys would find thoroughly outmoded were the proper means to shed on the merchants some of the glory of Jonson and Davenant, Carew and Townshend bestowed on Charles. So the printed version of the 1632 show, *Londini Emporia,* begins with a discussion of the word *Mercatura* and merchandise, pedantically developing a false etymology that justifies seeing Mercury as the god of merchants, a connection elaborated in the second show by land where the various classical functions of Mercury (messenger between gods and men, leader of the Graces, inventer of wrestling, deviser of letters, patron of eloquence) are turned to their mercantile equivalences and made to figure the enrichment of the world by the merchant-adventurers (p. 19). Though his pageants are always loosely and pedantically classicized in this manner—even more in the printed than in the acted versions[20]—Heywood always proceeds to clarify his mysteries directly, finding little value in keeping them "remov'd": "If a true Shepheard you desire to see, / Looke this way, for hee's embleam'd here in me," the shepherd of the first show by land tells the crowd; "But you gave *Praetor* rais'd to this high state, Hee whom as now I only personate," he addresses the mayor and proceeds to explain that the numerous throng is his flock, the city their fold, and so on. Peter Quince's group of rude mechanicals could ask for no more.

This clarity and efforts after it remain always a feature of the shows, as they must, if the crowd and the outdoor setting are acknowledged as determinative, as indeed they must be. But Heywood goes on treating his simple allegories in print as though they were "remov'd mysteries," adding to the printed texts etymologies and explications that unveil the already transparent as though it were in need of such elucidation, along the way adopting the masque's own snobbery: the succession of shows in 1633, as typically in Heywood's production, is interrupted before its millenarian conclusion by a fourth show that has no text. It is mere entertainment, a sort of antimasque, "for those whose ears are in their eyes," who could not appreciate poetry anyway. The mighty show then concludes its progress through the city with a Bower of Bliss, figuring England's future perfection, and an allegorical show of the theological and cardinal virtues presided over by Prudence.[21]

While there is little here that stands comparison with the courtly magnificence, the elegance and grace that Bacon praises in the masque—no revels, however much music—so that one can hardly claim for these the sort of organized participatory function that the masques entailed, yet the viewer is made one with the actors, is of the flock and engages in the same revelry that Shakespeare depicts in *Henry VIII*. The shows are the bourgeois parallel to the masques in being the ritual observance of communal hierarchy and governance whose goal is self-celebration. For all their mercantile internationalism, they are always nationalistic, not to say chauvinistic (no "petty Junks or wanton Gondolaes" are here to honor the "God-like" magistrate of London, but "Barges strong, / And richly deckt").[22]

Like the masques, they enlist classicism and Christianity, Mercury and the good shepherd, St. Catherine and Andromeda alternating toward the concretizing of their civic praise, spreading the courtly union of saint and god out into the masses, but doing so with a far greater emphasis on the saints, on the Christian moral basis of the marriage, than the court ever needed or enjoyed. It is part of the simplification of a broad public form that the elements of the union must be specified and directly stated, leaving no question in the mind of the observer that classicism is in service to Christian ideas. Platonism might serve as the visible ground of courtly art; visible Christianity could serve the same purpose for the City, leaving Heywood free to elaborate some blunt numerology in an awkward replication of a

Spenserian device. The scaturigo's speech enumerates for us the many splendors of the number twelve (Zodiac, Caesars, down of course to the Guilds), different in degree of aesthetic competence from courtly numerology, but not in kind. Throughout the century, civic pageantry borrows from the court such devices and techniques, adapting them to its far simpler stages, retaining its emphases in appropriate guises, elaborating its own mythology in which the interest in English history takes the form not only of Arthur and Brut but Sir John Norman and Simon Eyre, real mayors who became types of mayoral virtues in the popular mind—or at least in its most frequent manifestations. If the court could propose James as Soloman, the City could propose James's servant, James Pemberton, as Leofstane, as Munday did in 1611, or John Leman as Sir William Walworth in 1616.

Blunt and laughable they may have seemed to Pepys, yet the shows were an event that glorified the magistracy of the time in the same manner, through the same language, that the court was satisfied by in the masques; and this was quite conscious: Tatham in 1664 has Saint Catherine apologize to the King, after greeting him, "for shewing you no better sights, nor more." She continues:

> We hope Your Majesty will not suppose
> You're with your Johnsons and your Inigoes;
> And though you make a Court, y'are in the City,
> Whose vein is to be humble, though not witty.[23]

The verse makes obvious the unlikelihood that Charles would make such a supposition, yet he did go and no doubt received the recognition graciously, figuring for the crowd that interconnection of business and court that was rarely so literally expressed as in this year.[24] Over time, the shows present the organization of a culture into conformity with the interests and values of an altering ruling class, redirecting its revels toward the celebration of the City's power in the quasi-liturgical processions that in the printed versions, take up more and more of the text as the century goes on. The earliest shows printed, George Peele's of 1583 and 1593, give us first the device, then the pageant speech, to which fuller descriptions of the pageant cart and then the additional devices are quickly added. Soon the route through the city and the major participants are included. By the 1630s the order of the procession itself has pride of place, materializing the power of the City on the page as the allegorical figures did on the pageants.

It is in no way surprising that this would be so. Aside from the human propensity to prattle of what great ones do and to follow the forms of one's betters, the intimate connection between business and government had made Sirs and mayors of the most useful and able of the merchants over the Continent and in England throughout the Renaissance, so that the relative fluidity at the upper ends of the merchant class made it eminently reasonable that the guilds would picture themselves as part and parcel of the imperial myth.[25] They *were;* the livery companies' pecuniary grants to the crown began under Henry VIII, quickly becoming regular sources of revenue that the Stuarts, with their vast expenses and perennial financial problems, made vigorous efforts to control throughout their reigns.

But that is fact; the mythologizing that tries to affect the facts or at least make them palatable could make of the Court a medieval jousting place and of the City a morality play in which Saints George and Andrew oversee the strenuous prosperity of ironmongers and linen manufacturers. The moralizing of business like the archaizing of the nobility was a concentrated romantic effort after the glow of nostalgia that seems a permanent feature of the modern state and its inhabitants. The practical rationales underlying the specifics of court mythologizing (for instance, the establishing of the right to succession that accounts for the insistent Stuart propagation of British history and the descent from Brut) are no more distant from the form of their rationalization than the city's efforts to create for the upper bourgeoisie an honored place in England's past by reiterating year after year the history of London's mayors as rulers of Troy-novant and servants of a succession of kings wise enough to make place for the office.[26] The merchants celebrate their honored place in England's past to gain a place in the eternal present of mythological representation of England's glory. If Heywood's allegorical praise of the Lord Mayor is more humble and less witty than Jonson's of the King, it is cut from the same cloth, after the same pattern, and toward the same end.

Historically, it was completely successful, more successful in fact than the court's own parallel efforts, because its success had at least two facets—the dignifying of commerce and the assertion of communal validity for the principles of the leaders of this "money-gett, Mechanick age." Both perhaps speak for themselves, even through the quadrupally blunt expression of their modern demythologized form: "What's good for General Motors is good for the country." But we can find them, in far finer cloths, of course, in Carlyle's Captains of Industry who return again to the medieval world for their mythological expression, or in Shaw's *Major Barbara* that brings the feudal world up to date. It was a valuable and lasting myth. During the seventeenth century when its notions were still unsupported by mathematically acute political arithmetic, the dignity of commerce and the communal validity of commercial values continued to be asserted and sung allegorically at Lord Mayor's shows with only a break for the Civil War. They played their part in promulgating the honor of the London merchants and their proper hierarchic relation to king and country well enough that, even before the Restoration, they resumed, having lost little of their "lustre" in the Commonwealth's foreclosure. They hardly missed a beat in extending across the hiatus their nonsectarian generalized praise of king and country, a system that was broad enough to include almost everyone willing to honor the monarchy and the guilds. John Tatham, who wrote the City pageants from 1657 to 1664, also created the pageant, *London's Glory,* with which the guilds welcomed Charles II back to London on 5 July 1660. In it Tatham expresses what was probably the general sentiment of the City, which had regained—if it had ever lost—an absolute commitment to Charles and to the Crown. While the successive speeches of Time, Truth, and Fame, at their appointed spots along Charles's progress to the Guildhall[27] make it clear that the business of London is business, they are more concerned to insist upon the loyalty of the guilds to Charles, and they state their compliments well enough, directly and efficiently.

Tatham is a thoroughly inferior poet who did not waste his life writing City pageants. Nothing he versifies is not conventional, so his description of the course of the parade is now more interesting than the speeches of Time, Truth, and Fame—now, and then as well, for, as I have said, the descriptions of the procession had become more and more full and central to the printed text over the years. Tatham records the ranking and ordering of all the officials and soldiery, the budge bachelors and charity cases who lined up "from the Great Conduit to Temple Bar" amidst tapestries hanging and bands playing. The ranked companies, the sheriff and the "army" express the visible order of London far better than the verse can. Both Evelyn and Pepys remark on the pageantry, and from them we learn that the flags could not have fluttered as gracefully in reality as they do in Tatham's memory: despite all the efforts and expense of the guilds and their heartwarming affection for the king, it rained. Always the kinder and the more concerned for the spirit behind the letter, Evelyn gives the more gracious description:

I saw his Majestie go with as much pompe and splendor as any Earthly prince could do to the great Citty feaste: (the first they invited him to since his returne) but the exceeding rain which fell all that day, much eclips'd its luster: This was at Guild-hall, and there was also the Parliament men, both Lords and Comm: the streets adorn'd with Pageants &c: at immense cost.[28]

Pepys was kept walking all the morning at Whitehall by the rain, but he did see the king, dukes, and attendants "go forth in the rain to the City, and it spoiled many a fine suit of clothes."[29] Pepys stayed away from the show itself because of the rain, a move consonant with his usual practicality and also with his attitude toward such affairs. Of the Lord Mayor's show the same year, he says "We had a very good place to see the pageants, which were many, and I believe good, for such kind of things, but in themselves but poor and absurd" (p. 58).

For both Evelyn and Pepys, who were not annual viewers of the city's major affair as far as their diaries tell us, it is the cost, the display, the implicit connection of the King and the City that are worthy comment; the pageants as such are "poor and absurd," mere adornments, an attitude commensurate with Bacon's on the masque in both detachment and final evaluation. The magnanimity of princes and their organized, responding subjects is the point in 1660 as it had been in 1625. There is little reason to think that less sophisticated viewers than Pepys and less aesthetically responsive ones than Evelyn saw anything different. The message was known, the event was secular ritual, and the language was second nature, if a bit archaic, as Pepys' "poor and absurd" seems to suggest. The attitude shared by the three men is not far removed from their modern parallel's response to floats in Memorial Day parades. But there is, of course, one difference: for both Pepys and Evelyn, so long as the king is at the center, the affairs acquire an interest and real validity as expressions of social solidarity for which there is no modern parallel.

Allegorical representations of the virtues of good governance were, at any rate, being abandoned to that class of the vulgar gaper, to the non-Pepys and the non-Evelyns who leave no record. The Lord Mayor's Day was the Fourth of July picnic that, if we take the fifth act of *Henry VIII* as at all representative, it had always been. Its value as a retainer of meaningful allegoresis in the civic context was probably second to the sheer celebratory function of honoring the mayor as representative of the trade companies that, bringing London its pleasures and profits, helped cement a society. The evidence suggests that the class of the vulgar gaper included everyone and no one from the beginning. No one ever admits to having the slightest interest in what was said in either a masque or a lord mayor's show any more than in what was represented. And yet they were an expected part of everyone's life. The pageants drew a large enough crowd early in the century that Raleigh's execution was scheduled for that day to minimize *his* audience and, if Pepys is to be trusted, the crowds are still huge in the 1660s. The descriptions are published every year with fuller and fuller descriptions, first of the pageants, then of the procession, at last, with Thomas Jordan's tenure, of the dinner show at the Guildhall with all its music and satire.

We know that the significance of the masque for court dwellers lay less in what was said or shown than in the protocol of attendance. Reading the audience took far more of the participants' attention than reading the masque itself. Being there, seated according to your just deserts, was as jealously watched and noted as at any court function—just as where who rode in the procession was a concern of as much moment as the pageant allegories. The emblematic value of masque and triumph may have escaped the observers, but certainly not the emblematic value of the seating plan. Reality lay in the seating plan, which said a good deal more about real power than the wishful idealizations of rulers as Mercury or the good shepherd. That the idealizations were part of everyone's mental furniture helps explain the ease with which Dryden can speak of Charles as David; that they had become self-conscious—"poor and absurd"—perhaps explains his playful irony and theatricalizing of the role.[30]

Still, like Dryden, the devisors of these shows had a serious purpose, the same purpose that lay behind Charles V's initiatory fetes. Praise of the ruler is posited always on his unifying capacity, on his ability to bring a disparate world into cohesion, whether through Christian values or Platonic hierarchizing, economics or crusades. Like the masque writers, the City poets are hyperconsciously political men, fully aware of the forces they must imagine into cohesion. Take for example Tatham. Like Jonson in the fact that he wrote plays as well as fetes, he wrote plays rife with the conflicts of his time, understood as factional socioeconomic power struggles. Like Jonson, he took sides. While his canon begins in 1632 with a run-of-the-mill pastoral in pedantic couplets, *Love Crowns the End,* he moved, like his fellow Royalist Davenant, to *The Distracted State* in 1641, a topically relevant political drama, which was for some reason allowed printing in 1651. Its printing is strange because, while it is too bad a play to raise a rebellion, it does deal in awkward matter. A pro-Charles, anti-Scots diatribe against self-aggrandizing factioneers, its plot involves a usurping brother's eventual guilt-ridden suicide. In a typically thin disguise of topical relevance, the scene is set in Sicily with a quasi-

Greek cast, but a Scottish mountebank wanders through to provide the requisite target for anti-Presbyterian satire. The theme, "That crown can ne'er be fast that takes its rise from others' ruin," is developed in messy blank verse that keeps running out of feet, but the language has at least the virtue of being clear and prosaic, a quality that Tatham accounted a virtue, for, as he claims in the prologue to *The Rump,* "Truth doth need no dresses."

The Rump being a comedy is not apt to require "language three-stories high" or "star-tearing strains," as Tatham notes, remarking on comic decorum. Neither did its immediate predecessor *The Scotch Figgaries* (printed 1652) wherein Tatham again joined the campaign against the fading sect, continuing his berating of the Scots in ungainly dialect. Like *The Rump, The Scotch Figgeries* is a rather vicious play, telling us a great deal more about the ire engaged in in print and felt toward the Presbyterians in London in the early fifties than about human nature or the power of language. *The Rump* itself, if one can trust title pages at all, was not just printed, but acted "many times with great appleause at the Private House in Dorset Court," a direct subversion of the closure of the theatre that appears to have been more and more frequently overlooked as the fifties wore on. The play also sustained at least two editions, the first of which Pepys bought and the second of which righted all the names "suppressed" by reversal earlier (Lambert had been Bertlam, Whitelock Lockwhite, etc.).[31] That Tatham's royalism remained constant throughout his career is underscored by the fact of the indefatigable Mrs. Behn having made use of this play for her *Roundhead; or the Good Old Cause* in 1682. He is of the loyal party which, he is pleased to assure us in the prologue, is made up of "the better men." The worse men and their ladies are all travestied in the piece *in propria persona,* the chief object of satire being the parvenu Bertlams. Tatham's fear/hatred of the disorder attendant upon the ubiquitous appearance of upstarts he sees unleashed by the war and the death of Cromwell is typified in the treatment of Lady Bertlam for the particular and, for the general, a lively group of prentices calling for a free Parliament. Neither target is very artfully attacked, though the prentices have a scary dramatic vitality; yet art is far less important to Tatham than political effect. He was a perfect choice for City Poet over these years, representing its desire for a conservative, politically latitudinarian settlement, its social attitudes, its ongoing rejection of all extremes and its scapegoating identification of severe Puritanism with the evils of radical politics.

Tatham's own character emerges more clearly in a short piece of prose that he published "in the year that the saints are disappointed, 1660" than in the plays. Not that "The Character of the Rump" is inconsonant with the plays, but here he has the medium to express himself directly and enough rope to hang himself before posterity— enough space for gabbling on about "rumps" and "arses" (a type of humor that fills the plays, too, but there tied to character) and enough audacity, given the year, to take on folk he should have had the sense to avoid—Milton, Harrington, and Needham. Victory perhaps went to his head.[32] Throughout, Tatham's fear of change is uppermost. He regards the trio, and especially Milton, as dangerous because individualistic and novel, untried. His own royalism is protected by time-honored conservatism: don't pull out the crooked brick and risk bringing down the whole building. The people know their rights under monarchy; should they surrender these "and cancel their present happinesse which they are sure of, for the expectance of a better condition at the will and pleasure of new masters?"

I speak of Tatham not because he is an unsung literary giant—he surely is not. Yet he is the City Poet across the years of restoration, the singer of Charles and of the forces responsible for Charles's return. The Lord Mayor's shows resumed several years before the official return; *The Rump* was acted while Monk was in power; the City's power did not wait on the Crown's situation, but rather, as always, vice versa. Tatham was no hack, if what we mean by that label is someone whose pen is for sale to the highest bidder. He is absolutely consistent ideologically throughout his career, expressing the notions of the people who hired him to write city pageants, but also of himself. However ephemeral Tatham's work, it shows us clearly the attitude underlying Charles's resumption of power, and it shows that attitude to us in the forms and language of traditional epideixis. Tatham did nothing to expand or enliven those forms as in a few years Thomas Jordan would, with both music and social satire. In the seventies, the questions of the status of farmers, of the relation of County and City would be reopened; for now, praise is all that is wanted.

Some integrity Tatham did have. That he ever felt threatened, like Pepys, by the embarrassing emergence of an earlier flirtation with Roundhead ideas and associations seems all but impossible. He maintained better than many in London its conviction that venturing was adventuring, that the best government was one that allowed the venture to continue without innovation in its ordered, traditional, hierarchical way. This deplatonized code will play a fuller and fuller role in the literature of the second half of the century as other forms of hierarchy weaken under the pressure of Stuart error and social change. It will reach its apotheosis in the Purcell/Dryden *King Arthur,* an opera that elaborates the theme in the style kept alive throughout the century by civic fetes like the Lord Mayor's shows, whose banality the opera tries to transform by a witty conjunction of the shows with Davenant's style of idealization, to which I now turn.

── 4 ──

Conversion: Davenant

Whatever my defenses for Tatham, John Dennis would indubitably have put him in that class of "scribblers" he considered the inevitable poetic result of the political disruptions of the mid-century. He excepted from that large class a small group of "true Poets," most of whom had escaped to the continent and to most of whom history has not been so kind. Given Dennis's didactic, Longinian, and nationalistic convictions, William Davenant is not surprisingly prominent among them, for Davenant's poetic and theatrical efforts are highly affective, overwhelmingly pedagogic, and thumpingly British, as adamant services to the Crown as his nonliterary life itself. His commitments in the latter doubtless opened possibilities for the former, opera coming to England through the hands of a man who had, besides an abiding interest in musical theatre and indefatigable energy, the court connections without which no such endeavor saw success in Europe.[1]

Davenant was from the beginning primarily a comic dramatist and court masque writer, working from 1635 to 1640 with Inigo Jones to produce the final masques of Charles's reign: *The Temple of Love, The Triumphs of the Prince d'Amour, Britannia Triumphans, Luminalia,* and, at the end, *Salmacida Spolia.*[2] In both these and the plays he wrote before and after the Commonwealth, one sees not so much the follower of Shakespeare he advertised himself to be as the inheritor, however effective, of Jonson. Though Davenant did stage a laudable number of Shakespeare's plays after the Restoration, he did so in revisions that conceptualize the Shakespearean text along lines derived from

101

his preeminently Jonsonian sense of drama. The purpose of this chapter is to articulate that sense and to analyze both its rationale and formal effects. The ultimate goal is a better understanding of *The Siege of Rhodes,* a work that grows directly from his earlier experience both in the theatre and in life. Davenant's involvement in royalist politics works, on the surface at least, much to the detriment of what was, despite Dennis's testimonial, a limited talent. Still, that talent was the single most influential shaper of the early Restoration stage and ought for that reason alone to be better understood.

In addition, the products of his response to both Jonson and history are intrinsically important in ways that have been largely ignored or unproductively despised.[3] If we approach *The Siege of Rhodes* through an analysis of the masques, the quality of his response will, I hope, emerge as dramatically effective and culturally significant. It expresses that commitment to history that Walter Benjamin identified as definitive of the baroque theatre, where ultimate reality is sought not in metaphysical legend but in historical physicality and its allegorical interpretation. Benjamin's description of the central characteristic of the German *Trauerspiel* applies as well to the English genre Davenant instituted:

> It is not the conflict with God and Fate, the representation of a primordial past, which is the key to a living sense of national community, but the confirmation of princely virtues, the depiction of princely vices, the insight into diplomacy and the manipulation of all the political schemes, which makes the monarch the main character of the *Trauerspiel* [history replacing myth as the source of meaning].[4]

To understand how Davenant projected this conception we must look at his masques, where I shall stress the use of music, the treatment of comedy, and the quality of allegorization his works entail, using close comparison to Jonson to make Davenant's achievements clear. I shall then go on, with *The Siege of Rhodes* itself, to show how he altered drama toward the general characterization Benjamin formulates, alterations arising in part from the translation of courtly forms into the broader terms required for successful public appeal.

I

Commentary on the Caroline masque has inevitably included remarks on the breakup of its structure in the proliferation of the antimasques and the loss of any pretense to dramatic continuity. Coming to the masque when he did, Davenant is naturally included in these condemnations. Because I see little *dramatic* continuity in any but the very best (from this point of view) earlier masques, the more important definitive features of the late Caroline masques seem to me, on the positive side, what I have stressed in discussing Carew—the direct political and social satire—and, on the negative side, the poverty of the poetry itself. Aside from *Coelum Britannicum*, none of the masques after Jonson's was written by a poet of lyric distinction. That, more than any other quality, is what a masque requires to survive as a single, unified work of literature. Fine as the interaction of Momus and Mercury is, *Coelum Britannicum* would not be a great masque in our traditional terms were it not for the continuation of their themes in the lovely songs of Genius and Eternitie or the Chorus's lyric praises of the queen. No masque stands on the basis of comic or dramatic power alone. Even if we do read the masque primarily as a representation of Platonic politics, its aesthetic value still relies finally on the power of the songs to realize the symbolic meanings, to bring conventional notions to life. Davenant could not write songs, unless we except comic songs and drinking celebrations, of which he has several vigorous specimens. But his lyrical songs dwindle into banality and precisely that ungrounded profusion that condemned the masque to oblivion for years.

He could and did maintain the elaboration of the royalist iconography, as *Britannia Triumphans* well illustrates, if without the depth of classical reference Jonson commands. Through that iconography he develops the same audience-involving "drama" of social celebration, now close to a dream of resurrection, Gordon and Orgel have traced in Jonson. He remains as committed to the didactic ends that are intrinsic to panegyric, restating the *prius-nunc* trope over and over in his undistinguished poetry. Davenant's masques depend upon that iconography so absolutely that when its focus, the king, is absent, the entertainment dwindles finally into an imposing banquet.

I refer with the banquet to the *Triumphs of the Prince d'Amour* (1636), the masque with which the Middle Temple honored the visit of the sons of the old Elector Palatinate, now King of Bohemia, as Prince Charles-Louis sought to reacquire possession of the Palatinate. On this occasion the State was occupied by the princes, Rupert and Charles-Louis, "to whom this entertainment was only directed," and the Prince d'Amour, the Middle Temple's Lord of Misrule, who presented the masque. The king was not in attendance and the queen, who was, quaintly disguised her royalty in bourgeois dress, playing the role of citizen rather than exalted monarch: "the Queene was

pleased to grace the entertaynment by putting of [off] her majesty to
putt on a citizens habitt, and to sit upon the scaffold on the right hand
amongst her subjects."[5]

Perhaps the centrality of the eighteen-year-old Lutheran prince
helps to account for the slenderness of the masque, its lack of the
usual royalist effusions and the simplicity of its claims. No doubt
Davenant's own rather earthy attitude toward Venus accounts for its
directness. There is little here to puzzle over: he adapts the epideictic
movement from the disorder of incivility to the ordered world of
classicized hierarchy in a transformation "on a Sudden" from a set of
alehouses and tobacco shops full of drinking soldiers, sailors, roaring
boys, and impedimenta to a Temple of Mars, surrounded by a structured camp of tents. The first segment of the masque proper then is a
song by the priests of Mars of a battle won, its context "our bold
seditions." Having advanced to the State, the priests continue to sing
"to signify some battle lately fought." Oddly enough, this song is
devoted to the point of view of the losers, though the priests themselves are on the winning side. It is typical of Davenant to stress the
active, the physical, and the pathetic; the portrait of war in the song's
five verses is both graphic and pathetic enough to justify the Chorus's
unvaried repetition.

> Hark! Hark! some groan, and curse uncertain Fate,
> Which us for blood and ruin doth create.

And yet it remains strangely troublesome that the talk of victory and
Fame in the introductory song has led to this Darkness and "disorder'd fear," dejection and pursuit. We had expected celebration, and
Davenant has made room for war's horrors instead by empathically
taking the perspective of the losers.[6]

When the Knights Templar issue from their tents to dance majestically their first entry, they maintain the martial seriousness in ordered
choreography and then take part in an action that suggests that war
itself is under attack here. Cupid offers to sing so that Venus can
subdue Mars as in the old trope; warlike hearts must be "resigned" to
love. While the old Elector had been seen for years as the Protestant
protector and warrior extraordinaire, the Stuart masque generally set
the Stuarts on the side of peace, minimizing martial exploits: war
itself is not to be glamorized. Davenant accommodates both
ideologemes reasonably deftly here, through a Venus far more
graphic than Platonic.

One perhaps ought not be so literal in reading Davenant's iconography, for the masque, read too literally, takes an even stranger turn here, at least for modern eyes, less accustomed than the Caroline audience to accepting the work in terms of its hierarchically independent components. Cupid having discharged his arrows among the knights, the knights retire, the scene changes to a Venetian piazza, and the second antimasque, a parade of five national love humors, postures across the stage. The jealous Italian, the giddy Frenchman seem the knights transmogrified. They are, of course, nothing of the kind and are related to the knights not temporally but thematically. What may strike one now as discontinuity is the capacity of the drama of the time—and with it the masque—to employ contiguous scenes and modes that are related in terms of a conceptualized thematic, an emblem.[7] As such, the humors here act roughly and in a far less sophisticated manner the role of the Falstaff troupe in *Henry V.* In the masque context there is not the slightest chance of their intermingling with the masquers at all, because the masque is committed to their containment, their erasure. Only in developed comedy—and that rarely—do the figures intersect. The assumed barriers between the figures of disorder and the figures of hierarchy are absolute, so much so that antimasque and masque exist side by side in a perceived isolation that comes together only at the level of concept. When the knights reappear on the scene, they are identified by "several adornments, that might present them to every understanding for a troop of noble lovers." The two worlds of masque and antimasque never intersect, the antimasque setting off the beauties of the masque world as foils. The first antimasque's military leftovers serve as foil to the Knights Templar as warriors, the second to the knights as lovers. Together these constitute the cavalier ideal and its projected alternatives. To make these interact requires not masque conceptualization but mimetic drama, the mode of comedy. Though Davenant will turn to that in *Britannia Triumphans,* he does not in the *Prince d'Amour.*

Thus the conclusion of this masque can no more resolve dialectically than the bulk of Jonson's do. The masque overall enacts a repetitive parallel (Davenant's sense of form is always limited to similarly simple structures): perverted antimasque, ideal realization. The final movement superimposes on Mars and Venus, Apollo in his power-of-language avatar; the powers of love and war are united under poetry in its affective guise. The basis on which this is accomplished has little of the moral implication Jonson would attempt for the same purposes. Davenant turns from Apollo as wisdom figure to the literal Apollo as sun king, so literal the fruits of the sun's warmth are brought out to make up the banquet with which the whole will conclude. The triple union of the gods, Mars, Venus, and Apollo, is effected by fiat: the power of poetry is a given. Nor will Davenant resist the physicality of the god:

> Behold, how this conjunction thrives!
> His radiant beams Apollo strives
> So much to strengthen and increase,
> As growth and verdure ne'er should cease.

The conclusion extends this theme, praising plenty as the result of the Cavalier conjunction of powers, ending in the actual banquet, which apparently substituted for the general dance.[8]

I linger with this masque for several reasons. Its very conventionality is undeniably one of Davenant's usual qualities, as also its emphasis on the physical and the pathetic. Its interest for me lies, too, in its ideological similarity to Dryden's much more artfully developed *King Arthur*, years later, a point to be raised when we reach that work. In addition, its characteristics well illustrate my initial description of the Caroline masque. The reputed swelling of the antimasque is not in evidence here, where it is neither disproportionate nor unintegrated with the masque proper. The opposition of the satirically realized masque forms a tight union that banishes the forces of incivility with much the same insouciance, finally, as earlier masques had.[9] The piece suffers no discontinuity read in its own terms. The materialism of Davenant's presentation may distress, but it is hardly more escapist than Jonson's Platonism. Their real difference lies in the nature of the poetry and in the stronger recognition here of opposing forces.

The Jonsonian masque with which the *Prince d'Amour* has externally most in common will help substantiate the point. *Lovers Made Men* (1617) is the only Jacobean masque known to have been continuously set to music, as this is the only Caroline one. They share as well noncourt performance, *Lovers Made Men* having been one of Lord Hays' masques, performed at his home for the French ambassador, Baron du Tour. Like Davenant's, Jonson's lacks the usual regal compliment and centering. Quite possibly most significantly, neither was staged by Inigo Jones. Nicholas Lanier created the setting for *Lovers Made Men* as well as the music; Herbert tells us that "M. Corseilles made the scenes" for the *Prince d'Amour*. Whether through the lack of Jones or noncourt performance, both masques modify heavily the spectacular component, strong in the masques to either side of them in both writers' production.

Internally, they have less in common—the subjects are only partially similar: the resignation to love that forms the second element of Davenant's subject is the whole motive in Jonson. Jonson's Cupid is a figure of Platonized eros that transforms lovers drowned in oblivion into the reveling active figures of "airy parts, / Tried and refined" who dance the first entry. The contention of Mercury and Cupid, wit and eros, resolves in the sparkling eyes of the ladies of the audience. There is no antimasque in this light, lyrical elaboration of old motifs. Davenant's own "Prince d'Amour" refers not to Cupid (who does appear briefly), but to the Middle Temple's Lord of Misrule, the presenter. The title's topicality is part of the masque's realism, the game involved in gentlemen of the Middle Temple taking all the roles here, including the antimasques'. The self-identification with the ordered world of the masque proper is put aside for the jocularity of misrule's topsy-turvy. The masque, in fact, crosses two of the Renaissance's great rituals: court self-projection and the parodic Lord of Misrule. In such a context, claims for the seriousness with which the masque was taken dissolve, the preference is given to satire and to a consciously theatricalized presentation of time-honored themes, that rely far less on lyricism than material argument for their realization. In place of the light Jonsonian pseudo-argument of Mercury and Cupid, we have the enticing physicality of Venus pitted against the pathetic scenes of Mars; in place of Jonson's ironically Dantesque parade of poetically realized lovers,

> Only one
> There is that walks and stops and shakes his head,
> And shuns the rest, as glad to be alone,
> And whispers to himself he is not dead . . .
>
> (ll. 43–46)

we have Davenant's staged lovers, given physical rather than verbal presence in their pantomine. We have neither the music for *Lovers Made Men,* nor the complete music for Davenant's masque, though what we have indicates that Lawes matched the declamatory quality of Davenant's poetry with a declamatory musical style. One can surmise, as Sabol does for Jonson, that the general conception is choreographic rather than literary, and so it is not surprising that the effects remain essentially declamatory in keeping with their discrete emblematic projection.[10] An emblematic rather than emotionally convincing recitation and song is the musical effect.

The references to *stilo recitativo,* as in *Lovers Made Men,* remain obscure, the extent to which Lanier or Ferrabosco may have tried to implement their Italian counterparts' advances quite unclear. But the place of music in the symbology of the Jonsonian masque *is* clear and, in large part, obvious. The extensive music generally accompanies the masque proper, the harmonic world, and takes the form of strophic and through-composed songs. The antimasque, when it uses music, does so often in the form of antic dance, as in *The Masque of Queens* (1609) or indeed in the first shadow of an antimasque in *Hymenaei* (1606) where the four humors and four affections interrupt Reason and Order to Ferrabosco's "kind of contentious music." Mary Chan, who has given us the fullest explication of the music in Jonson's emblematic theatre, can find in the music to which this description is applied little sign of a formal "contentiousness" and posits the likelihood of antic mimicry accompanying the singing.[11] If this is true, even where music accompanies the antimasque, its disorder is visually realized; that is, the choreography rather than the music per se creates the emblem. (This remains true through Purcells' *Dido and Aeneas*, which bears many other memories of the emblematic theatre as well.)

As Jonson's comedic passages enlarge, they do so by moving away from music, by enlarging the use of verbal comedy—dialect speech, a deaf tirewoman travestying Venus, conversation between a cook and poet reflexively examining the whole question of the antimasque's relation to the masque.[12] It is a medium overwhelmingly verbal, most often prosaic. The antimasque music usually remains confined to parading dances that exemplify vices or aberrations, one by one, as in *The Golden Age Restored* (1615) or, in a masque that Davenant may well have had in mind as model to his entertainment for the Elector, Jonson's penultimate, *Love's Triumph Through Callipolis* (1631), which begins with a long parade of national affectations in love "after the manner of the old *pantomimi*."

Tropologically Jonson frequently enough makes music part of the contention between order and the disordering *affetti*, suggesting the struggle that will be resolved by the overwhelming sudden appearance of Light, Wisdom, Reason, or another appropriate opposition. The music itself depends on "antic gesticulation and action" for its communicative function and merely underscores what is given in the other media. It is part of the emblem but as the order of memorialization of the creators of the masque insists, hardly a primary part.[13] This is, of course, not true of the masque considered in its participatory function, since the dance is the means by which the audience becomes one with the masqueraders. The extent to which music remains an emblematic italicizer is dependent on developments within music, of course, but more importantly, so far as music in the theatre is concerned, on developments within the conventions of the uses of music. The roots described here, though, are never lost.

There is a fairly obvious connection between early and late seventeenth century uses of the particular tropological device I have been speaking of here. Jonson created within the antimasque several motifs of disruption that would reappear in altered guises after the Restoration: the Vulcan and Cyclops of *Mercury Vindicated* reappear in Shadwell's *Psyche*, the frozen lovers of *Love Restored* in the brilliant ice masque of *King Arthur*, the witches of *The Masque of Queens* in *Dido and Aeneas*. All of these motifs recur after having undergone some modification in the French theatre, modification that has made them in some cases more dramatically integral, less purely tropological. The fact may be as much a loss as a gain; nonetheless, once the mythology elaborated in Jonson—the essentially magical nature of Platonically conceived regal power that orders the world by sudden metamorphoses—has departed the field, the justification for its antidramatic, metamorphic broken sets goes with it. The substitutions are not always effective, the conventions often hollow, yet in growing out of the comic context Jonson gives them into the drama conceived as a whole action, united and dramatized as integral, rather than an evil or aberration simply to be dispelled, they achieve a flexibility largely absent from the masque in its pure state.

Jonson himself moved in this direction, and Davenant followed him. A masque like *Time Vindicated* (1623) leads more or less directly to *Britannia Triumphans* (1637). By 1623 Jonson had, as we know, made the comic element of the masque the home of not simply an opposition to the courtly ideal but also miniature dramas in their own right, comedy evolving out of the antimasque toward drama, asserting mimesis against allegoresis. Allegory frequently enough wins, as in *Time Vindicated*, where Ears, Eyes, Nose, and Fame give us in conversation a picture of the envy-ridden gossip at St. Paul's walk. None of the characters acquires any definition beyond his moralized abstraction, nor does he need it; they all interact moralistically in much the same manner as the somewhat more fully conceived Cook and Poet of *Neptune's Triumph*.

The difference is largely one that springs from the greater breadth enclosed in vocational types as compared to monolithic moral ones. The developments in comedic expansion during Jonson's masquewriting career produce isolated strong comic interludes separate from the business—and the body—of the masque proper. They unite to it primarily in the thematic and broadly symbolic terms we have seen also in the *Prince d'Amour*. In themselves they develop into comic gems in their own right, pulling against a tropological relation that is at root unchanged.[14]

The fate of the tropological was greater and greater submergence throughout Jonson's career—the gradual early abandonment of Ripa and Alciati, the general simplification of allegory, the intensification and expansion of the comic antimasque—to the point that it is difficult to consider it as antimasque in function any more than in form. At the point that the comic exists in its own right, functioning as the entire entertainment, or all but the compliment and the revels— Christmas of *Christmas His Masque,* Captain Cox of the *Masque of Owls,* the addition to *Pleasure Reconciled to Virtue* of the separately conceived and complete *For the Honor of Wales*—a point Jonson reached more and more frequently as the years went by, he is abandoning masque to a splendid and often surreal array of comedic possibilities and, as often, to mimetic comedy. This is the point Davenant goes on to mine in *Britannia Triumphans,* a masque that retains the complimental function, shows the root tropological relation (of disorder to ordering éclat), but evolves its comic drama with far less regard for masquing than for mimetic drama. Both Jonson and Davenant have joined what I called in chapter 1 the Ariostan line.

Here, after an opening contention between Action and Imposture to which I will shortly return, the work takes on the shape we expect in Stuart masques and follows the usual tropological pattern: Merlin brings on a series of antimasques illustrating the social vices of the day—mountebanks, parasitical courtiers, rebellious leaders— standard stage types. The series of six ends when Bellerophon rides in on Pegasus "most timely, and by inspiration sure," out of the blue. But Bellerophon does not dismiss Merlin's shows immediately. The mountebanks and apemaster depart to be replaced by another show designed to illustrate that it is not only fools but wise knights who are taken in by appearances. It is a scene out of Ariosto, or some far lesser *romanza,* wherein medievalized lady, knight, Saracen, all historically dressed, are involved in a travesty of chivalric romance, labeled by Bellerophon ("How trivial and lost thy visions are!") and dismissed to clear the stage for praise of Charles (Britanocles) and Henrietta Maria (Galatea). By 1637–38 the transformations were not so immediate as they had once been, but just as absolute.

The struggle to retain the transformations is as politically motivated as it is politically revealing. *Britannia Triumphans* encodes Charles's response to the Ship Money fiasco of 1637, to his necessary capitulation to economic and national interests. The Puritan satire in the figure of Imposture, which looks to us now so mild, was strong

enough to be remembered in 1698 by the anonymous partisan of
Collier who in *The Stage Condemn'd* expended nineteen pages of invec-
tive on it.[15] Davenant had carefully and disingenuously defined Imposture as not a Puritan at all but a pure figure of dissimulation and
dissension, who, in creating factions, destroys the possibility of peace.
He seems as much, from our distance, a stock Jesuit as Puritan, but
this hypocrite, like Tartuffe in the climate of his context, clearly was
incendiary. One must imagine Davenant as remarkably naive to think
protestations against such an identification would stand against his
opening emblem: young and lovely Action standing with his willow
and laurel opposite crabbed Imposture, with his angling rod and bag
and horn. If the Puritans chose to see their faces in the type, though,
it was their choice and not Davenant's, who is as careful as Shakespeare had been with Malvolio to limit his reference. If the masques
had become more desperate politically, it was because the times were
politically far more desperate than they had been in 1608 or 1619.
Davenant's masques did not, at any rate, run aground on sheer
panem et circensis (as Shirley's antimasque of cripples and beggars in
The Triumph of Peace [1634] can be said to have done), but on ideology.
Creating a masque that presents Charles as the hero who reigns o'er
seas "reducing what was wild before" to order, in front of a backdrop
of a small fleet that grows before one's eyes greater and greater was
probably only slightly less incendiary than the Puritan Imposture.

In the elaboration of the ideology, the opposition of Cavalier Action
to Puritanic Imposture, the masque adumbrates questions about the
implications of its medium, questions that remain intrinsic to spectacular forms throughout the century. The long colloquy between
Action and Imposture, abetted respectively by Bellerophon and Merlin, has as its subject not the political situation pure and simple, the
moral state of the English people, factionalized and led astray by the
desire for self-interested power, but also, as the names of the principals suggest, the art of the theatre, the art of dissembling and of
feigning. "Wisely," Imposture tells Action,

> the jealous sceptics did suspect
> Reality in every thing, for every thing but seems,
> And borrows the existence it appears
> To have! . . .
> That universally shall take which most
> Doth please, not what pretends at profit and
> Imaginary good.[16]

Action is naturally unconvinced. He knows that

> Fate takes not so little care of those
> For whom it doth preserve the elements,
> For what is chief within us should be quite
> Deprav'd, as we were only born to aim
> At trifles here, like children in their first
> Estate of using legs, to run at sight
> Of bubbles and to leap at noise of bells.
>
> (191)

How to tell the true shows from the false, the mimic apparitions of a cozening magician from the fair displays raised by the offspring of heaven, is left to our reason and the revelation of the faith that guides Action and Bellerophon. But raising the question gives Davenant an excuse—and a good one—for the alternative displays of Merlin's knight versus Saracen and Bellerophon's bringing on Fame and the closing compliment: Britanocles (played, of course, by Charles) clears away the misty clouds of error. Being the ultimate satisfaction of all the senses, he brings them into accord with divine harmony:

> Since all the odour, music, beauteous fire,
> We, in the spring, the spheres, the stars admire
> Is his renew'd and better'd every night!
>
> (159)

The Platonism that supports the regal compliment perhaps has worn a little thin and certainly has a short future, but the questioning of the appeals to the sense doesn't. It will remain a problematic motif of operatic events throughout the seventeenth century. As a sophisticated theatre seems led by its very nature to question, tease out, elaborate the reflexive themes of appearance, dream states, life as a play, so spectacular music theatre is led to elaborate the same theatrical themes with a special emphasis on the fallibility of the senses and their conflict with rationality—the Platonic, the Boethian themes. As we know, Davenant certainly did not invent them, nor even introduce them to the Caroline masque, Townshend having developed his comic material expressly around the Platonic theme in 1631, but Davenant develops them creditably here, granted that his own audience was perhaps more interested in the topical level of negative satire easily wrung from the show. They probably felt the same way about Malvolio. Davenant had at least a sardonic enough sense to allow Imposture a telling remark on Bellerophon's reality:

> Cry mercy, Sir!
> You are Heroic virtue, who pretend

An embassy from heaven, and that y'are sent
To make new lovers here on earth.

(197)

Of course, this is the voice of Hypocrisy, so one should not wonder "what makes you any more real than Merlin's ladies 'of yore?'" But one does. One hears not merely tropological opposition, but the non-Cavalier resistance to the whole enterprise of masque. Dryden will ask the same question in *King Arthur*, without the convenience of a Neo-platonic reply—or of a Charles to play the role of Britanocles.

Three points need stressing: simplest, that the iconography that the masques implement remains identical with that of the Jacobean years; second, that the proliferation of antimasques is as much a response to the social realities of the 1630s as to the audiences' desire to be distracted with foolery; and finally, that Davenant's interest in the perceived unreality of the theatrical argues against a capitulation to the illusionism fostered by Jones's Italianate advances of the stage.

On the first point I have nothing at all to add to what the iconographers have told us. I raise it here only to stress continuity and refer the reader to Strong on *Britannia Triumphans* and Gordon on *Salmacida Spolia*. Gordon takes Davenant as typical enough to use *Salmacida Spolia* as his exemplary text in an essay formulating the ways and means of Renaissance roles and mysteries. The code was by now endemic to the form.

On the second, I would reiterate that the increase in antimasques, if we are speaking of the antimasque proper, those entries that the times themselves called the antimasque, merely continues a development well under weigh by the 1620s. If we speak instead of the broader, more amorphous tropological opposition of disorder to ideal reality, we can note, with Orgel, with how much greater effort the harmony of Jonson's later masques is asserted than of the early. Generalizing on the quarter century of Jonson's masque production is a precarious business, yet I think a reading through the masques will not deny Welsford's old sense that the antimasque becomes destructive to form, if not adventitious. What is for Welsford formal destruction is for Orgel a more herculean educative effort. In either case, one is seeing the impinging of social reality on absolute idealization. If the masque itself encodes the Court's own vision of its power and the antimasque its raison d'être, we can expect the proportions to shift as the years go by. They did in the social drama and, unless the poets were as blind as Gordon assures us the Court was, that ought to be reflected in society's expression of itself, however displaced. The same concern emerges, as I have said, in the City pageants where Heywood's 1639 *Londini Status Pacatus* hopefully, wishfully presents the horrors of war in the comforting guise of its Continental and not English occurrence, taking the occasion to exhort the populace to compare our blessed peace to our neighbor nation's "throwes."

The essential point on which Jonson's masque content differs from that of his successors is his resistance to the strings of separate emblematic entries in the antimasque proper, though it should be noted that most of those strings constitute together one gigantic disruption per masque. The sense of disorder that results from first, mountebanks, then monkey trainers, then drunken sailors is no doubt the sense desired, the weight of that confusion the ideal world is threatened by in the 1630s. That the confusion is presented visually rather than verbally is, of course, to the disadvantage of the later masques considered as literature, though it makes its point about the inarticulate irrationality of the enemy rather well. Jonson's great advances in the integration of mimetic comedy into the masque world— always finally subverted, forcibly contained with idealism—are continued by his successors in the clever conversation between Publius and Platonicus in *Albion's Triumph,* in the marvelous leaping prose of Momus in *Coelum Britannicum,* in Davenant's Imposture.[17] In all of these, with their varying responses to the functional necessity of the form, the symbolic subversion of comic energy is awkward finally only because the mission itself is awkward.

Of the third point, one may say that the masque, being the most elaborately artificial form of its day, could hardly be unaffected by the pressure toward icastic imitation exerted by and on all Renaissance art forms and especially in the theatre, which, in the Jacobean years in England, achieved a degree of "reality" that still takes one's breath away. But like the visual arts, the theatre, even when it had created that degree, chose not to surrender either its freedom from the merely real nor its capacity to order nature according to its desire. These are the terms in which the Renaissance itself would see the choice, in even so ambivalent a view as Bacon's. He warns so strenuously against mistaking the patterns of the mind for the patterns of nature, because he recognizes the power of the desire to do so.[18] That choice, and the unavoidable consciousness of having made it, strengthens in the face of the developing illusionism of the theatre.

Throughout the later sixteenth and the seventeenth centuries, the theatre commented on itself as the non-real, not only Platonically to call the real itself into question but also to establish its own representational claims. No serious writer who worked in idealizing modes avoided—or sought to avoid—the implications of his subjunctivity. Before he wrote *Le Cid,* Corneille wrote *L'Illusion Comique,* which differs from a modernist version of the same theme, from, for instance Pirandello, by insisting on arresting the regress, on coming to a final, known resting place, where the hall of mirrors reflects finally not another mirror, but the true. It is because of the arrest that the work of idealization can proceed without cynicism, and it is also because of the assurance that arrest is possible that the ludic undetaking can go on. The topos *theatrum mundi* is as old as Western theatre, but at no time was the stage as assured of its own perfection and concerned for the solidity of its ontological basis as during the Renaissance—and therefore as committed to playing its self-symbolic games. We know from Shakespeare studies since at least Anne (Righter) Barton's *Shakespeare and the Idea of the Play* how extensively Shakespeare pursued this theme and from Jackson Cope's *The Theater and the Dream* how widespread its theatrical elaboration was.[19] It seems now eminently natural that the masque world and the burgeoning operatic stage, with their intense artificiality should have taken it up, and they did—sometimes to amusing ends, sometimes as merely a prologue trope, but always with the nervous effect of a self-consciousness registered, a confession made, no amendment to follow.

II

The result of the confession may seem negligible—until we turn to Davenant's second political venture, the heroic play, where such self-consciousness is not immediately visible and therefore the artificiality of the genre subject to a kind of attack the masques themselves averted by second-guessing. It has always been clear that the heroic plays, which Dryden traced to *The Siege of Rhodes,* were not interested in mirroring life by photographing it. It has been less clear what they instead wanted to do and succeeded in doing for the audiences that for a brief while loved them. If they seem foolish in their unreality now, so did they then, for it is on precisely those grounds that Buckingham et al. satirized them parodically in *The Rehearsal,* a step that would have been wasted on the pointedly artificial, nonmimetic masques.

It is relevant that a member of the court produced the parody. Overall, the heroic plays are recognized as being time bound and time explicable. Their vogue coincides with the euphoric years, heady but short, of the boisterously hopeful attitudes attendant upon the Restoration proper. That they were always preeminently a royalist form is only emphasized by their parodic attack coming from within the charmed circle, a version of allowed foolery. When substantial attacks on the theatre are mounted, they will come from without, and they will have none of the sophisticated good nature of Buckingham's self-assurance. What Buckingham was attacking, other than the egos of individual writers, is already evident in *The Siege of Rhodes,* though there it exists in far too chaste a manner to have called up *The Rehearsal.* The superman, the fustian, the otherworldly single-mindedness of the actors will become far more pronounced in the years and plays to follow, but they all exist in embryo here, where, as Parsons pointed out, one is confronted not by people but by masquelike abstractions, by Honour, Love, Magnanimity, and Jealousy personified, who act out the clear and simplified plot line—rather, the situations—of a masque, a fact Davenant is well aware of when he calls the figures chessmen in the prologue to the second part.

As with most of the masques, the music does not survive, so it is no longer possibe to know what music may have contributed to complex-ifying the characters, turning them away from masque, toward drama. We do know that Henry Lawes and Matthew Locke, the best theatrical composers of the mid-century, supplied the music for three of the five entries, and we can conjecture from their surviving work what that might have meant. But the likelihood that it would have changed the nature of the figures rather than the intensity of their expression seems slim. Locke's music for the masque in *The Empress of Morocco* and for *Macbeth* brilliantly underscores the emotional content of the text, heightens it by objectifying it, but it does not change it in the direction of complexity.[20] For that to happen, the possibility of the music changing the text must exist—adding, subverting, commenting ironically: there is little reason to think from Lawes's or Locke's extant theatrical music that they would have done so. That they would have heightened and intensified the text in a declamatory mode seems more likely, making the emotions and their conflict stand out in even higher relief. What modulation of feelings, blending one into the next, what positing of conflicted emotion palpably realized may have been accomplished must remain hopeful speculation.

Davenant, at any rate, apparently did not consider such possibilities the value of music setting; in his indirect comment on *recitativo,* through the musician in *The Play-House to be Lett,* he defines its use with the same commonplace Dryden was to repeat in the introduction to the *Instrumental Music for The Prophetess:*

> Recitative Musick is not compos'd
> Of matter so familiar, as may serve

> For every low occasion of discourse.
> In Tragedy, the language of the Stage
> Is rais'd above the common dialect,
> Our passions rising with the height of Verse;
> And Vocal Musick adds new wings to all
> The flights of Poetry.[21]

Perhaps it is because of the commonplace nature of such pronouncements that Davenant's seriousness about using music has remained suspect over the centuries. Nethercot and Harbage, the major authorities on Davenant since the thirties, were quite convinced that *The Siege of Rhodes* was conceived as a play, the music added later to subvert Puritan censorship. Thus Harbage will say of the work that it was "conceived originally as a musical drama to be rendered in *stilo recitativo*" (243), yet he consistently treats the music as a subterfuge to get around the censors (e.g., 123–31). Dent shares the literary scholars' sense and makes the case that *The Siege of Rhodes* was written in couplets as a heroic play and then subjected to cut and paste to be allowed production. This would explain for Dent both its metrical irregularities without one's having to assume *stilo recitativo* composition and also what Dent considered its peculiarity as drama: a succession of short episodes wherein nothing happens.[22]

Though we do have Dryden's word for the Dent/Harbage view, we also have his rather different explanation of the work's metrical "irregularity": according to the "Essay of Dramatic Poesy," it is a Pindaric, with no suggestion of cut and paste. Since Dryden's memory has been known to slip on other occasions, succeeding scholarship has been willing to overlook his testimony and try to take the work at face value, as I do here. That effort was spurred first less by the perceived intrinsic value of the work than by the recognition of forgotten external facts. John Freehafer brought forward both the theatre patent granted Davenant in 1639, as evidence that his interest in bringing music to the stage far antedates *The Siege of Rhodes,* and the patent of 1660, which Fruehafer claimed *required* that Davenant adapt Shakespeare. Freehafer's claim has been called into question in a way that itself asserts motives for Davenant's works that tend to dismiss the old sense that all difficulties with Davenant are referrable to his status as exploitative entrepreneur, and we are left with the clear question of the rationale of the work.[23]

Among critics as well as historians there has been some effort recently to see *The Siege of Rhodes* in a kinder light than it has enjoyed in years. Most effective, I think, is Philip Parsons' essay, cited earlier, which recognizes Davenant as a consistent theatrical writer and *The Siege of Rhodes* as substantively the culmination of his prewar intentions. One can reject Parson's "total theatre" notion without demeaning his presentation of Davenant's value and its specification of Davenant's debt to the masque.[24] The old claim, fostered by Davenant himself, that he is the conveyer of the Elizabethan acting tradition from Shakespeare to Betterton should not be extended to character conception and should not hide from us either his Jonsonian roots or what aspect of Shakespeare he successfully promulgated in a new age, his greatest success being the adaptation of *The Tempest* he shared with the young Dryden. While adaptation may or may not have been required, surely Raddadi is right to assume that what form the adaptations took tells us something about what Davenant found theatrically attractive in Shakespeare. Those features, I would argue, are such as assimilate most readily to an essentially conceptual style, the style of the masques and of the heroic plays whose interest lies in the verbalization and visualization of abstract ideas analytically conceived rather than in the mimetic representation of complex psychological entities. As a result, the "Shakespearean tradition" that Davenant carried on for the British stage could bear at least as much resemblance to the French theatre of his more recent memory—to Corneille and Mairet—as it did to the Elizabethans as we understand them now. It bore even more to the Jonsonian masque and comedy—in its conception of character, its abstraction of design, and its production values.

This is consonant with the consensus of criticism now on Restoration drama, which, for all its disagreements and variety, acknowledges the relevance of baroque rubrics, emphasizing momentary passional tableaux, affective and analytic in conception and intent, qualities clearly visible in *The Siege of Rhodes'* serial nature that troubled Dent so. Character analytically conceived and serial structure go hand in hand because, as I argued in speaking of *Henry VIII*, they subvert causality, creating a world—and reflecting a world—that must be referred to providence. Serial construction is well adapted to both passional tableaux and analytic plot treatment for the obvious reason that in addition to emotional concentration it abets the scenic isolation of concepts. What we lose in cumulative force we gain in developmental clarity of ideas—the feature that led Brecht to reject Aristotelian plot as he did Aristotelian identification. Brecht's motives were, after all, not very different from Davenant's in the sense at least that both are essential ideologues who, like Dryden, found the honor of the writer's calling in its didactic function and the primary function sociopolitical. I mention Brecht because it has been too easy and too generally ready a response to see baroque effect standing alone, assaulting the sensorium in the effort to reproduce homeopathically the desired emotion from the audience. There is truth in Parsons' argument that such efforts ultimately took over the stage—that passional tableaux gave way to passionate drama, to melodrama, and that in the hands of Settle and Lee the route struck by Davenant led to a kind of "total theatre" that enlists all the media toward the quasi-Wagnerian effects Parsons analyzes so effectively. But it is reductive to read Davenant's intentions back from Lee. It is particularly so if it requires one's reading out Dryden, as Parsons does, on the grounds that, unlike Settle or Otway, Dryden was constitutionally incapable of allowing emotional effect to reign supreme and *thus* departs this theatre.

What did Davenant ask of music? If we take him at his commonplace word, simply that it add wings to the poetry, in that presumably unexamined homeopathy where "our passions" refers to both the actors' and the audience's. Music is a further means to objectify the emotions, much as Davenant's declamatory poetry, with its stolid materialistic tropes and figures, does, a means of putting before the audience the objective realization of the subjective state. It is not strange that Davenant would look to music for this service since we know, from the preface to *Gondibert,* that he considered music the legendary act of completion of heroic poetry, the act that assured its affective force. There, too, the intention is politically didactic. We remain in the commonplace—not particularly exciting yet no less considerable for our purpose, understanding Davenant's enterprise.

Superficially Davenant gave *The Siege of Rhodes* the appearance of opera as he understood it—that is, as masque or *ballet de cour*—by dividing it into entries rather than acts. We can pass this by as superficial musicalizing to get by the censors, as is so often done, or we can note that the entries are our first indication that we are dealing in serial form and the avoidance of causal plot. The entry implies not, as the act does, a segment of action, but simply the appearance of the performer as performer for his segment of the unified emblem. Typical of the conscious artificiality of the forms that employed it, the "entry" points to the performer as performer, just as the "act" points at the action as a unified image of enacted life. The second part of *The Siege of Rhodes* abandons the label, assuring those who see Davenant subverting censorship that they are right. Perhaps they are. It is the case, certainly, that the second part is more a "play" than the first.[25]

In fact, the history of the play's text records its steady movement away from the initial experiment through the addition of Roxolana in the second quarto and the addition, therefore, of the marital involvements she brings into the play. Similarly, the elaborate scenic descriptions of the first part are eliminated from the text of part two, giving it, at least on the printed page, a far less operatic appearance than part one. At a level below the purely mechanical, part two also abandons a second and less superficial operatic quality: its acts, unlike part one's entries, are not organized toward climactic musical events.

In part one there are five entries, each one enclosing the display of a public, then a private virtue and its attendant emotion, closing off in a chorus that comments ironically (intensified in the later text) on what has been staged. Honor, Love, and Magnanimity are presented in various guises, Alphonso, Ianthe, and Solyman respectively being primarily identified with one virtue, though Ianthe and Solyman, the two paragons of the piece, are given situations to display all the virtues one by one. The remarkable fact about the work is not so much what Dent was bothered by—its serial presentation of inaction—as its lack of conflict, absent until the third entry when Jealousy at last enters. Before Roxolana was added to the text, Jealousy itself had little presence, represented in the practically perfect Alphonso. We are accustomed in Renaissance drama to the background political action environing and giving rise to a foregrounded private action whose significance it resonates. Something like that may be what Davenant had in mind here—the dissension posited behind the Christian forces perhaps paralleling the dissension caused in the love interest by Alphonso's jealousy. But because the political dissension is merely posited (it exists back in Europe) and not enacted (the united nations of Christian soldiery is more unified in the opera than in *Henry V*), the parallel has no force, and any that it might have is dispersed in the virtual death wish that unites the army and separates the lovers. Here, the nature of Davenant's own royalist dreams obtrudes, the heroes of lost causes becoming splendid in their willingness to die, the glory of absolutism declaring itself in subverting that desire.

What saves the lovers and, for the nonce, the army is the Magnanimity of Solyman, whose commitment to exactly the code of honor that holds Alphonso and the Christians, rescues them against their wishes. As in political romance generally in the Renaissance—in Ariosto, in Tasso, in the Moorish novel—the internationalism of the moral code overrides the nationalism of the specific themes. Only the glory of extraordinary men rises above the generic splendors of the code. Because this is an opera, not an epic, that glory is located essentially in the two male figures, Alphonso and Solyman, and their feminine counterpart, Ianthe. The rest of the dramatis personae are potentially equally noble, but too vestigial to crowd the spotlight or the score. In part two, Davenant will gesture toward real conflict, suggesting a triangular love interest on the Christian side with the Admiral's desire for Ianthe; but because perfect virtue cannot be disturbed in the Christian camp, the Admiral consciously displaces his love in Iago-like gestures against Solyman, and the triangle never develops. As a second effort in the same direction, the successive rewritings of the piece led, by the reissue of the second quarto, to the addition of a new interest in Roxolana. Her role creates one of those "double Walks" that Davenant called the "chief ornament belonging to a History Dramatically digested," but that the length of recitative performance and the limitation of available performers had prevented him from using initially.[26] The addition of Roxolana changes nothing in essence in the printed text, since she is purely a parallel to Alphonso, tightening the symmetry of the work but fading on the printed page to mere chiasmic duplication. Pepys admired her so inordinately that one must assume that she added a great deal to performance, more probably, than a new soprano voice to the ensemble.

The dramatic digestion of a history was, in Davenant's mind, an emblematic process, as his metaphors reveal: "Turns and Counterturns . . . double Walkes, and interweavings of design." To make a drama of historical material is to cast it in a visual pattern that reveals its placement and movements in space. More a dance than a drama, it has little need for conflict to sustain it, but for pattern and symmetry, proportion and rhythm—for musical qualities whatever the specifics of the opera's actual score. This description of drama applies to all of Davenant's dramatic works, though he develops it here in the historical context. Asking for character in the usual sense makes as little sense as asking for choreography in a Flaubertian novel. While the text's history records, as one of the effects of performance reception, a move toward the comic thickening of character interest, character here generally accords, even after the changes, with emblematic visualization. Ianthe does most pointedly in her famous veiled entry:

> *Mustapha.*   This is *Ianthe,* the Cicilian flower,
>   Sweeter than Buds unfolded in a Shower;
>   Bride to *Alphonso,* who in Rhodes so long
>   The Theam has been of each Heroick Song;
>   And she for his relief those Gallies fraught;
>   Both stow'd with what her Dow'r and Jewels bought.
> *Solyman.*   O wond'rous virtue of a Christian Wife!

> Advent'ring lifes support and then her Life
> To save her ruin'd Lord! Bid her unvail!   Ianthe *steps back.*
> *Ianthe.*   It were more honor, Sultan, to assail
> A publique strength against thy forces bent
> Than to unwall this private Tenement.
>
> (2. 2. 70–81)

Succeeding discussion elaborates the moral emblem. This emblematic conception and elaboration connects Davenant's plays to his masques as absolutely as the distanced abstraction of their meaning does. The physical objectification of form is continuous from masque to play and rigorously limits any illusion of extemporaneity. As each entry alternates between the two loci, the public political situation and the private love story, it moves between two sets of images that rigidly encode the same notions in the same form.

In calling the two levels "public" and "private," I use misleading designations, though they are Davenant's own. There is little that is private about the personal action, as public in its conception and enactment as the historical plot. In both cases what we see is the emotion engendered by the situation depicted, and whether the case be personal or public, the response is unvarying. Having conceived his jealous conviction that Solyman's kindness to Ianthe and himself is motivated by Solyman's desire to acquire Ianthe, Alphonso faces her in what is their most personal encounter:

> *Alphonso.*   Had Heav'n that Passe-port for our freedom sent
> I would have chosen some better Instrument
> Than faithlesse *Solyman.*
> *Ianthe.*   O say not so!
> To strike and wound the virtue of your Foe
> Is cruelty, which war does not allow:
> Sure he has better words deserv'd from you.
> *Alphonso.*   From me Ianthe, No;
> What he deserved from you, you best must know.
> *Ianthe.*   What means my Lord?
> *Alphonso.*   For I confess, I must
> The poyson'd bounties of a Foe mistrust:
> And when upon the bait I look,
> Though all seem fair, suspect the Hook.
> *Ianthe.*   He though a Foe, is generous and true:
> What he hath done declares what he will do.
> *Alphonso.*   He in two Days your high esteem has won:
> What he would do I know; who knows what he has done.
>
> (4. 2. 27–44)

The scene goes on to discuss and display Alphonso's jealousy in further fits of sarcasm till Ianthe is left alone on the stage to lament

the fall from honor entailed in this loss of trust. Her lament is rhyth-
mically quite fine; it is one of the sections of the work one would love
to have Locke's setting for—in part for the sheer pleasure and in part
to know to what extent music would offset the thinness of Davenant's
verbal imagination. That imagination seems incapable of arising to
the melodramatically rich situation conceived for this woman committed now to death in the face of the dishonor of her lover's suspicion. Opera has for generations thrived splendidly on precisely such
moments, usually with precious little need of help from the libretto's
fabric.

But we haven't that music and so note that what is remarkable
here—and peculiar to mid-seventeenth-century serious drama—is
neither the lament nor the irony. Hamlet could be more sarcastic with
Ophelia, DeFlores with Beatrice-Joanna. What is remarkable is the
extent to which the public and the private share precisely the same
limiting language. Characters like Alphonso and Ianthe, Solyman and
Roxolana need only one vocabulary because they have only one "set"
on the world, only one perspective in terms of which they apprehend
all their experience and in terms of which we therefore apprehend
them. That is the perspective created by their exalted and absolute
values, realized on the stage or page in their linguistic univalence.
Because they speak in one mode only, and that a rigid one, there is no
conflict between their public and private being. All their essential
values are in complete harmony.

Such conflicts as exist in the play do so because of misapprehension
of the motives of others or because of external conflicting goals. The
loss of personality in such characters is not, as is often claimed, a
result of the character's lacking interiority. Alphonso's jealousy is certainly Davenant's representation of an interior life. It is rather that
the interior life is in full harmony with the historical world, with
public life, a state we find hard to take seriously. These are Chapman's
"whole men" and women who, facing a situation wherein public requirements and personal desires create a potentially conflicted situation, experience remarkably little difficulty in choosing the public by
bringing the personal into line with it. They are the descendents of
Henry V. If there is a struggle, it is usually suppressed as in one of the
grandest examples, the Infanta in Corneille's *Le Cid,* whose splendid
visceral emotionality is simply abandoned as the play draws to its
conclusion. Corneille created for her the sort of situation in which we
want to see worked out the struggle between her love for Roderigo
and her public necessity. The circumstances are not unlike Cimena's
own: her lover her father's slayer, now the national hero and her fated

husband. Each of the women could have given Racine material for a tragedy that would have resolved their situations in monumental despair. Corneille leaves them both unresolved, concluding the play in a tense ultimatium that each should find herself in duty's execution.

In England, for twenty years and more, characters presented as particular representations of the human and not as representations of individual identities, characters as generic as Descartes' description of the passions, where individual difference is deviance, create a world in which those characters who achieve literary individuality are extreme enough types to seem *sui generis*—Maximin and Saint Catherine in *Tyrannic Love,* for instance, but no one in Davenant. In his heroic plays there is no conflict between the demands of the world and the demands of the self; *The Siege of Rhodes* elaborates emotional states, but not conflicted states. This is what makes Davenant's work so strange, so particular in the history of drama—and what he handed on in varying degrees to his successors. Later heroic plays would present us with less absolute characters, especially among villainous females. Dryden would depart the field altogether precisely to adapt one of the most remarkably conflicted gentlemen of the stage. And yet not one of the serious Restoration plays, including *All for Love,* succeeded in creating images of the human that later years could believe. Their virtues remain their artificiality, their success in positing analyzed emotion and effectually portraying it in its analyzed forms. Their appeal is effective largely with those—the number has never been great—who can enjoy the distance such analysis implies. On these grounds I would argue against the opposition of affect to reason. An appeal to the audience's emotions is not an assult on the sensorium if the appeal is conceptually clear. It remains so in Davenant, as in Dryden. This is a question I shall discuss in detail in the next chapter, when Dryden is my subject, but it is, I think, relevant to make the point here.

In place of conflict embodied within a character, *The Siege of Rhodes* gives us the same conflict that the masques had, though it is pushed off to the side, or rather, to be literal, down to the end—the ends of each entry. Here the choral passages are given their chance to react to the events within the heroic tale. A range of possibilities is elaborated, all having one thing in common—they call into question the relevance of exalted virtue and *virtu* to common life. Davenant follows out the usual masque formula by proposing the educative function, the model nature of the long-suffering virtue of an Ianthe, the martial valor of an Alphonso. Yet the staged pupils seem less than model students. Instead they bring us down to realistic expectations, soldiers pumping up their own morale or wives telling the husbands who have just suggested Ianthe be their model:

> You that would teach us what your wives ought to do,
> Take heed; there's a pattern in town, too, for you.
> > Be you but Alphonsos, and we,
> > Perhaps Ianthes will be.
> *Men.*　Be you but Ianthes, and we
> > Alphonsos a while will be.

At the end of each entry (this is the third) Davenant manages thus to take another perspective on his heroes without specifically satirizing them. In doing so, he introduces another voice to the work, rescuing it from the monodic. The resolution of the conflict between *l'homme moyen sensuel* and Solymanic magnanimity in model making is, of course, intellectually suspect, resolving as it does little of the true question, which was raised by Williams in *Henry V,* but the impossibility of answering it means the death of heroes, and Davenant—and a sizable audience—still wanted heroes.

That desire commits Davenant to an epipoetic and therefore antinaturalistic style. His commitment to ideal imitation and its politically didactic uses was, Dryden would agree, well met by that style. And yet the question, what has this to do with real life, continually obtrudes in his work. That is perhaps the strongest mark of an intellectual integrity in the man. When Laura Brown sees his choice of an aristocratic heroic action as imposing on his work a necessarily limited aristocratic form, it seems to me she has taken the action itself as the whole of the work and skirted its true form, which springs from a theatrical tradition, aristocratic but not unself-conscious, and not uncritical of its own values. In the end, it is true, Davenant chooses aristocracy, as his audience also did for a number of years. The best explanation for why that choice found the form it did seems to me to come not from literary studies alone, which can explain masque sources and Corneillean influences, but from the historians and anthropologists who try to look at culture before literature has mediated it, "impossible" as that may be.

For many of them, the experience of Charles's beheading and the events leading up to it ought to have produced exactly Davenant's career. For Victor Turner, conflict responses in the real world take the form of "social dramas that universally display an agonistic pattern of four phases: breach, crisis, redress, and reintegration or recognition of schism."[27] While it is obvious that Turner's scheme has not itself escaped literary mediation, it is useful to understanding the experience of the Stuart courtly world in a universal context:

> Social dramas occur within groups of persons who share values and interests and who have a real or alleged common history. The main actors are persons for whom the group has a high value priority. Most of us have what I call our "star" group or groups to which we owe our deepest loyalty and whose fate is for us of the greatest personal concern. It is the one with which a person identifies most deeply and in which he finds fulfillment of his major social and personal desires. (P. 149)

The "breach" that sets the social drama into perceptible motion is an incident of infraction of a rule of morality, law, or custom in some public arena; an incident that may be deliberate—a challenge to entrenched authority or a spontaneous emergence "from a scene of heated feelings." The crisis precipitated exposes "the current factional struggle within the relevant social group" and "beneath it there becomes slowly visible the less plastic, more durable, but nevertheless gradually changing social structure, made up of relations which are relatively constant and consistent" (p. 151).

In Turner's view not only the response to crisis, "the adjustive and redressive mechanisms brought into operation by leading members of the disturbed group up to and including the performance of public ritual," but also the enactment of the breach and crisis itself are governed to some extent by the learned narratives of the culture that give the actor a frame of procedure for initiating, extending, and bringing to conclusion the crisis. Turner developed his paradigm from the study of Ndembu culture, but it is clear, as he acknowledges by reference to the *Poetics* (p. 153) that the paradigm itself is a Western and literary construct pertaining at least as well to *Antigone* as to Ndembu history. The universality of the claim need not trouble us. Unlike the anthropologist, the English literary historian is considering a culture that he shares with his subject. Insofar as the Turner paradigm is a Western construct, the actors of the seventeenth century share it with Aristotle and with Turner as Turner's classic example, the conduct of agons of Thomas Becket with Henry II and the bishops, makes evident. The story of the fall of the Stuarts, with its crisis that turned out to be a catastasis, is a second, equally clear example. Or rather, a protracted series of examples, eighty-five years of history containing a long series of social dramas and not a single identifiable event. What I am interested in here is the place of literature in the series. For Turner "it is the third phase of the social drama, redress, that has most to do with the genesis and sustentation of cultural genres, both 'high' and 'folk,' oral and literate." Among the Ndembu, when conflict exists that is not amenable to rational settlement—when, that is, "claims are advanced under different social principles, which are inconsistent with one another even to the point of mutual contradiction," sorcery and ultimately rituals of reconciliation are performed (p. 155).

Michael Walzer saw in the beheading of Charles as of Louis XIV just such a ritual as the anthropologist posits here and saw it in terms harmonious with both Marvell's "Horatian Ode" and Geertz's "model of" and "model for," the distinction I relied on in chapter 1. It is a ritual generating changes in the social order and its governmental expression that are fulfilled by succeeding history on "Christian" models of order. Geertz himself objects to Walzer's sense that the ritual of king-killing altered French and English life irrevocably, "that is, that the rituals were availing."[28] But specifying the degree of efficacy of ritual in a sophisticated culture is highly problematic. It is in such societies that ritual is displaced into other forms of poesis, into tragedy, comedy, epic, and less-distanced forms—the masque, the City pageant, the heroic play, whose connection to the rite is more immediate and more dependent than that of fully displaced forms. The death of the masque as masque, its evolution into musical entertainment coincides with the effective death of ritual even as ceremony, when the resolution of suprarational conflict passed fully from symbolic reenactment to the legalistic rationalism that has struggled with it ever since. In a sophisticated society, which no longer believes in the real efficacy of ritual, its place is usually taken by other forms of poesis. But seventeenth-century England was not yet clearly such a culture. The hold of the forms of ritual within its framework is attested by not only Christianity but the very literary forms we have been concerned with.

The desperation of the masque in the 1630s is indeed the last gasp of that form's ritual efforts. When the masque returns after Charles's beheading, it is no longer ritual in any sense, but an essentially musical dramatic form, its participatory revels, memory. New forms could be expected to emerge with the reemergence of the "star group" in the late fifties, its triumph in 1660, so long as critical conditions obtained. The form emerged in the heroic play. These plays, with an appeal now so difficult to understand, enacted something resembling an exorcism of the Interregnum demons—of rebellion, of individualism, of antimonarchism—and thus their close and problematic relation to Hobbes and Hobbist themes, even when written by anti-Hobbists. As "model for" the heroic plays offer the Hobbist answer to cultural disarray—the single mighty sovereign; as "model of" they are far more conservative than Hobbes, insisting on a picture of order that emanates from one rational heroic center, who holds the destiny of the culture in his own hands, which are not those of the individual, but the heroic type. The literary model is of course Aeneas, but the cultural need is the Civil War.

Davenent's own canon is illustrative. In 1634 he wrote the play *Love and Honor,* frequently pointed to as the nascent heroic play, largely one must believe, on the strength of its title.[29] The play involves a bewildering array of little conflicts, none of them love and honor, all practically unmotivated displays of altruistic love contingent on the capture of the princess of Milan. This is played off against the purely self-interested desire with which the comic subplot is rife—and where such life as the play has exists. If one could imagine *Tyrannick Love* without Maximin and with its Christianity displaced by familial devotion, one would have a good sense of what *Love and Honor* has to offer. But one cannot, of course, imagine *Tyrannick Love* without Maximin any more than without Saint Catherine. The saint is Dryden's own necessity; the central superhuman male Davenant's post-Caroline addition.

The extent to whch the Court was more than willing to encourage the self-enactment that Davenant's idealizations involve is clear in Downes's report of the revival of *Love and Honor* for the opening of Dorset Garden:

> The play was richly cloath'd; the King giving Mr. *Betterton* his Coronation Suit, in which, he acted the part of Prince *Alvaro* [the philosophical, pure-hearted heir to the throne]; the Duke of *York* giving Mr. *Harris* his, who did Prince *Prospero* [the right-minded, but naive warrior]; and my Lord of *Oxford* gave Mr. *Joseph Price* his, who did *Lionel,* the Duke of *Parma's* son ["so young, and fill'd with thoughts so excellent / That they surprise my wonder more than love!"]; *The Duke* [senex of the piece, converted in the end by miraculous identity discoveries] was acted by Mr. *Lilliston,*

predictably with the aid of no one's coronation suit.[30] We are practically back in the masque world at this public celebration of royalism and its new theatre. Yet everything has changed. It is only the King's suit and not the King himself that will parade across the stage, the vestments and chasubles, not the body. But I think we make an error if we mark this down as simply one among many instances of the aristocracy giving its old clothes to the theatre. Coronation suits find their way to museums today presumably because back in some shadowy time they contained magical power—consider saints' relics—which became symbolic value, which then became the purely historic interest they have now. In 1661 the value was still at least symbolic, or the careful distribution of the costumes would have been otiose. Davenant, at any rate, continued to celebrate Britanocles in Solyman and Alphonso, though he had to do it in the body of a Betterton or a Captain Henry Cook.

The short-lived success of the vogue has been attributed often, as I have said, to the euphoria of the Restoration. In the heroic play that euphoria created, a displaced ritualistic form; that form—both when it is and when it is not practically (that is, theatrically) effective—is always "a cultural statement about cultural order as against a cultural void." Moore and Meyerhoff continue in *Secular Ritual:* "Ceremony is a declaration against indeterminacy. Through form and formality it celebrates man-made meaning, the culturally determinate, the regulated, the named, and the explained. It banishes from consideration the basic questions raised by the made-upness of culture, its malleability, its alterability."[31] For the anthropologist Turner it is precisely the determinate nature of ceremony that separates it from true ritual, which "does not portray a dualistic, almost Manichean, struggle between order and void. . . . It is rather a transformative self-immolation of order as present constituted, even sometimes a voluntary *sparagmos* or self-dismemberment of order" (p. 164). Charles I, who had vigorously involved himself in theatrical castings of the drama of his life (the most famous, of course, being the suit to the Spanish princess that turned masque into fiasco), found himself finally in the position to enact true ritual, a self-immolation, a *sparagmos* less than voluntary, but so remarkably effective that the writer of *Eikon Basilike* could create of the role the most effective ideological statement of the Civil War, one that Milton could try to counter only by subjecting its narrative to a rigorously demystifying exegesis, destroying its Christological pretensions in the revelation of its borrowings from French romance.

Or rather, attempting to destroy. Reason might say Milton's hermeneutics were devastating, but the general will among star groupers, not just Tatham, moved otherwise, and the "king's book" remained a talisman. By 1660 there were few in London who did not count themselves among the star groupers, few who were not, like Pepys, nervous about the surfacing of any earlier associations with the Puritans in a climate that reasserted the essential orthodoxies of Church and Crown. Benjamin considered absolutism definitive for the continental baroque—for its general style as well as its theatre. The English baroque reasserts absolutism on the stage in precisely the guises he stresses: tyrant and martyr as the two faces of sovereignty; Maximin and Don Sebastian are only the greatest examples. *Tyrannick Love* is, I suppose, the purest of the type, but it has a remarkable number of lesser fellows, works whose effort is to contemplate absolutism in its most extreme forms—the Eastern potentate, the late Roman emperor—and to find it winning a *lieto fine* in domestic virtue, either early in its heroic center or later in its ingenues. Davenant's pattern, based on the idealized relation of Charles and Henrietta Maria, stressed equally her valor and her chastity and established a pattern that led, it seems now ineluctably, to the bourgeois end wherein private, individual happiness must fill in for empire and every dramatization of history be supplied with an underwalk of private emotionality whereby the failure of the public world can be redeemed or its successes celebrated. Davenant's second thoughts were to make Solyman not simply a great Eastern potentate, but a married man. If Roxolana is no Xantippe, still she rules the bedroom and threatens the peace of the world ruler as lineal antecedent to Dryden's domesticated Cleopatra and many other more licit ladies. Solyman's awareness of and caution before her threats of nocturnal dissension are the stuff of comedy, and the intrusion of the politics of the bedroom into the play, adumbrated in part one's additions and fully developed in part two, mark a turn away from the emblematic conceptual of the heroic to the bourgeois domestic of comedy on Davenant's part, a break he continued to move between in his next work as well. It is perhaps a trivialization, one that Dryden tried to make right in a series of women as potent as Solyman himself—Nourmahal and Lyndraraxa—but he came round at last to *his* Cleopatra via such heroines as Berenice of *Tyrannick Love.*

The domestication of the imperial hero is always a difficult business, as act 5 of *Henry V* makes patent. At no point does the intrinsic undercutting of the heroic myth by mere reality come closer to the surface than in marriage. The perspective of the wife, like the valet's, cannot be given on the heroic center if he is to remain pure in his absolutism. By the end of *The Siege of Rhodes,* Solyman has become in one sense a person even as you and I, but not because he has fought a war—rather because he has Roxolana. It is significant for the times that she and not he was the beloved character who gave her name to her impersonator—and that twenty years before domestic drama won the boards. It was in domestication and the ironic choice of the Chorus that the act of conciliation was dramatized in the recognition of the distance between the life of the common man and the imperial heroes. Humor is in most cultures a potent weapon of redress; it finally, and shakily, integrates the two worlds of the masque here.

── 5 ──

Dryden's Recapitulation

During the 1650s and 1660s, Davenant's musical stage productions move between two poles: some are clearly masque-descended, political and continuing the general effort of *The Siege of Rhodes* to celebrate a great leader in a peripherally demotic context; some are far more closely connected to contemporary French theatre, either by way of direct borrowing of texts or through the adoption of its ballet. Since the *ballet de cour* is the French correspondent of the English masque, similarly staged and shaped and equivalently intended, the poles tend to come together, making Davenant's interest in the French not difficult to understand. There seems little indication in his work that he tried, like Richard Fleckno, to go to the Italians for his musical theatrical ideas. Fleckno recognized that the Italians were the masters of recitative and the leaders in devising musical means to dramatic representation, but he had none of Davenant's court connections, and therefore his knowledge, in effect, lay fallow. Davenant, either because his masque background made the French more assimilable or simply because he did not know the Italians, persisted along the Jonsonian line.[1]

The outcome of his cumulative ventures, which I shall briefly characterize, was to give England two forms. The second, the ambigué or semi-opera, was even less favorably viewed by later times than the first, the heroic play. A sense of its generic success is available in the fact that its most popular example, *The Beggar's Opera,* is, like *The Rehearsal,* a parody of its kind. These semi-operas, which in their serious manifestations seem so odd now, were as ambivalently received in their own day. Roger North was certain they all sustained "a fatall objection: they break unity, and distract the audience. Some come for the play and hate the musick," and some vice versa. No one is satisfied. On the other side, a partisan, like George Granville, who wrote one—*The British Enchanters*—believed North's vice a virtue: ambigués allowed *vraisemblance* in the action while retaining music's lyric potentiality, making these operas the "highest delight" of public spectacles.[2]

North traced the form to Settle's *Empress of Morocco,* forgetting or ignoring the fact that the Davenant/Dryden *Tempest* antedates it by at least three years.[3] In fact, it is to Davenant that we owe the genre. Since it is the form, as North noted, ushering in fully sung opera, and since virtually all of that was imported from Italy, the ambigué is as close as England managed to get to the real thing, barring that handfull of sports *Albion and Albanius, Dido and Aeneas, Venus and Adonis.* Given the number of them produced, one can also say that, fatally flawed as they may be, the ambigués had an appeal far broader and longer lived than the heroic play, whose plot they usually borrow. Given the plot borrowing, they are very closely related to English drama's most troublesome rara avis and extend its life on into the eighteenth century, quite possibly because, despite Granville's conviction of vraisemblance in the spoken part, they are so honestly unreal. Whatever else it does, the music makes them far more varied in their realization than the naked heroic play could hope to be and frees them from some of the pressures of imitation.

Variety, the freedom to experiment, is the signal quality of Davenant's post-*Siege of Rhodes* productions. Before he discovered in the adaptation of *The Tempest* what was to become a far more prolific formula than a spoken *Siege of Rhodes,* he mounted a group of plays that explore what both music and the French have to offer his new theatre: *The History of Sir Francis Drake* (1658), *The Cruelty of the Spaniards in Peru* (1659), and then *A Playhouse to Be Let* (1663). This last work is homologous to Davenant's whole project of 1656 to 1663. It combines the two earlier works with two farces in a compendium of tryouts all staged as just that—tryouts of the public taste for the newly opened theatre. About the farces, a free translation of Molière's *Cocu Imaginaire* and a travesty of the Antony and Cleopatra story, the less said the better, though Maidment and Logan considered the latter estimable as the first burlesque drama in England, holding the boards into the eighteenth century.[4] The farces show us one of Davenant's estimates of the audience, and the latter's success proves he was not wrong. They bracket two far more interesting works, all four strung together on the premise of a playhouse vacant for rental during the

Term vacation. The premise gives him that standard conglomeration of theatrical types who watch the tryouts and respond mundanely to the hopeful applicants. Davenant's prologue probably refers to this frame when he claims of his "disjoyned and yet united" members that "in the whole contexture they agree." The frame conversations, reminiscent of Jonson's entr'acte discussions (for example, *The Magnetic Lady*), very lightly tie the mass together and allow us the sort of view of theatrical matters I cited in the last chapter.

The works of interest to me here are musical and political. Malone decided (and Maidment and Logal follow him in thinking) that *The Cruelty of the Spaniards in Peru* is an opportunistic piece, allowed production because of Cromwell's hatred of the Spanish. Gosse was as certain that it reflects Charles's anti-Spanish stance. It is, in either case, a striking example of masque techniques adapted to the public stage for clear political purposes, whatever the specific topical motive, which need not detain us. The play is proffered by a dancing master and consists of six ballet entries. Each entry has its emblematic set, before which a dumb show is enacted, the whole explicated by the Priest of the Sun; the theme of his speech is followed up in a song and dance. The burden of the piece is, naturally given the form, historicopolitical, tracing the Incas' decline from a golden age of innocence and peaceful harmony under natural law—Montaigne's, not Hobbes's state of nature—through the internal breakup of a kingdom split among rival claimants and the attendant introduction of the profit motive. The new motive makes the Spanish conquest easy, gold having replaced honor as the motivating force behind public action. In the final entry, the British bring the promise of delivery.

Dent described *Cruelty* as reminiscent of Davenant's first Commonwealth theatrical, *The First Day's Entertainment at Rutland House* (May 1656)—a sort of lecture-recital of declamations with music for whose form he could posit no French (despite the dancing) nor Italian (despite the music) source.[5] While Hedbäck took Dent efficiently to task on the same point with regard to *The Siege of Rhodes*, her claim that the Italian opera does provide parallels is thinly supported and, I think, unnecessary. The principles involved here are all available in the English masque once it had turned, as it did during the thirties, from an expressly moral into an expressly political medium. Again, as Benjamin insisted of the baroque, the historically based abstractions of the piece are imagined physically. *Cruelty*'s plot, even more diagrammatically developed than that of *The Siege of Rhodes*, is a historical frame for the material representation of conceptualized conflict. It puts before us in the most complete form Davenant could imagine allegorized, rationalized values, the music employed as emblematically as the sets, everything aimed at concretizing the abstract point of the scene. So, for example, the fifth entry opens with "A Doleful Pavin" played over the scene change "which represents a dark Prison at great distance." Engines of torment are farther off and

> Two Spaniards are likewise discover'd, sitting in their Cloaks, and appearing more solemn in Ruffs, . . . the one turning a spit, whilst the other is basting an Indian Prince, which is rosted at an artificial fire. This object having remain'd a while, the Priest of the Sun enters.
> (P. 111)[6]

And moralizes the picture in a speech that makes nonsense of the Spanish claim to bearing its share of the white man's burden:

> What Race is this, who for our punishment
> Pretend that they in haste from Heav'n were sent,
> As just destroyers of idolatry?
> Yet will they not permit
> We should our Idolls quit,
> Because the Christian law makes converts free.
>
> (P. 111)

The condemnation of the Spanish is, of course, the justification of the British, as it continued to be for several centuries. The gestures toward selective internationalism reflect, to be sure, general European statecraft as much as Charles's or Cromwell's particular policies and are duplicated in *The History of Sir Francis Drake.* In both, Davenant is fully aware of the financial basis of international policy and its mercantile connections, and in *Drake,* as in *The Siege of Rhodes,* he stresses the need for cooperation against—as in Shakespeare's Lancastrian plays—a common enemy.

Davenant, too, in his far more limited way posits a single great man whose charisma generates order on a limited scale. His sense of the poet's task in this regard is stated most simply in the Epistle Dedicatory to *The Siege of Rhodes* where, having justified the simplicity of his characters as efforts " to render the *Ideas* of Greatness & Vertue" both pleasing and familiar, he goes on to excoriate those who attack hierarchical stage models:

> My Lord, it proceeds from the same mind, not to be pleas'd with Princes on the Stage, and not to affect them in the Throne; for those are ever most inclin'd to break the Mirrour, who are unwilling to see the Images of such as have just authority over their guilt.
> (A₂ v)

As hierarchy is a necessary postulate of the social order celebrated in all Davenant's emblematic political theatre, so it is a necessity of the form in which that order is enacted. We see this most obviously in the pitching of solo voices against the massed voices of the common men: as the working out of international cooperation is based on a common enemy to unite factions in terms of their own self-interests, so the working out of internal order is based on a common enemy—the gross desires that run unchecked among the common men. Drake does not so much control his predatory and voracious troops as allow them their natural bent in order to get the work done. Where the *Siege of Rhodes* was carefully organized toward choric resumes of the model potential of the heroic centers, the solo voices, *The History of Sir Francis Drake* allows the commoners' songs to overflow the play, both undermining the model affect and effectively parodying the heroic concept a dozen years before *The Rehearsal* did its more destructive job. Drake himself remains a mirror, expressing "the *Ideas* of Greatness and Vertue," but his context calls the Ideas' value into question. One begins to wonder if there is any saving the common man. The writers were always aware of the irony that question produced.

I

Dryden picks up precisely this point in his two operas two and three decades later.[7] *Albion and Albanius,* originally intended as a prologue on the French model, quite probably for *King Arthur* in some lost original state, is in its own terms simply a fully composed masque. It is one of Dryden's bitterest and most painful works, bitter in its content, painful in the way of bad art. What began its life as a frank prologue, praising Charles as Quinault praised Louis in those slightly displaced pastorals that filled the Jeu de Paulme with light, dancers, and *gloire*, became with the death of Charles, a theatrical version of Rubens's Whitehall ceiling, a fictive apotheosis. It unfortunately spends decidedly too much time on the enemy: the antimasque Tyranny, Zeal, and Democracy create the usual royalist bugaboos of factionalism and disorder, though Thames and Augusta early assure us that "A Commonwealth's a Load / Our old Imperial Flood / Shall never, never, never bear again" (1.1.114–6).[8]

The poetry rarely rises above that level, though Dryden did supply his composer, Grabu, a few good songs and one outstanding theatrical occasion: act 2 scene 1's gory Hell and its lines that ring ironic reversals on Milton's fallen angels. The devils get to laugh in chorus, and if, as Franklin Zimmerman in praising them admits, "the effect

falls considerably below that achieved by Purcell in the witches' chor-
uses in *Dido and Aeneas*," they are at least as chilling as the Lully/
Quinault satyrs of *Les Fetes de l'Amour et de Baccus* (1672), one of the
best of their sources.[9] The laughing devils have as little chance of
winning their conflict as masque evils ever do, yet they are emblematically fine, far more attractive than the depressingly tired crew, Tyranny, Zeal, and Democracy.

The substantive praise of Charles that goes beyond reiteration of
the Stuart Imperial iconography is aimed at his services to trade and
the navy that supports it. While James's accession to the throne before
the opera reached its final form may explain the stress on the navy,
the emphasis on trade is endemic to the whole—and unified—
conception. Mercury, the god of trade here as in Heywood's City
pageants, opens the opera before the Royal Exchange and sets up a
series of nautical and mercantile symbols that buoy Albion's progress
to the imperium and his country's escape from democracy. To measure the distance between Jonson's version of the Imperial dream and
Dryden's more mundane one, one need only make the comparison
Earl Miner suggests when he declares Dryden's treatment of this
theme comparable to that of *Neptune's Triumph*, conflating Jonson's
health and peace with Dryden's wealth and peace.[10] The conflation
seems to me a disservice to both writers, ignoring the hopeful moralism of the one, and the beseiged realism of the other.

The theme is elaborated much more fully in a far better work, *King
Arthur*, and honestly elaborated as well, a feat in the context of these
epideictic theatricals. It is in this work that Dryden brings to its logical
conclusion the masque line of the theatre, if we consider the masque
from the point of view of its epideictic function. *King Arthur* is the
fulfillment of Dryden's and Davenant's and, I daresay, some of Jonson's intentions, even perhaps down to the spectator becoming "what
he watched."

II

The major difficulty in semi-operas is the one that even Granville
was aware of: the integration of two disparate and distinct modes and
media. In the case of the sort of musical comedy integration that
became the rule after the turn of the century, speakers turn into
singers as the occasion arises, so that even in fully composed pieces,
in, for instance, Congreve's *Semele* or Addison's *Rosamund,* the characters move directly from apparent speech to song. The tendency is
inevitably toward the comic, toward, in fact, farce.[11] Those lines that

can lead easily and smoothly into song are apt to be themselves rather easy and a little too smooth to embody either serious thought or intense emotion. The German *Singspiele,* the most successful combination of spoken text and song, is by and large comic, up to and probably including *Die Zauberflöte.* Molière's collaborations with Lully are similar; and even in that remarkable meeting, Quinault was called on to write the song texts with that simplicity he had mastered in the *ballets de cour.* Left to themselves, Congreve and Addison, the best of the writers who tried the form, created creditable works, but works that had no success at the time or later.

Congreve follows a *tragedie lyrique* model and competes emotionally with the French for two acts, but lacking recitative competence, his isolation of the text to sheer emotion unsupported by action or lyrical conviction creates the true insipid by the third act. Congreve may not have intended "When I languish with Anguish, / And tenderly sigh, / Can you leave me, deceive me / And scornfully fly?" to be funny, however many internal rhymes, but it is, even if it were not coming from the mouth of Jupiter. Addison quite recognized this and made *Rosamund* a parodic comedy from beginning to end, and a good one, in a broad way. It is the sort of comedy that has Sir Trusty, Knight of the Bower, undercutting every word spoken by the high characters and every romance device Addison can work in. It is the sort of comedy that first comic opera and then vaudeville have thrived on ever since, deriving half their laughs from the absurdity of strutting Catos breaking into song.[12] Sir Trusty's response to Rosamund's scene 2 plaint is a perfect example of Addison's procedures:

> What savage Tiger would not pity
> A Damsel so distressed and pretty!
> But hah! A Sound my Bow'r invades   [*Trumpets flourish*]
> And Echo's through the winding Shades;
> 'Tis Henry's March! The Tune I know:
> A Messenger! It must be so.[13]

Little surprise that Rosamund is resurrected to a convent after her draught of the Queen's poison while Sir Trusty simply wakes up, fulfilling tragedy, and comedy, and moral didacticism in one prop.

But Dryden was in search of something quite different in *King Arthur.* While the work is not solemn—not even sober, its overall intention is consonant with the function of its intended prologue. It is regal praise of the masque sort: intense, absolute, and fully self-aware. The monarch has changed since the initial conception, but not the poet's role. Drama here is absorbed into masque, extending Jonson's and

Davenant's own procedure with a latitude that would perhaps have stunned his predecessors. The more usual course, deriving from the Davenant/Dryden *Tempest,* had been to accomplish the integration of spoken and sung drama in precisely the opposite order. By creating a dramatic situation in which the principles could conceivably be expected to watch a masque, the writer would supply precisely that. Vraisemblance would not be violated, and music and machines would flood the stage. *The Empress of Morocco,* the Betterton *Prophetess,* Shadwell's *Tempest* all use this maneuver. It was a particularly useful way to update the old plays inherited by the two companies in 1660. In reversing the procedure, Dryden was following out the most fully articulated conception of opera produced in England at the time. It is a ceremonial conception and a festive one. It relies, as *King Arthur* itself does, on a thoroughly conceptual tradition, hardly removed from allegory, still closely tied to the stark emblematics of the masque iconography and, as such, opposed to the psychologically mimetic representations then crowding it off the stage, in both Shakespearean imitation and she-tragedy. The tradition suits Dryden's ideal imitation as it did Davenant's; it answers not to realistic mimesis but to concept and to the didactic function that justified epideictics from the beginning.

Thinking of opera in generic terms, as he did all literary forms, Dryden devised a *translatio studii* in the preface to *Albion and Albanius* that ascribes to opera a purpose that, if it is reductive, is also basically historically accurate: in Italy the "first operas seem to have been intended for the celebration of the marriages of their princes, or for the magnificence of some general time of joy"; to illustrate the purpose, he instances the general practices of the carnivals of Venice, Rome, Savoy, and Florence, "and at Turin particularly, was performed the *Pastor Fido* written by the famous Guarini, which is a pastoral opera," whose prologue has given the French their ubiquitous design, "a compliment to the sovereign power by some god or goddess; so that it looks no less than a kind of embassy from heaven to earth" (p. 3).

He attaches this purpose to a famous descriptive definition: "An *Opera* is a poetical Tale, or Fiction, represented by Vocal and Instrumental Music; adorn'd with Scenes, Machines, and Dancing. The suppos'd Persons of this musical Drama are generally supernatural, as Gods, and Goddesses, and *Heroes,*" "Heroes who are supposed to be their peculiar care," he adds a page later, but the value of the supernatural he develops almost immediately: "The Subject, therefore, being extended beyond the Limits of Human Nature, admits of that sort of marvellous and surprising conduct which is rejected in other Plays

. . . because where gods are introduced second causes are out of doors" (p. 3).

We have then three points: opera's function is (1) to be a public celebration in (2) the form of a scenic musical fiction that (3) involves the supernatural. Of the three, the musical medium proves the most dispensable in Dryden's practice, though he apologizes for its loss: the mixed mode of a work like *The Tempest* or *King Arthur* "cannot properly be called a Play, because the action of it is suppos'd to be conducted sometimes by supernatural means or Magick; nor an *Opera*, because the Story of it is not sung" (p. 10). Turning from *Albion and Albanius* to *King Arthur*, he gave up much of the singing, but not the freedom from probability that music implied. His description of Corneille's *Andromede* in the "Essay of Dramatic Poesy" repeats the same principle.[14] Nor did he abandon public celebration, as act 5 makes palpable. I want now to look closely at each of these three points both as the work exemplifies and as Dryden's relevant prose elaborates them, in order to clarify Dryden's intentions and to show how the work fulfills and, in fact, exceeds them.

In emphasizing the supernatural, Dryden was accepting as definitive the one element shared among plays of the time that made them opera for less theoretically interested observers—the machines.[15] For Dryden this had a special literary significance, since he had already spoken in warm defense of the epic machines and now, in opera, found the perfect stage for their appearance. It was virtually impossible to implement them in a Christian epic, Dryden would note with sadness eight years after *Albion and Albanius* in the "Discourse Concerning Satire" and again in the letter to John Dennis, but on the operatic stage the only condition on their use was propriety. They are one of the wings that poetry had added to prose and that music now can add to a poetry fettered by the demands of probability. Agreeing with Boileau that the loss of the machines eliminated a major source of the "strength and beauty" of the classical epics, Dryden speaks immediately in both the "Discourse" and the letter of his own "hint" to retain them by combining Platonic notions of the spirits with the Christian idea of national guardian angels; he also had in mind two likely subjects: King Arthur's defeat of the Saxons and the Black Prince's defeat of the Spanish. And while he was never to write his Christian epic, he had by this time already written his epopoetic opera. Yet in *King Arthur*, though he availed himself of the freedom from probability the form implies, he brought a god onto the stage only in the illusory ice masque of act 3 and reserved the rest until the final triumphant masque when the action had been concluded. They never touch the action. Mars would apparently have seemed as indecorous to Dryden as to us, acting in a play with King Arthur and Merlin, even if he were doing his traditional job, in complete propriety, as Mercury does in *Albion and Albanius*'s fully sung world. Such guardian angels of the nations as might appear in the Christian world of Arthurian romance must be other than classical gods. They also must be handled in such a way as to avoid the problem that Dryden found most troublesome in Tasso's and Ariosto's treatments of the marvelous: the dramatic and moral implications that arose from heroes displaced by supernatural forces. He cites as instances St. Michael in *Orlando furioso*, Cant. 14, and the same angel in *Gerusalemme liberata*, Cant. 9, where the implicit foreordination of the outcome not only destroys the suspense of the drama, but also calls into question the moral nature of the heroes:

> What pleasure, what entertainment, can be raised from so pitiful a machine? where we see the success of the battle from the very beginning of it? unless that, as we are Christians, we are glad that we have gotten God on our side, to maul our enemies, when we cannot do the work ourselves?[16]

What sort of substitutes for the classical gods will retain their beauty and yet skirt the problems? Dryden contends that "Christian poets have not hitherto been acquainted with their own strength," which lies, for his purposes, in the Book of Daniel and its "doctrine almost universally received by Christians" of "guardian angels appointed by God Almighty as his viceregents, for the protection and government of cities, provinces, kingdoms, and monarchies." If this ecumenical notion—and its ecumenism is of obvious value on the public stage in 1691—were only "accomodated with the principles of Platonic philosophy as it is now Christianized" the result would be as strong "an engine for the working up heroic poetry, in our religion, as that of the Ancients has been to raise theirs by all the fables of their gods" ("Discourse," pp. 88–89). What Dryden had in mind as the process of accommodation is further clarified by his discussion of the genii in his "Life of Plutarch." There, in an interesting passage that begins with Dryden insisting on the rational open-mindedness of Plutarch to spiritual notions, he turns to the Greek's explanation of the cessation of the oracles: "He seems to assert the *Pythagorean* Doctrine of the Transmigration of Souls" when he assorts under a single almighty power "Genii, or Daemons, of a middle nature, betwixt Divine and Human." Dryden's description of these genii continues as a close parallel to what he depicts in Philidel and Grimbald, who are the positive and negative aspects of spirits who have "purg'd off the grossness and faeculency of their earthly being" and "from thence either rais'd higher into an aetherial life, if they continue virtuous, or tumbled down again. . . . after they have lost that purity.[17]

Dryden's digression on the genii concludes with a discussion of Plutarch's describing the activities of the genii of the British Islands of the Heroes, certain that Plutarch means "our *Druydes,* who were nearest to the *Pythagoreans* of any sect; and this opinion of the *Genii* might probably be one of theirs" ("Plutarch," 256). Thus the appearance of genii in *King Arthur* would be justified to Dryden on native historical grounds, neither an anachronism nor without propriety. Anglicized Platonism becomes the means to Christianize syncretically the machines of both the classical and the barbaric fables. Dryden concludes the excursus with his own reasonable explanation of the cessation of the oracles: they had been the result of "Enthusiasm" caused by "natural vapors," and, as the vapors diminished in strength, so the oracles were "decreas'd by the same measures." Personal genii cannot, of course, be accounted for in this materialist manner; they are, as in the case of Socrates, "no more than the strength of his imagination; or to speak in the language of a Christian *Platonist,* his Guardian Angel" ("Plutarch," 257).

These personal guardian angels may seem of little concern in the mythic plot of *King Arthur* since the angels Dryden refers to in both texts dealing with his epic machines are pointedly identified with the national guardians described in Chapter 10 of Daniel. And it seems likely that the conversation among the Britons that opens the opera, setting the date of this last battle between Saxons and Britons as Saint George's day, refers us to the true guardian angel of whom Merlin is the romantic avatar, directing and protecting Arthur and his forces in explicit conflict with the Saxon's parallel magus. They conflict in exactly the manner proposed in "A Discourse Concerning Satire," evil spirits contending with the good as allowed forces within divine discretion (pp. 90–91). Saint George himself appears only verbally in the opera when Honour sings of him in the final revelation of the Order of the Garter. The personal genii as expressions of "the strength of his imagination" are of concern, however, in realizing the mode of activity of the supernatural powers of the opera. They literally translate us from the plane of history, however mythic, to the plane of the imagination, from the world of the word to the world of the ear and eye, from verse to music.

The apotheosis of this power of movement occurs in the final act, where once again Daniel is a source. For Daniel supplies, along with as

guardian angel notion, the apocalyptic framework that the closing act
of *King Arthur* appropriates. Where the rest of the operatic episodes
of the play are integrated, with a high degree of success, with the
spoken action from which they emerge, the final masque—swollen to
gross proportions on the face of it—is relevant to the preceding action
only as a vision offered Arthur by Merlin of the history of the land he
has founded by defeating the Saxons. In the tradition of epideixis and
like the angel in Daniel 11–12, Merlin presents a prophecy of the
triumph of British power and glory which, unlike Daniel, pretty well
ignores the difficulties the nation shall suffer through on its way to
ultimate success.[18] Arthur, in one of his few obvious displays of wisdom, deduces their omission.

The nature of his hero is unavoidably affected by Merlin's power,
despite Dryden's consciousness of the implicit difficulties. Anxious to
avoid what had troubled him in Tasso and Ariosto, he made several
efforts to forestall the impression of foreordination, to retain suspense and protect his hero's force, both physical and moral. None of
the efforts is entirely successful, from the point of view, at least, of a
mimesis at all realistic, the point of view that his remarks on the
Italians implies. Thus in act 4 when Arthur faces his illusory temptation, thoroughly warned of the illusory nature of the place and protected, as the audience knows, by Philidel, he has a speech that
attempts with minimal effect to call the outcome into question—or at
least to dramatize his apprehension. Thus too the final act of the play,
a single combat between Arthur and Oswald, is almost irrelevant to
the action, unnecessary though not unprepared for. It is an occasion
to create momentary suspense and to return active force from Merlin
to Arthur, but it does not really work—in part because we continue to
believe its ending is foreordained and in part because the magi are
still there, interfering every step of the way.

The most important effort toward avoiding Tasso's problem is, of
course, the one Dryden offered in the "Discourse": the inclusion of
evil spirits who "have a permitted power from God of acting ill"—
Oswald, as in the single combat, and Grimbald, who employs that
power of cunning and fraud Dryden admired so much in the Uriel
incident in *Paradise Lost* (Watson, *Dramatic Poesy,* 2 : 91). In act 2, Grimbald presents himself to Arthur as a shepherd and tries to lead Arthur
and his men to destruction in a bog. The scene is one of the best
musical passages in the opera, an echo song that expresses both the
capacity of evil to take on the appearance of good and the ordered
confusion Arthur's troupe is subjected to as Grimbald and Philidel
contest for their belief. And yet, dramatically the scene is defused, for

before it occurs we have been assured that Merlin knows exactly what is going on. The trial is more a test of Arthur's ability to read signs (or conceivably, his preparedness for grace) than a complication in the action that requires unraveling or creates tension.

This is for us a common difficulty of early music drama, and all Dryden's efforts and theorizing do not save *King Arthur* from it. One unavoidable result of the seductive machines is precisely that suppression of human agency Dryden thought Tasso could have avoided simply by giving the faithful "more courage, which had cost him nothing" ("Discourse," Watson, *Dramatic Poesy*, 2 : 88). It is apparent, I trust, that the reason for Dryden's "failure" here is my conflation of genres. What is relevant to Tassonic epic is for Dryden irrelevant to opera understood as masque. It will have been obvious to anyone acquainted with the Stuart masque that my discussion of *King Arthur* has not mentioned the pertinent fact of the opera's elaborating yet again that piece of Tudor-Stuart historiography mined by both regimes for its ideological value as a succession argument: the Brute story, which traced the Stuarts back through Arthur to the Britons' Trojan origins. The masques refer to the story frequently; the prophecy of Merlin that ends this play had been often repeated early in the century by Jonson and others in their efforts to describe James I as the new Arthur Merlin had promised England.[19] In returning to it now, Dryden is perhaps consciously archaizing, perhaps simply enjoying a good story; he is certainly reminding his audience of old myths as myths, comforting to Jabobites, enjoyable to anyone.

The operas generally release into magic and mythology, into lightly held providentialism, the will that would be held accountable in drama or the epic. "Where gods are introduced second causes are out of doors." The Dryden/Davenant *Tempest* and the Tate/Purcell *Dido and Aeneas* are examples of the same situation. Where Shakespeare's Prospero remains in control of the action throughout, Dryden/Davenant's has become so merely a second cause, one among equals, that Ariel, "unbid," as he tells us, and all unassisted, solves the crux of the plot that Prospero's various manipulations have so masterfully created. Aeneas's subjection to magic is so complete that Wilfrid Mellers manages credibly to see him as an "un-hero" and to give the opera over to Dido's feeling feminine passivity.[20] In all three cases, as in all the situations of *King Arthur* that I have referred to, the dramatic as we conceive it as sacrificed to the emblematic, the psychologically forceful to the allegorically meaningful. In the process purposive activity—on the part of the humans—falls away, subject to some greater will.

III

Purcell's *Dido* is the signal reminder of the lost opportunities of the musical stage of the time. Except for momentary isolated songs, Purcell was never given the occasion to create equivalent drama. More ink has been spilled over this catastrophe than over any other musical fact of the last decade of the century, little indication though there may be of Purcell's having shared the grief. He instead wrote the occasional and occasionally integral music for a succession of plays beginning with *Theodosius* and on through *Diocletian,* the one that brought him to Dryden's attention as a possible collaborator for *King Arthur*—and presumably led to the radical shift in Dryden's sense of the relation of the poet to the composer: from "'Tis my part to Invent, and the Musicians's to Humour the Invention" (Preface, *Albion and Albanius,* 10) to (what every musician and musicologist wants to hear) "because these sorts of entertainments are principally design'd for the ear and eye . . . in reason my art, on this occasion, ought to be subservient to his."[21] Given the fact that *King Arthur* is a spoken play with intercalated music, this deference of the poet to the musician is far less important to the achievement of a unified dramatic work than it is to the theoretical implication that Dryden was willing at least to entertain the notion that music had communicative value—that its affective power could be capitalized on in the course of developing a drama.

"In a play house," Dryden had said in the epistle dedicatory to *The Spanish Friar,* "everything contributes to impose upon the judgment; the lights, the scenes, the habits, and above all, the grace of action, which is commonly the best where there is most need of it, surprise the audience, and cast a mist upon their understandings."[22] Music's "principle Intention being to please Hearing rather than to gratify the understanding" (Preface, *Albion and Albanius,* 4), it too is one of those impositions upon the judgment that are the theatre's stock in trade, though here aural rather than visual.

If we accept D. T. Mace's argument that the Saint Cecilia Odes are a significant step in the seventeenth century's transition from the "mere" harmony of numbers to the "power of numbers" (in the depiction of the *ethea* in "Alexander's Feast"), from harmonious proportion as a rational ideal to rhythm's value as an analogical representation of the inarticulate passions,[23] the argument substantiates the notion that Dryden sees music as an assault on the understanding, casting a mist upon reason. But it puts that notion in a positive frame. The idea becomes, as Mace asserts, part of the historical effort of the seventeenth century to invent a language for the passions, "one not wholly articulate but one which could represent by movement the very contours of the passions themselves" (Mace, 292).

Viewed in this way, Dryden's remarks on opera seem less deprecations of the form, as they are usually taken to be, than quite realistic, if limited, recognitions of its potential. In "Defence of an Essay" Dryden described the goal of the dramatic poet as "to affect the soul, and excite the passions, and above all to move admiration. . . . The converse therefore . . . must be heightened with all the arts and ornaments of poesy." On these grounds prose is inferior to poetry as the medium of a serious play. "And as poetry is a rise above prose and oratory, so is Musick the exaltation of poetry." The addition of music is the addition of a means to "affect the soul and excite the passions, and above all to move admiration." We have heard Davenant recite essentially the same idea. That is to say, the potentiality of musical affect is not limited to mimesis—to Mace's analogical capabilities of the *ethea*—but includes audience response in a more direct (and potentially manipulative) fashion. It is a medium understood to be subjective as well as objective in its latent effects, and, hence, to be supremely capable of generating the epic response, admiration.[24]

On the question of audience response, there is a sense in which Dryden wanted to have his cake and eat it, too. And because of that desire he can implement fully the baroque reliance on the sensory at the same time that he insists upon the primacy of the reason. All the citations adduced above balance the ear and eye against the judgment and understanding, the merely sensory against the rational. And yet he is quite willing to enlist any means available to court the ear and eye, to "endeavour an absolute dominion over the minds of the spectators." For Dryden this was not the contradiction it may appear to us. For behind all these statements lies an implicit understanding of the fictive, which he makes explicit now and again: "You are not obliged, as in History, to a literal belief of what the poet says; but you are pleased with the image, without being cozened by the fiction."[25] The statement about the poet's endeavoring dominion continues, "for, though our fancy will contribute to its own deceit, yet a writer ought to help its operation."

There is no confusion in Dryden's mind, nor did he anticipate one in the audience's, between the literally true and the fictions we engage in. The primary goal of the poet is to satisfy our desire for "the pleasures of the fiction" by creating that mystification that is proper to each of the arts in turn: comparing the pleasures of poetry and of painting he claimed the means of each to be "by deceit. One imposes on the sight, and the other on the understanding. Fiction is of the essence of poetry, as well as of painting." One can by implication justly add, and of the spectacular episodes that enlist music together with poetry and painting to create the fictional image in *King Arthur*.[26]

If we turn now to specific musical episodes, we can see how music is part of the image-building power of the drama in its capacity to depict scene and emotion as well as to generate a sensory/emotional response—from the principals and, it is implied, from us. The clearest exemplification of the limits of art is the ice masque in act 3. It is also, but for the closing masque, the most fully elaborated musically and visually and became the most famous episode of the opera, performed separately through the eighteenth century. It is the first encounter of Emmeline, just released from blindness by Merlin's art, with the charms and temptations of the theatre: innocence encounters sheer seduction as Osmond, the evil magus of the Saxons, tries to thaw Emmeline's frosty heart by example. The beautiful display, lovely in itself if perverse in intent, shows Cupid arousing the frozen *genius loci* to praise of Love, heaven and earth's source, the eldest of the gods. He then, waving his wand, extends the perspective back to the full company of singers and dancers. They recreate the cold in musical *tremolo,* the sort of scene painting variously praised and condemned by theorists of the opera from Vincenzo Galilei onward. Purcell has a model for the frozen lovers' musical depiction in the Lully/Quinault *Isis,* where the same device is quite as attractively used. The difference is not so much musical as poetic, since *Isis* has nothing resembling the steady elaboration of the theme, illusion, that Dryden develops throughout *King Arthur.* In the Lully opera, the illusions of the form are never directly questioned and therefore the frozen lovers exist on exactly the same plane as everything else in the work, rather like Jonson's *Love Restored*'s lovers, though in Lully they are part of a full drama. In the self-awareness of *King Arthur,* the levels of reality implicated in the form itself become part of the temptation theme, making the emblematic displays of masque integral to the experience the principals undergo.

The show is as delightful to Emmeline as it would be to us, could we ever see it:

> I could be pleased with any one but thee,
> Who entertained my sight with such gay shows,
> As men and women moving here and there;
> That, coursing one another in their steps,
> Have made their feet a tune.
>
> (3. 2. 179–80)

Arthur himself faces several far more confusing illusory displays. But Emmeline's response can be directly glossed by "The Defense of an Essay," where the relation between Reason and Imagination is analyzed:

> Imagination in a man or reasonable creature is supposed to participate of Reason; and when that governs, as it does in the belief of fiction, Reason is not destroyed, but misled, or blinded: that can prescribe to the Reason, during the time of the representation, somewhat like a weak belief of what it sees and hears; and Reason suffers itself to be so hoodwinked, that it may better enjoy the pleasures of the fiction: but it is never so wholly made a captive, as to be drawn headlong into a persuasion of those things which are most remote from probability: 'tis in that case a free-born subject, not a slave; it will contribute willingly its assent, as far as it sees convenient, but will not be forced. (Watson, *Of Dramatic Poesy*, 1 : 126)

Emmeline's response to the ice masque indicates roundly that her Reason will not be forced; as an audience to Osmond's show she can imaginatively participate just as far as she "sees convenient." If, like Eve's, her first response to sight, "the mother of desire," was narcissism as she gazed into her mirror, her response to external temptation is to graduate to virtue. Her education in between these two events was again like Eve's, though its ultimate issue so different: saved from the self-absorption of the narcissist by the replacement of her image in the glass with Arthur's, she finds in him the model whose image, having defeated self-love, is hardly tested by Osmond, though that gentleman is foolhardy enough to make the comparison:

> My pent-house eyebrows, and my shaggy beard,
> Offend your sight, but these are manly signs;
> Faint white and red abuse your expectations:
> Be woman; know your sex, and love full pleasures.
> (3. 2. 176)

Emmeline's notion of full pleasures does not include pent-house eyebrows.

To stage the temptation of the hero and its opposite effect, Dryden implements more explicitly the earlier Renaissance epic, moving back to Spenser and to Tasso. The means of the temptation remain the same, though they are no longer given the victim as shows: black magic creates first a Bower of Bliss, second a Mount Olivet episode. Arthur walks within them, forewarned of their illusory nature. While a pair of lovely sirens do affect him as they sport naked in a fountain singing a limpidly seductive song, he has little trouble maintaining his pursuit of love and honor. He tells us that

> A lazy pleasure trickles through my veins;
> Here could I stay, and well be cozened here.
> But honour calls. . . .
>
> (4. 4. 183)

The seduction continues through a minuet on "How happy the lover," whose lively beauties don't confuse Arthur either ("And what are these fantastic fairy joys, / To love like mine?"), but momentarily illusion in a simpler form, the "love like mine," the direct mimetic representation of his beloved encased in the tree he is cutting down, stymies Arthur, who has to be saved by grace, the genius Philidel, unveiling not Emmeline at all but the disguised Grimbald. Not before Arthur has abandoned Reason, though, in a splendidly sophistic apostrophe:

> If thou wert made for souls,
> Then souls should have been made without their bodies.
> If falling for the first created fair
> Was Adam's fault, great grandsire I forgive thee;
> Eden was lost, as all thy sons would lose it.
>
> (4. 1. 187)

Simple mimesis thus can be the trap of reason, at least when it ensconces the sum of one's desires, as Grimbald/Emmeline does Arthur's. Suprahuman agency is as necessary to true sight in that instance as Merlin's magic was to Emmeline's literal visual recovery. Opulent sights and sounds that introduce desires alien to one's nature have proved far less misleading than pure, albeit romantic, verisimilitude, the fictive foisted upon desire as reality. Imagination, the power enacted physically by the operatic genii and their engines that bring on stage all those delights of ear and eye that Emmeline during her blindness of the first two acts has such difficulty defining and understanding, is as dangerous as the will allows it to be. It remains essentially, whatever form it takes, that power of the mind that classically, from Aristotle through Hobbes, raises the pleasures of the senses to mental acts and is, as in Hobbes, in itself without specific moral implication. If this seems an ingenuous notion, it has at least a long and illustrious lineage.[27]

IV

While Dryden's conception of the imagination is clear enough, the implications built up around it by the opera's treatment of modes are less transparent. The power of imagination is embodied in the magi and their agents, figures compacting the national and personal genii—Merlin and Philidel on the one side, versus Osmond and Grimbald on the other. Grimbald and Philidel are, of course, the only figures who both speak and sing, who exist in both worlds, an "intermedial kind of life, partaking of them both" ("Plutarch," 253), and it is they who, at the behest and under the direction of Merlin and Osmond, subject the principals to the world of the imagination or free them with its visions, much as Merlin's magic restores Emmeline's sight. That world is neutral in principle, enslaving or enlightening depending on the motive of the guardian angel and on the will of the character acted upon. But overall, given the fact that the plot is based upon defeated temptations, the emphasis falls on the imagination's power to mislead.

The opera contains nine musical episodes, six of them direct or indirect presentations by the figures of imagination to the principals as audience, a common shift of music drama in the period, made integral here through its thematization, as I remarked in the *Isis* comparison. In these episodes Dryden (and Purcell) most clearly "endeavour an absolute dominion over the minds of the spectators," as the magi do over the minds of the characters.[28] Yet while the incidents themselves are clear about the status of music and spectacle in the drama as a whole, Dryden's treatment of the major modes of the opera creates difficulties in his positioning of the hero in relation to society. If we understand the grammar of the opera as having, quite traditionally and in accord with Dryden's definitions and Davenant's masque-founded procedures, associated music with the sensory and illusive world and verse with the world of reason (and reasonable faith), we notice as well tht the main characters as figures of reason and the spoken word seem more pitted against than crowning society at large, the common men and women who along with Grimbald and Philidel make up the sensory world of the musical segments. If anything unites them, it is love, the opera's one ubiquitous value; but love is usually conceived in the musical segments as a sexual common denominator, though in the heroic action it figures as the valorizing motive for the heroic activities of both Arthur and his adversary, Oswald.

We are so accustomed to think of music as what Dryden called it, that step above poetry that leads to the suprarational, we are surprised when the expectation is reversed here. In the one musical episode where what would seem to follow from Dryden's remark does occur, the scene of religious emotion expressed in Woden's worship by the Saxon army in act 1, the worshipers and the worship are shown to be palpably misguided, antiquated believers in barbaric gods motivated by a bogus spirituality. Elsewhere, the musical episodes that are not products of the magi's powers of illusion are fairly direct antiheroics. We think of the troops in *The History of Sir Francis Drake* when the Briton's victory song counters the Saxon search for honor, fame, and glory with British common sense:

> Now the victory's won,
> To the plunder we run:
> We return to our lasses like fortunate traders,
> Triumphant with spoils of the vanquished invaders.
> (1. 2. 151)[29]

The Kentish "lads and lasses," who divert Emmeline in act 2 with "Let not your days without pleasure expire; / Honour's but empty," lightly questions the major virtue of the play by pitting it against momentary self-interest. It seems quite natural that a traditional *carpe diem*, with its customary refusal of purposive action, would appear in this context, women waiting for their soldiers to return from battle. The song is sung by the customary shepherds and shepherdesses, "of all Callings the most innocent, the most happy, and who by reason of the spare time they had, in their almost idle Employment, had most leisure to make Verses and to be in Love" (Preface, *Albion and Albanius*, 6). But for all their innocence, leisure, and love, the shepherds and shepherdesses are quite hardheaded souls: the men engage in an extended play on phallic flutes, the women refusing to join in until some marriage contracts are signed—compact theory wittily invading the theoretically timeless world of pastoralism. These episodes are all set in music that is dramatically apposite to the moment, and if they do not, as some musicologists note, come together to achieve musical coherence, they make dramatic sense, painting their subjects quite positively for precisely what they are: the delights of the unheroic flesh.

These delights and the commitment to them become over time half of a subsidiary conflict in the opera, the conflict implicit in the design of the work inherited from masque. In accepting the absolute modal break between hero and commons, king and society, Dryden perhaps spoke truer than he intended. The opera makes palpable what so often hovers in the background of the heroic plays. But here the curiosity of heroes not singing and the common man being raised into song, the voice of the gods, constructs a tentative bridge between two modes of being, effectively equalizing a discrete and disparate society. The break may, of course, be quite unintentional, the casual concomitant of doing the action in spoken verse and the shows in music, as if to follow out the advice of Corneille, who wanted nothing sung of the action that needed to be understood, and of St. Evremond, who to a large extent agreed.[30] But intentional or not, the break has at least two effects: because they have none of it, the music cannot serve a mimetic function considered as expressive of the emotional lives of the principals, the Vossian route that all later opera was to take. Insofar as the music here is descriptive of the inarticulate passions, it realizes the emotions experienced by the mass and proffered to but ultimately rejected by the principals. Through this fact of design, the essential dramatic conflict—love and honor, Arthur versus Oswald for the hand of Emmeline and the throne of England—is displaced by a subsidiary conflict inherited from the masque between the heroic world and ordinary life.

Before we decide that this is simply a masked way of admitting that Dryden's play could not survive on its own terms being turned into an opera, we should look more closely at the heroic side of the tentative bridge. Arthur, a figure answering to the doctrine of ideal imitation, is never presented to the audience as a man with whom it can identify, the sort of figure whose emotional life need be realizeed therefore, in the manner of less idealized characters. He is an Aeneas, exhibiting "the beauties of a god in a human body." Nothing makes clearer the effect of the distance that stands between the ideal hero and the Aristotelian conception of identification than Dryden's various remarks on Aeneas: "Where a character of perfect virtue is set before us, 'tis more lovely; for there the whole hero is to be imitated."[31] Arthur, the Britsih Aeneas, perfect in his virtue, is designed to be a model to aspire to, a model who turns the opera's delight into learning on quite the same ideological grounds for which Dryden congratulated Virgil.

> The Roman Commonwealth, being now changed into a Monarchy, Virgil was helping in that design, by insinuating into the people the piety of their new conqueror, to make them the better brook this innovation.[32]

As model, Arthur must exhibit his valor, his capacity for love, his wisdom, and, above all, his rationality—which he does, through the plot and his verse speaking. Through the musical episodes, the value of these virtues for the country at large is exemplified, as it always had been in court masques. And here the failure for a modern audience emerges. It is not a failure in the handling of genre—for King and commons do become integrated, after a fashion, something the masque rarely tried—but in the political terms of the integration. For in the course of *King Arthur*, Dryden transfers the masque associations of symbolic power from the King to a double sovereign—King and "sceptered subjects"—from the King in his traditional role as an embodiment of sacramental order to the King and country as an integrated economic order, symbiotically self-sustaining.[33] We the audience are genially expected to share the values of the opera's commonalty, to admire Arthur and assent to his emblematic values. The King and his company of heroes (the Order of the Garter enskied in the final display) make the civilian pursuit of pleasure possible. The civilian's pleasure will produce new soldiers and new sailors. In *King Lear* such knowledge is cause for tears; in *King Arthur* Dryden tries to make the best of it, calling it in effect the basis for communal cohesion.

While in the body of the action both Arthur and his future consort have been associated with the wealth that proves their worth, their closer association with the spiritual war between the guardian angels has kept the identification of hero and wealth in abeyance. In the fifth act it emerges in full force. Its emergence is of course assisted by the impersonality of Arthur. Whether because of heroic idealization or those concessions to Whiggery Dryden felt called upon to make by depersonalizing his hero, the result is the destruction of the very possibility of a national hero unsullied by the monetary values that fill the vacuum created by the king's personal demise.[34] Kings and heroes are not seen as discrete personalities who actively achieve great ends but as masque models, inspiring figureheads who hieratically sustain the community as models of noble virtue, models for whom a more particular relation to the common man is not at all easy to discern.

The relation seems at best ensconced in those pragmatic ideas that had, after all, sustained Charles, too, when he was there: Britannia ruling the waves around the island fortess, a good balance of trade, a peaceful harvest, and full barns. Pan and the Nereid sing of no Arcadian shepherds and the joys of love until they've sung of "pleasure mixt with profit," British wool more famous than Jason's because it is "growing gold." I find it difficult not to imagine a certain Mephistophelian pleasure on Dryden's part in translating the Horatian *utile dulci* into this materialistic context with Shetland wool outstripping Jason's fleece, a traditional set of symbols displaced by its modern equivalents. But if Arthur becomes now for us the bright penny of reified wealth rather than an emblematic figure of more traditional values, this is surely so in large part because the musical spectacle has been devoted throughout to realizing not, as the spoken text has, his god-relation, his valor, even his wisdom, but the pleasures these protect. And the musical spectacle is stronger finally than the romantic allegory's power to assimilate it, or than reason's power to control it.

Yet for earlier audiences, the final spectacle must have been the means of assimilating all difference, for in it Purcell and Dryden achieve a splendidly practical coup, perfectly designed to capture the gentry at the same time that it resolves their opera. They turn court masque into City pageant, or rather, insert at the point where refulgent masque with its aristocratic associations is anticipated, a celebration from Lord Mayor's day, with all its bourgeois connections. If Dryden wanted, as he claimed in an epigraph, *celebrare domestica facta,* he could have found no more appropriate means. As I have shown, the Lord Mayor's pageants had been proclaiming for years the nascent mercantilism that Dryden shared, and they did it in a language that accepted, indeed depended on, the imperial hierarchy of Tudor, then Stuart mythology, the same mythology that made Brut to Arthur so important a line to be resurrected, refurbished, and made to glow. We can extrapolate from the annual event an ideal form that encloses its essentials: a praise of the Thames or some other personification of England's "wat'ry power," a pair of pageants on the new mayor's civic and commercial virtues, an episode of tumbling, folk music, or misrule parallel in function to the antimasque, and a culminating vision of the future perfection of England. Each pageant is quite discrete, the theme of prosperity and national well-being running through them all. When Dryden and Purcell move from Aeolus to Pan and the Nereid, on to Comus and the folk attacking tithing, then out to Venus and the great display of the Order of the Garter, they are following the same route from the Thames along the Great Conduit to the Guildhall that Peele, Munday, Dekker, Tatham, Settle et al. traveled, station by station. Dryden even borrows their literary devices: the Golden Fleece as the type of British wool, profit and pleasure as purely materialist notions are from as early as 1603 constants of the pageants that allowed the amalgamation of commercial virtues with the more exalted cultural values encoded in classical motifs.

In their musical and scenic realization, *King Arthur's* pageants are of course dependent on the masque. They resemble more than a little the masque with which Shadwell closes his *Tempest*. But in their content and succession they depend from the civic pageants. In bringing the two together—the courtly fiction of the imperial dream, the British Aeneas and attendant Gods, and the City fiction of the virtues of commerce, Dryden gave London a means to celebrate itself fully and ecumenically, whatever he may have thought of William, man and king, himself. The audience is invited, as in the old masques, to "become what they have watched," a social group intent upon not merely their ideal, figured in Arthur, but their own communal revelry and self-congratulation.

V

If the grand and undateable post-Renaissance shift from a theocentric to an egocentric world view finds its modal shift in the arts in the movement from allegoresis to mimesis, Dryden and the opera of his day are caught in the receding wave.[35] Epistemes aside, all the operas, tragic or comic, Whig or Tory, involve themselves heavily in the world of myth and its allegorical representation, whether the myths be political *(King Arthur)*, psychological *(Psyche)*, familial *(Circe)*, or religious (all of them). The English operas are also all self-consciously reflexive artifacts, thematizing more or less fully their own self-awareness in the subjects of illusion and the dubiety of the senses, toying with the audience's awareness of the overwhelming appeals directed to it. When the work is beyond the control of the author, as it was in the case of Charles Davenant and *Circe*, what is produced is a scramble that teaches one how much there is to manage in such undertakings. *Circe* is an outpouring of every piece of Greek mythology for which Davenant could muster up the shadow of a connection, every filial, governance, and marital mythic moment in Bulfinch, laced together by the "power of music" motif and culminating in a universal self-destruction that burns up the stage. It may be "total theatre" or a precursor of *Götterdämerung*, but it surely is inchoate and rather awful. Yet Dryden was interested enough in either the idea or William's son to write a prologue for it. One suspects, given his stress on Charles's youth and the virtues of forgiveness, that the second is the motive. If *Circe* had been any good, it could have shared a place beside *King Arthur* as a musically conceived original. As it is, one can only say that Charles tried hard to fulfill the family's commitment to musical theatre.

Though *The Tempest* and *The Prophetess* retained their viability on the stage longest, *King Arthur* seems to me the best of these Purcellian works.[36] It does so because it is the only one that succeeds as a unified whole. Where *The Tempest* and *The Prophetess* never lose the marks of their origins as complete plays with music added later (as true of the Fletcherian play, which few of us hold in memory, as of the Shakespearean one, which we all do), *King Arthur* develops out of the world of illusion and suprarationality that is its medium and does so fully, with nothing supererogatory. When Shadwell brings *The Tempest* to its closing masque, he uses the shift of the impresario, as Shakespeare himself, after all, had done. Propsero says:

> Now to make amends
> For the rough treatment you have found today,
> I'll entertain you with my Magick Art.[37]

The scene changes, music emanates from the rocks, and Neptune, Amphitrite, Oceanus, and Tethys appear. The impresario device is not in itself objectionable, but the total irrelevance of what emerges is. Dryden avoided Shadwell's irrelevance and Charles Davenant's hysteria by choosing the mythic world of Arthurian history as his subject and the celebration of English national pride as his goal. Together with Purcell he turned the operatic resources of their time to an end they could serve and masterfully did. It was not our end, and it was not repeated. It brings to a successful conclusion the emblematic masque devolution of public praise; epideictics gave way now, on the stage as in print, to satire. *The Dunciad* was its future. Yet the operatic theatre in England pursued the potentialities unlocked by epideictics for several decades. The next two chapters will conclude this study by examining some of the best examples after having considered the theoretical bases on which the extensions were founded.

___ 6 ___

Representation in Contemporary Theory

*I*n talking of Dryden, I have glossed over several issues whose fuller discussion will be fruitful in understanding where the early opera fits in a broader picture of seventeenth-century theatre. My oblique and limited rejection of Mace's contentions on Vossius, my characterization of Dryden's attitude toward affect as "wanting to have his cake and eat it, too," my treatment of his use of music as a technique of characterization—all of these need a firmer foundation and fuller explication to stand as reasonable explanations both of his practice and of its relation to the theatre in general. To formulate such an explanation, I must at this point consider some of the theory behind the practice in larger terms than Davenant or Dryden give us and in a wider context than my focus on them has allowed thus far. I intend by this means to elucidate as well some of the primary connections of the works we have been considering to their less narrowly conceived fellows. I shall try to move toward the whole question of the place of music in Dryden's theatre, the reasons for his attack on Settle's *Empress of Morocco,* and the implications of that attack. Explaining these large issues as fully and accurately as I can requires my entering the murky waters of discussion of the passions, because this is the notion that ties together what seem to me the "primary connections" I mentioned: character and its techniques of representation; its relation to plot; authorial presence in the work. Many readers will have felt that my attention to the figural tradition has stopped the discussion short at precisely the point at which masque becomes opera: where the dramatization of passionate experience becomes the fundamental concern of a work. I need to explain why I think that has been just. To do that, I must begin with psychology and thus with Descartes.

I

When Robert Hume tried to discern a consistent theory underlying the serious drama of the Restoration, one that would explain to us what the intentions, at least, of the writers might have been, he decided that beneath the widely varied descriptions and incomplete statements of the period lay a few assumptions too abstract and general in their language to commit the writers to any very specific clarification of techniques. They speak constantly of imitation and the passions, of affect and its uses, but never tell us exactly what is being imitated or how, nor how the affect sought is supposed to be achieved.[1] Ultimately to one seeking descriptive explanations of the practice of the dramatists, the theory appears a wasteland of "falderal" and "muddiness" that does very little to explain what the writers thought they were doing.

On the question of affect which so involved them, we are left finally, as Rogerson had said in a similar context, with the notion that a faithful copy of the outward signs of an emotion would "by a sort of contagion . . . evoke a corresponding emotional response" from the audience. This situation is particularly trying to Hume, whose commitment to an affective view of Dryden naturally leads him to seek out evidence of a clearer understanding of the "contagion."[2] If it is legitimate to taxonomize drama in terms of affect sought, the major analytic question must become *how* the work can imitate the world in order to achieve those affects; but, as Hume remarks, singularly little is said among the theorists about "the processes and mechanisms by which the spectator was affected and then responded" (p. 158). He attributes the omission to the fact that we "are looking at *legislative* criticism, that concerned with how an author should write. Explanatory or appreciative criticism, that written with an audience or reader in mind, was in its infancy." He looks forward to Addison for its arrival and must content himself with an unlegitimated taxonomy.

The question that Hume raises and that, he convincingly argues, vitiates the theoretical lucubrations of the last third of the century is not a question peculiar to aesthetics. It is a problem, from our point of view, in the history of psychology. It exposes for attack the adequacy of the period's understanding of the subjective response, or rather, the inadequacy of a psychology that has yet truly to recognize the need to account for subjective responses. While it is true that, as

Hume so ably demonstrates, the end of the century is replete with
contradictory and half-baked notions of the various passions relevant
to the various generic categories in terms of which such talk was
carried on, and equally full of contradictions about the ways to work
those passions, it seems thankless now to denigrate literary critics for
their apparent incoherence, that is, for having no better understanding of psychology than Descartes or Hobbes.

One point does seem clear from Hume's survey of the evidence:
their criticism does not give us terms we can accept as adequate for a
clear rationale of the serious drama because the idea of an analyzed
subjective response was not available to the critics, nor did they create
one. Lacking that, we must try to understand better how their own
terms explained for them the kinds of questions we speak of now
quite differently—how their terms filled the gap that we now fill with
"subjective response." I turn to Descartes not because he created the
terms, but because *The Passions of the Soul*, both directly and indirectly
through French theatrical examples, does effect the Restoration
dramatists and states the most influential and most fully developed
analytic psychology of the mid-century.

Descartes does not assume unchanging universality in passional
effects; in fact, he assumes that he must account for differences
among responses. But his sense of particularized subjective response
is limited as deviance, implying a universal norm behind human be-
havior. Thus in part 2, article 136, "Whence come the effects of the
passions peculiar to certain men," he explains particularity as the
result of associations from prior experience—all the way back to the
womb:

> I shall content myself with repeating the principle that underlies
> everything I have written about [the passions], namely that our soul
> and our body are so connected that once we have joined a certain
> bodily action to a certain thought, one of them never presents itself
> to us later without the other presenting itself also, and that the same
> actions are not always joined to the same thoughts. This will suffice
> to give a reason for anything we can observe as peculiar to ourselves
> or to others in this matter, and which has not been here explained.
> For example, it is easy to conceive that the strange aversions of
> some people which make them unable to endure the smell of roses,
> the presence of a cat, or similar things, come only from the fact that
> at the beginning of their life they were made to suffer by such
> objects, or that they sympathized with their mother's feelings when
> she was made to suffer by them while she was pregnant.[3]

Thus the variety of individual responses can be explained empirically
while the passions in general can remain universal and thus, along

with the cogito, the unifying fact of human experience. By such epicycles Descartes's psychology remains comformable to classical literary theory while creating for itself applicability to a range of emotional experience wider and potentially more particular than earlier explanations of comparable breadth and specificity allowed.

I should be more precise about my understanding of Descartes's analysis in order to clarify these claims. In *The Passions of the Soul,* Descartes differentiates among the passions, their objects, and the intellectual emotions. The passions are effects in the soul of actions in the body caused by the perception of objects either material or a part of the soul itself (1. 17). The passions of the soul are related properly only to the latter (1. 25). His description of each of the soul's passions in terms of its physiology—how the blood and animal spirits move, what routes they take, what expression they cause, how they are all controlled by the movements of the pineal gland—constitutes the materialism of his analysis. Consistent with the advances of medical science, it is a materialism of startling applicability for the arts in formulating conventions of representation for the passions. But it does not exhaust what Descartes has to tell us about emotional life. If the passions are immediate and unalterable responses to stimuli in respect of the immediacy of bodily actions, yet intervention is possible through those functions of the soul that are not encompassed in its passions, but rather constitute its other thoughts—all those functions of the soul that are not "caused, maintained, and fortified by some movement of the spirits" (1. 27). These include the intellectual emotions. The simplest example of this differentiation occurs in Descartes's definition of Joy:

> Joy is an agreeable emotion of the soul in which consists the enjoyment that the soul possesses in the good which the impressions of the brain represent to it as its own. I say that it is in this emotion that the enjoyment of the good consists; for as a matter of fact the soul receives no other fruit from all the good things that it possesses; and while it has no joy in these, it may be said that it does not enjoy them more than if it did not possess them at all.

In this manner consciousness of itself is necessary to all the effects of the soul: not to know them is not to have them. He continues,

> I also add that it is of the good which the impressions of the brain represent to it as its own, in order not to confound this joy, which is a passion, with the joy that is purely intellectual, and which comes into the soul by the action of the soul alone, and which we may call an agreeable emotion excited in it, in which the enjoyment consists

which it has in the good which its understanding represents to it as its own. It is true that while the soul is united to the body this intellectual joy can hardly fail to be accompanied by that which is a passion; for as soon as our understanding perceives that we possess some good thing . . . imagination does not fail immediately to make some impression in the brain from which proceeds the movement of the animal spirits which excites the passion of joy. (2. 91, slightly altered from Haldane and Ross in the final clause)

Shortly Descartes will apply this differentiated joy to the theatrical events that bring us joy out of the painful through our consciousness of excitation (2. 94). Titillation, the enjoyment of experiencing passions "not being able to harm us in any way, seem pleasurable to excite our soul in affecting it." The pleasures of theatrical representations are paralleled to our general response to "pleasurable stimulation":

But the cause that brings it to pass that in a general way joy follows pleasurable sensation, is the fact that all that we call pleasurable sensation or agreeable sentiment is simply due to the fact that the objects of sense excite some movement in the nerves which would be capable of harming them had they not strength sufficient to resist the movement, or were the body not well disposed; and this produces to the brain an impression which, being instituted by nature to give evidence of this good disposition and this strength, represents that to the soul as a good pertaining to it, inasmuch as it is united to body and thus excites in it joy.

The ugly and the painful are turned into pleasant experiences not so much by the agitation that accompanies all passion, but by our consciousness of that agitation.[4] What we enjoy is our awareness. Descartes is more precise about the place of consciousness when he reassesses the aesthetic situation in terms of the initial differentiation:

I shall only add here a consideration which, it seems to me, we shall find of much service in preventing us from suffering any inconvenience from the passions; and that is that our good and our harm depend mainly on the interior emotions which are only excited in the soul by the soul itself, in which respect they differ from its passions, which always depend on some movement of the spirits. And, although these emotions of the soul are frequently united to the passions which are similar to them, they may likewise often be met with along with others, and even take their origin from those which are contrary to them. . . . And when we read of strange adventures in a book, or see them represented in a theatre, which sometimes excite sadness in us, sometimes joy, or love, or hatred, and generally speaking all the passions, according to the diversity of the objects which are offered to our imagination; but along with that we have pleasure in feeling them excited in us, and this pleasure is an intellectual joy which may as easily take its origin from sadness as from any of the other passions. . . .

And, inasmuch as these inward emotions touch us most nearly, and in consequence have much more power over us than the passions from which they differ, and which are met with in conjunction with them, it is certain that, provided our soul is always possessed of something to content itself with inwardly, none of the troubles that come from elsewhere have any power to harm it, but rather serve to increase its joy, inasmuch as, seeing that it cannot be harmed by them, it is made sensible of its perfection. (2. 147–48)

Thus Descartes has created that space for the intellect that granted Dryden and his peers the freedom to exercise the senses as fully as they chose without encountering charges of mere manipulation, and thus the recipient and not the exciting object has become the potential central focus of the system artist-object-receiver that any aesthetic theory must take into account. Where in the past the focus remained always the object, with Descartes the receiver achieves centrality, Descartes's entire discussion of the passions being based on the formulation that the perception of objects and not the objects themselves create that agitation of the soul that we call a passion (1. 27–28). The world of emotional experience becomes the world of the self perceiving objects that are related to the self through desire.[5] The will can effect the passions only by altering the representation of the desired object, in light of its other perceived goods (l. 45).

Though the depiction of the passions on stage can constantly refer us back to Descartes's descriptions, it would be years before the full implications of his theory would be effectively applied to aesthetics.[6] My selection of citations may create the false impression that Descartes was himself, in this work, interested in such problems, but he in fact raises the arts only as examples in dealing with the larger issue, the functioning of the passions.

Even the notion of the place of self-consciousness, the idea that ultimately leads on to Kantian aesthetics and expressive theory, remains only an addendum by the time Dennis was writing. Dennis's discussion of the Enthusiastic passions, in *The Advancement and Reformation of Modern Poetry* (1701), concludes its recognition that not only "Things" but "Ideas of the Things" produce enthusiasm with "Add to all this, that the Mind producing these Thoughts, conceives by Reflexion a certain Pride, and Joy, and Admiration, as at the conscious view of its own excellence."[7] The separation of "Things" and the "Ideas of Things" from our consciousness of the effects being wrought explains what I earlier spoke of as an anomaly in Dryden's own aesthetics: his insistence on the availability of the sense of artifice to the viewer or auditor coupled with the steady effort after emotional affect and the awareness of drama's capacity to overwhelm the spectator. Given the place of self-consciousness in Cartesian analysis, there is no anomaly; we *can* have our cake and eat it too, being affected by the emotional world put before us and at the same time conscious of our consciousness, spectators at not merely the play, but at our own involvement in the play. Where post-Kantian thought, our thought, would turn this spectatorship into a play of ironies leading to the eternal regress of mirroring structures of mediation, Cartesian self-consciousness, in its transparency (Cogito, *ergo* sum, not cogito cogitans), avoids the ironies caused for us by the division Kant perceived between naturalness and the mediating structures of self-reflection.

Dryden of course accepts Descartes's transparency: Adam entering *The State of Innocence,* says

> What am I? or from whence? For that I am,
> I know, because I think; but whence I came
> Or how [he does not know innately][8]

so reasons to a divine power in nine lines, from the beauty of his surroundings and his own physical capabilities, and most importantly, his mental abilities. These he both comments on and illustrates, sounding a great deal more like Descartes throughout than like his Miltonic predecessor, whose lines his are tagging.[9] For Dryden, as for Descartes, the fictiveness of the work is our guarantee of full consciousness at the same time that the work is thereby granted autonomy without a loss of relevance to our lives, the structures of consciousness being reflections of reality and not of our minds themselves. There is no need here for an expressive theory in the post-Kantian sense, that is, an expressive theory that develops from the displacement of the world by the mind of the creator. Such a theory can and usually will see the work as an expression of the writer's personality, revealing itself, ultimately, quite apart from the author's intention. Here instead, the writer's place and control remain as fully conscious and artful, as artificial, as in classical rhetorical theory. Expression is an attribute of dramatic character or lyrical persona bestowed by the writer according to his desires for the work, which persists in mirroring not the mind of the writer but the world, though new weight has been given to the receptive mind of the audience.

That mind, it can be assumed, given the universality of the cogito and the passions, is identical in operations with the minds of the writer and of the play's characters. They are the same in their operations and their mechanisms of response. Thus, inducing an effect in an audience should require simply exposing it to the same experience that the character is exposed to. Effect and affect are one, the character's experience and the audience's.[10] At the same time, a play, given its limited time structure, cannot hope to accomplish that literally, though it can try: Davenant, Dryden, and others were fond of the *tabula rasa* character—the man who has never seen a woman, Adam, Galatea, blind Emmeline—characters whose entire experience can be staged for the audience, as it were, *ab ovo*. More frequently, in fact ubiquitously, we encounter one of the awkward heroic play's most awkward moves for projecting the passions, the virtual description of the mechanisms of emotional response as the character takes us through his consciousness of affect, step by step. It is a kind of dramatic shorthand, skirting the problem of temporal limits in recreating for the audience the character's emotional life so the audience, too, will feel it.

Over and over, these plays will describe emotional response as if to answer the question, *how* does someone feel when an object of desire strikes his consciousness and how does this feeling get expressed. They answer it not as a true classicist, a good Aristotelian, would want, through an action that encodes a moral choice nor as a romantic a hundred years later would like, through a speech that implies an entire particular life encountering unmediated experience, but rather by giving us an analysis of what I am feeling now. This is literal mimesis with a vengence. The character tells, that is, of his consciousness of his own response to the object. He puts before us not so much what would reveal to us expressly the moral response of the speaker as what Descartes has told us in detail goes on in the soul when it is confronted by an object that moves it:

> *Zanger.* Ah, Prince! much more indeed; for had you seen
> The Griefs and Beauties of the Christian Queen,
> You would have felt the Trouble which I had;
> These did to Pity, those to Love persuade:
> They helped each other to perform their Part,
> Grief soften'd, and her Beauty seal'd my Heart;
> . . . .
> When she her Royal Infant did embrace,
> Her Eyes such Floods of Tears show'r'd on her Face,
> That then, Oh, *Mustapha!* I did admire
> How so much Water sprung from so much Fire:
> And to increase the Miracle, I found
> At the same time my Heart both burnt and drown'd.[11]

Or, more simply, Brutus in Tate's *Brutus of Alba*, explaining in act 4 his reelings in ecstasy to the Queen of Syracuse, while she explains hers to him. Virgil, Tate's source, had needed neither, nor, happidly, did Purcell when he turned Tate's play into *Dido and Aeneas*. But Dennis did for *Rinaldo and Armida's* second act display of Armida's "greatness of soul," a quality that appears to be a large capacity to feel and to describe the workings of those feelings to us. Rinaldo himself is more taciturn, telling us briefly just after Armida has analyzed the softness in her soul as not compassion, but "something softer"—love,

> Ha! The Queen!
> Now, where are all thy feeble Resolutions?
> One Glance has humbled thy Aspiring Thoughts,
> Pleasure flows streaming from those Lovely Eyes,
> And with it's [*sic*] Sweetness overcomes my Soul.[12]

Or we could turn back to King Arthur's response to the naked nymphs. Or to Settle's *Empress of Morocco* when Laula counters the young queen's Love and Obedience:

> Let those, whom pious conscience awes, forbear,
> And stop at Crimes because they Vengeance fear.
> My deeds above the reach and power aspire.
> My bosom holds more rage, than all Hell Fire.[13]

The Empress, who is in various situations of duplicity throughout the play, rarely displays her true emotions for us, but analyzes those, both real and imagined, of the other characters and of her fraudulent self-projections. She entraps Muly Hamet with the convincing depiction of her response to his attempted rape. Appearing as she sat pensively paying tribute to her husband's fate,

> The sudden objects did new thoughts produce;
> My Griefs suspended, lent my tears a truce:
> For then I otherwise employ'd my Eyes.
> Whilst in his aspect I read Victories.
>
> (3. 1. 125)

She progresses here through a description of the external manifestations of passion in Muly Hamet, less detailed than the one she elaborates for the young queen after poor Morena has been tricked into stabbing her own husband in a masque, but no less attentive to the stage representation of passion that she gives there:

Alone I saw her in a posture set,
As if she thought of something high-and great—
Strai't with a more than common rage enflam'd,

She   mov'd—star'd—walk'd—storm'd—rag'd—curst—rav'd   and
damn'd
With a distorted look she tore her hair—
Unsheath'd her dagger—and gave wounds to th'air—

(4. 3. 155)

The analysis of the passions throughout these moments, as of their
imagined—and probably factual—theatrical depiction could serve as
textbook examples of *The Passions of the Soul*. This is not to suggest that
the dramatists had all read Descartes, but rather that the conventions
of emotional projection that developed in the Restoration theatre are
parallel to the most advanced thinking on the emotions of the day,
whether it entered the stage by way of Descartes himself or of the
French theatre. In Dryden's Adam, the first seems the more likely
source, but sources seem less important to me than the fact of the
intelligent effort undertaken here. The attempt is in kind not unlike
the Freud-laden dramas of the 1920s and 1930s and helps, perhaps as
much as specific political and sociological considerations, to account
for the subjects and their treatment in the heroic plays.[14] The subjects
must be emotionally extreme and involve the sorts of characters who
can believeably be expected to display their emotions for us. Character has such importance in the drama of the period not only because it
was extreme in that extremity that pulls the modern reader up short,
making us look for parodic explanations, but also because, if we re-
vert to theory, character not action had become the center of thinking
about the serious drama on the grounds of its importance in the
recreation of the passions conceived as states of soul directly com-
municable to the audience, independent of the shape of the action.

II

I take Dryden as typical on this point. He tells us, in the "Essay of
Dramatic Poesy," that if Beaumont and Fletcher did outsell Jonson
and Shakespeare two to one in the late sixties, it was because of the
accessibility of their emotionality—the gaiety of their comedy and the
pathos of their more serious plays—expressed in a language less obso-
lete than Shakespeare's by characters conceived not as Jonsonian
humors, but concerned with love. If Jonson was the putative model
for the comic dramatists of the time, yet the heavily emotional turns
and crises of Fletcherian drama pleased the audience more and
weighed more heavily on the serious plays. Eugenius, early in the
"Essay," had claimed as one of the virtues of modern over ancient
drama the depiction of love, valuable for its universal affective app-

eal. Having allowed that sudden gusts of passion are not loquacious and to make them so were to break verisimilitude, he adds,

> But there are a thousand other concernments of Lovers, as jealousies, complaints, contrivances, and the like where not to open their minds at large to each other, were to be wanting in their own love, and to the expectation of the Audience; who watch the movements of their minds, as much as the changes of their fortunes. For the imaging of the first is properly the work of the Poet; the latter he borrows from the Historian.[15]

Though it might seem unlikely that Dryden, the defender of Jonson's structural powers, would have made as free with plot in propia persona as he allows Eugenius to do, unanswered, here, yet the "Essay" throughout, even in the Examen of *The Silent Woman*, focuses heavily on character and minimizes plot consistently. The poet is repeatedly described as one whose concern is with imaging "the movements of the mind" even where plot is not consigned to the historian. As a result, the emphases that Lisideius's opening definition of a play proposes are maintained: "A Play ought to be, A just and lively Image of Humane Nature, representing its Passions and Humours, and the Changes of Fortune to which it is subject; for the Delight and Instruction of mankind."[16] Crites, the only participant who, as spokesman for the ancients, will defend action, objects to the definition on logical grounds (you speak for all genres), but allows the definition to pass, even with its embedded character-centered definition of plot pushed to the penultimate clause. No one denies that "the soul of Poesy" is the "imitation of humours and passions," the final arbiter for Neander of everything, outweighing the rules, outweighing the problem of the mixture of tragedy and comedy, outweighing the injunction against underplots. States of emotion as depicted in the heroic plays are the definitive materials of drama.

These become the described emotions that make up the play's colliding passional field. Dennis speaks for the heroic genre when he says of his opera, whose plot and characters combine Tasso and the heroic play, "I design'd not only to move Passion, but as many Passions as I could successively, without doing violence to my subject." The adverb is telling. As Dennis conceives it, a play is an occasion, a container for the evocation of a discrete but consistent series of passions "successively"—the audience is to receive those emotions "contagiously" (in Rogerson's terminology), one by one, and the conception of character necessarily becomes less a conception of character as we recognize it than of vehicle, a vehicle now for emotional states, rather than ideas alone, but still an inherently allegorical conception, as in the masque, as in Davenant.[17]

Little wonder that the story per se so often seems disconnected from the particular characters and their interest, and so rarely seems the source, but rather the occasion of the characters' feelings. The whole play has appeared to more than one critic a kind of grid on which evocative moments are arrayed. The procedure is quite opposite to any suggested by Aristotelian theory: "They do not, then, act in order to represent character, but in the course of their actions they show what their characters are."[18] Aristotle describes character morally rather than emotionally conceived, and therefore action *can* be the play's soul in a manner totally foreign to the Davenant line's way of thinking—about plot, about character, and about emotional response, however much that final concern owes to the cathartic end Aristotle posited for tragedy. Their conception is far more immediate than Aristotle's in its equation of the stage's represented emotional life and the audience's. The unbroken continuity assumed between the two is grounded on the universality of emotional life as shared reactions to stimuli, whereby the means of mediation of the passion never need be discussed insofar as those means rely on a "contagion" that can be positively understood as a given of the stage's continuity with real life. It is not an entire plot as the imitation of an action that will stage the stimuli, but individual and, if need be, discrete actions, each projecting its stimulus.

The point I would stress here is the apparent externality of the dramatic procedures resulting from this understanding of affect. If the Cartesian analysis of the passions helps to clarify the rationale of the dramatists' methods by explaining their continuing assumption of "contagion," still it does not make them contagious any longer. Ideally we will experience along with the character both the "sudden object" and the "new thought produc'd," the "Pleasure streaming from those Lovely Eyes." But generally we in fact do not. Ideally, the theory should have produced the most immediate of theatrical experiences, uniting us with the innermost reaches of the most extreme emotional moments of the characters' psychic lives. But over time, it has not. Even those who have acquired a taste for the heroic play most often defend it as consciously artificial, praise its distancing, and honor its unreality. Those qualities are certainly not what its writers ever claim for it. Admiration may be here, as in Descartes, the single emotion beyond desire, impersonal and purely intellectual, but it is engendered not by the unreal, only the "rare" (*Passions* 2.70ff.). The writers instead thought they were entering deeply into, as Mace has insisted, the movements of the soul, and thought they were doing precisely what the truly great dramatist—a Racine, a Shakespeare—did, having found a way to make drama's necessarily externally perceived and presented characters reflect and project their interior lives.

A comparison to the case in comedy may make my point clearer. The home of ethos as tragedy is of pathos, comedy never turned to the elaboration of the inner self as its *raison,* never abandoned external portraiture as its means as well as end, and it therefore thrived throughout the languors of the serious drama, a point Dryden makes himself in the "Defence of an Essay." The two generic groups are separated on the Restoration stage and in its criticism on just this distinction. When Dryden speaks of the serious drama, he leaves no question about whom he values and why: Shakespeare is the greatest depictor of the passions any stage has had. Where classical characters fall short as stage representations of passionate experience, Shakespeare (along with Fletcher) describes pathos in perfection, through the exercise of wit. This single fact raises Shakespeare above all other dramatic poets in Dryden's eyes, excusing all his blunders and awkward naivete. I take this to be a typical and consistent position throughout Dryden's career, whatever else changes.[19]

For comedy, the emphasis shifts from emotion; we hear less about the truths of the heart—and more about Jonson. Passion is subsumed under the rubric manners, always a primarily external notion, though a descriptive, revelatory one: "Both [Ovid and Chaucer] understood the manners; under which name I comprehend the passions and, in a larger sense, the descriptions of persons, and their very habits" ("Preface to Fables," Watson, *Of Dramatic Poesy* 2:278). Manners are the visible expression of passion as of type, of status, of role. Dryden's comic emphasis falls from early to late, from the "Essay of Dramatic Poesy" to the "Preface to Fables," on the external representation of character in terms of a visible typology, though a typology particularized well beyond mere abstraction. The variety of humors in which Jonson (and Chaucer) excelled are understood as "some extravagant habit, passion, or affection particular . . . to some one person, by the oddness of which he is immediately distinguished from the rest of men." Complex comic character, as in Falstaff, "the best of them," is "a miscellany of humours or images." The materials of comedy, worked up most masterfully by Jonson, are immediately visible expressions of excess, recognizably human, not merely stock types defined fully by age and station (the limitation of Attic New Comedy), but particularized distinctly "not only in their inclinations, but in their very physiognomies and persons."

So far, then, as comic character is concerned, Neander claims this particularization of the old stock types as the Elizabethans advance beyond classical comedy, giving to the stage what Dryden would claim in "Preface to Fables" Chaucer had imparted to narrative poetry, granting the general character universal to mankind a local habitation and a name. It was in such externally perceived and presented characterization that the Restoration made its own advances as well, and because its principle was, after all, sound—because we *can* know character in drama through its external manifestations—on the basis of this principle the Fopling Flutters and Mirabells, the Lady Wishfort's and Maskwell's peopled the stage in greater numbers and to greater delight than at any other point in English stage history. When Dryden acknowledged his audience's preference for comedy, that ought not to have been a complaint, but praise for the audience's recognition that this is what the Restoration stage could do, given the success of its external procedures, the relative failure of its efforts after the inward soul and the affect that governed those efforts.

The primary device to achieve those affects, authorized in a far different context by Aristotle (*Poetics* 50a33), relied on in theory and in practice throughout the Restoration, was a device of action, those turns and counterturns that create the shifts in mood expressed in the Cartesian self-explications I have pointed at.[20] There is thus a great deal of pressure on the poetry to make those shifts effectively and directly convey turns not simply of the action but of the psyche. While heroic poetry has seemed a splendid vehicle for argumentation, at least in the hands of Dryden, it has seemed less capable of conveying those emotional peaks and passionate effects Dryden wished it to embody. The reason lies in Dryden's treatment of metaphor, itself typical for the period, creating that sense of externality and distance that separates us from the character at precisely those moments we ought to be entering his experience most fully. Here the desire for control, for authorial power, defeats the desire for affect.

One can locate the problem in the attitude toward action and the relation between character and action that results from that attitude.[21] I think it is also heavily influenced by the interpretation of a Horatian apothegm that Dryden connects significantly to metaphor. "*Si vis me flere, dolendum est/ Primum ipsi tibi,*" Horace had said, echoing Aristotle's suggestion that "the most persuasive poets are those who have the same natures as their characters and enter into their sufferings; he who feels distress represents distress and he who feels anger represents anger most genuinely" (*Poetics* 55a22).

Such classical advice issued effectively in the Renaissance in those rhetorical catalogues of tropes posited not on their usefulness in making handsome, sensuous poems but their efficacy for creating significant and affecting figures.[22] However far into abeyance the catalogues of tropes and figures had fallen by Dryden's time, he turned to a Longinian rhetorical reading of Horace in defending the style of heroic verse:

> If you can enter more deeply, than they [the most learned and the judicious] have done, into the causes and resorts of that which moves pleasure in the reader, the field is open, you may be heard: but those springs of human nature are not so easily discovered by every superficial judge: it requires Philosophy, as well as Poetry, to sound the depths of all the passions; what they are in themselves and how they are to be provoked: and in this science the best poets have excelled. Aristotle raised the fabric of his *Poetry* from observation of those things in which Euripedes, Sophocles, and Aeschylus pleased: he considered how they raised the passions, and thence has drawn rules for our imitation. From hence have sprung the tropes and figures, for which they wanted a name, who first practiced them, and succeeded in them. Thus I grant you, that the knowledge of Nature was the original rule; and that all poets ought to study her, as well as Aristotle and Horace, her interpreters. But then this also undeniably follows, that those things, which delight all ages, must have been an imitation of Nature. . . . Therefore is Rhetoric made an art; therefore the names of so many tropes and figures were invented; because it was observed they had such and such effect upon the audience. Therefore catachreses and hyperboles have found their place among them; not that they were to be avoided, but to be used judiciously, and placed in poetry, as heightenings and shadows are in painting, to make the figure bolder, and cause it to stand off to sight.[23]

Dryden exemplifies his point with close readings of passages from Virgil, Horace, and Cowley and adds further practical criticism from Longinus, all of it tending to the conclusion that bold figures "work their effect upon the mind" best in the depiction of passion, "for then, Si vis me flere dolendum est primum ipsi tibi. The Poet must put on the Passion he endeavors to represent."

Dryden's translation summarizes neatly the distance between his interpretation of Horace and what a post-Kantian expressive theorist would make of the same lines:

> The passion that is traced before us has glowed in a living heart. . . . He speaks forth what is in him, not from any outward call of vanity or interest, but because his heart is too full to be silent. . . . This is the grand secret for finding readers and retaining them: let him who would move and convince others, be first moved and con-

vinced himself. Horace's rule, *Si vis me flere,* is applicable in a wider sense than the literal one.[24]

Meyer Abrams cites Carlyle here to make the observation that Sincerity's elevation to eminence in the pantheon of poetic virtues, a corollary of the idea that "feeling is the essence of poetry," has quite put out perceptible artfulness as the source of satisfaction in poetry. To translate into Dryden's own language, sincerity has displaced that "coolness and discretion which is necessary to a poet" and been replaced by "a heart too full to be silent." The loss of the discretion necessary to a poet for Dryden results in such fiascoes as *The Empress of Morocco.* Dryden argues in his attack on *The Empress* that Settle has completely misunderstood the meaning of "poetic license," which ought to be only verisimilar poetry:

> Fancyfull Poetry, and Musick, used with Moderation are good, but men who are wholy given over to either of them, are commonly as full of whimseyes as diseas'd and Splenatick men can be: their heads are continually hot, and they have the same elevation of Fancy sober, which men of Sense have when they are drunk . . . so meer Poets and meer Musicians, are as sottish as meer Drunkards are, who live in a continual mist without seeing, or judging anything clearly.[25]

While Dryden, Crowne and Shadwell do not grant Settle enough success in his play to suggest that he effectively besots his audience, their extended criticism of the play's plot and language takes up in detail the play's insults to reason, its defeat of discretion in pursuit of the grand. The attack on Settle is carried out through close readings—in some cases literal-minded reductions of the extremest sorts, in some cases thoroughly just objections. The effort is to expose both plot and language for its excesses and awkwardnesses. The objections illustrate the same attitude toward metaphor that Dryden reveals in that other essay on poetic licence, the "Apology for Heroic Poetry." There his poetic examples of hyperbole are such as immediately appear striking and improbable, perhaps striking because improbable, yet on closer scrutiny prove rationalizable. Thus he gives us his defense of Cowley's depiction of Goliath and of Longinus's example from Herodotus of the Lacedaemonians at Thermopylae. It is just, finally, to portray the passionate, occasions when we speak "more warmly" and "with more precipitation," but not in the portrayal to abandon "the coolness and discretion which is necessary to a poet." Rationality is thus not a predicate of a play's characters; it is an attribute of style; again we are at that intersection of artifice and imitation wherein the authority of the artist is asserted as control. A play's conversation is not "a composition of several persons speaking *ex tempore*" as Howard had claimed; rather, it "is supposed to be the work of the poet, imitating or representing the conversation of several persons" (*Defence of an Essay*, 114), a principle that explains a great deal more than the capping couplets Dryden is specifically defending here. Settle's abandonment of that authority, the voice of the poet behind the several persons speaking, is his authorial sin.

In yoking excessive music and metaphor with the drunkard, in the passage cited above, Dryden identifies both as techniques that move easily into the irrational, appealing to, presumably, the viscera, away from clear judgment in an abandonment of Descartes's intellectual emotions. When I remarked earlier that the Restoration dramatists thought they were accomplishing with their Cartesian declamations what Racine or Shakespeare achieved in the way of projection of the soul, I assumed the obvious objection to the comparison in any reader's mind would be less the discrepancy between more and less fully integrated senses of plot and character than an incommensurability in the poetry. The willingness of Shakespeare, and to a lesser extent Racine, to sacrifice the authorial voice, to allow metaphoric logic to carry them—and us—beyond clear judgment into regions less amenable to rational analysis, regions that have a good deal in common with the one music opens for us as well, is not a quality for which the latter half of the seventeenth century admired any poet, even including Shakespeare. The three men responsible for the attack on Settle were among them responsible as well for the major operatic works of the Restoration—Crowne's *Calisto*, Shadwell's *Tempest* and *Psyche*, Dryden's *King Arthur*. All three share a thoroughgoing rejection of the capacity of music to do exactly what we most value it for, creating for us, as metaphor also does, access to areas of mental experience inaccessible to rational analysis. This is as evident in the works cited as in the attack on Settle; all of them are based on temptation stories wherein the resistance to sensuosity is thematically central, its compatibility with reason a primary problem.

There is significance, I think, in the fact that *The Empress of Morocco* has been proposed of late as the hidden gem of the musical drama of the period, a significance that extends well beyond the intrinsic value of Locke's and Settle's work. From quite different perspectives and to thoroughly disparate ends, both Curtis Price and Philip Parsons have praised *The Empress* for the integration and dramatic effectiveness of its embedded masque.[26] They have considered it a successful implementation of the musical resources of the stage, concentrating on the ironic plot turn accomplished through Locke's masque. That this is a point that Dryden et al. submerge or failed to recognize can detract from its value no more than their failure to see the relevance of the walking gentlemen to *Henry VIII* detracts from Shakespeare's multiple perspectivism in that play. Rather it points up the tyranny of cultural limits, which are functional in both directions here. Structural irony had nothing like the seductiveness for 1674 that it has had for the twentieth century, and it could never have made up for drunken Fancy if it had. Unlike modern readers, Dryden would not see around the irrationality of language and action, the abdication of responsible control, of discretion, he saw in Settle's work.

In the 1752 Dublin version of *Henry VIII* published in Dryden's name, a version devoted to the monarchical epideictics on which Shakespeare's play is structured, everything that relates to the undercutting of epideictic forms has been eliminated—the opening ambiguities around the Field of Cloth of Gold, the circling whisperers and eavesdroppers, the multiple interpretations of the acts undertaken. Buckingham's role is cut to pieces and the comic characters—the Old Lady and the Porter's Man—are retained via Restoration comedy: she is the racy gossip and he distinctive lowlife, in clear masque-line contrast to the now much more carefully focused conflict between parvenu Wolsey and the King. The final prophecy, having dropped the lines referring to James I, is a historically defensible, demystified praise of England's promise. We can mourn the losses as oversimplifications; we can also recognize that pseudo-Dryden achieves a tighter, clearer "tragedy" (his label) and, from at least one point of view, a better play. Forced to choose between the two today, we would doubtless take Shakespeare's version, for its rich ambivalences, its unresolved ironies. But perhaps we need not simply choose. Perhaps we can see pseudo-Dryden's enterprise as more than the bare assertion of reason and authority, clarity and praise. We can see it instead as an effort to present those as coherent goals, making this play-version less the expression of a lost time than a fully conscious choice of materials. It recognizes that the cessation of James's claims leaves the tragedy the subtitle describes, despite perspectival "subterfuges" (as I fear Dryden himself would call them).[27] The work, in all elements of its style, ought finally to be comfortable to reason, understood broadly, as a play as rich as *Don Sebastian* makes evident; not life, but the drama that interprets it, is answerable.

This is what finally defeats the heroic play. In pursuit of affect, employing the most extreme characters, analyzing the passions carefully and at length, its entire *raison* a pursuit of emotionality, it could not forgo rationality for a moment in its practice, so that all its content is, in a very real sense, in conflict with its embodiment. When the self-defensive insistence on reason and artifice has been put aside, a twentieth-century critic can find as much to admire in *The Empress of Morocco* as in *Tyrannick Love*. Settle begins to look like us, post-Freudian, in touch with a subconscious life we recognize. We can respond to that in a way that Dryden would have found first despicable, then mystifying, much as Dennis felt when he watched the Italian opera take over the English stage.

One feels, in retrospect, that music ought to have been among the means that writers of the heroic play and its related texts employed in their efforts to project the emotions of their characters. And music does appear more insistently on the stage now than ever before, though never in a more fully integrated manner than in *King Arthur* and therefore never primarily in the role of character projector at all. That, of course, is precisely what opera had been invented for in the first place, though Dryden, with his functional emphasis, ignores the fact in his Preface's *translatio studii*. There, as in practice in *King Arthur*, he treats opera as an accoutrement of fete and music in a suitably figural sense, imitative of the passions and effective on the audience, though always distinctly divorced from the expression of the principals themselves, objectifying their temptations, distancing their involvement with the temptations in the analytic manner of the masque tradition. The tradition Dryden recognizes does emerge from the princely fetes, the Medicean parallel to the Tudor and Stuart masques, though as opera it had long before Dryden's time separated itself from those functions. Dryden chooses to view opera reductively when he avoids the fact that makes it the closest theatrical sibling of the heroic play. For opera per se, at the point at which it emerges from the fetes, was designed not merely to praise princes, but first to move the passions, and to move the passions on the same classical rhetorical principles that govern the Restoration serious drama, though without the aid of a Cartesian specificity. In stressing the source rather than the sequent product that existed in his own time in France as well as Italy, Dryden was, consciously, I believe, following the same route that he had with metaphor. Put more broadly, I want to suggest that the English dramatists rejected opera as we know it not simply because of economics (the management was willing to go to great lengths to pay for the Italian operas when they came over) nor because their tradition of spoken drama was too strong to be unseated, but because music like metaphor threatened the commitment to explicability, to authorial rationality, to controlled artifice.

III

The conflict between emotional affect and rationality had been instrumental in defining the route of opera's development from the beginning—or at least, in defining its polemics. The impulse behind the theory of those Italians Dryden refers to in his Preface was affective and expressive to a fault, for a professional musician like Artusi, but it accorded perfectly with dramatic theory and satisfied the literary amateurs among whom opera was created. The Camerata sought a drama that could vie with the ancients for affective power by the moving depiction—or perhaps rather, recreation—of the emotional experience of the subjects. Caccini, Peri, Galilei—all the initial composers take as a given the idea that music's end is to "delight and move the affections of the mind"[28] an idea which was not, of course, the property of these "moderns" in the struggle that ensued over their practice.

Artusi, one of the most vociferous of the opposition, insisted too that delectation was the end of music.[29] The quarrel was over means. Artusi argued that the new practices were not "founded upon some reason which could satisfy the intellect;" the dissonant relations in which the new music abounds "can in no way be a harmonic relation" (p. 42) and effect, when they do, by deception of the mind, which harmony ought rather to satisfy (p. 39). The "perfection of their music" is a result not of knowledge of music (they have *not* read Boethius and Ptolemy on the fallibility of the senses), but of extramusical mimicry ("they are content to know how to string their notes together after their fashion and to teach the singers to sing their compositions, accompanying themselves with many movements of the body, and in the end they let themselves go to such an extent that they seem to be actually dying" [p. 42].) Instead of appeals to the intellect, to the knowledgeable understanding of text and score, the new music, according to Antusi, appeals directly to the senses through passional mimicry and exemplifies the vice of mere sensuous appeal.

Monteverdi, naturally in 1607, responded by copious citations to Plato and Boethius in defense of his famous position that the words are mistress of the harmony and that to judge of his compositions, as Artusi does, without reference to the words is to deprive them, in quite the language of Jonson, of their soul—that is, "the disposition of the soul itself," quoting Ficino's translation of *Republic* (398 D). The argument over the seconda pratica is a technical argument about theories of harmony and the dissonances unnecessary to my point, which can be made, I believe, from the polemic I have been citing.

Behind Artusi stands Zarlino's authority and conviction that music is its own subject; it need imitate nothing at all. The rational order of music creates its own materials. Behind the Platonist Monteverdi's response is no lesser claim to reason, but a shift in goals. "I have reflected," he tells us, "that the principle passions or affections of our mind are three, namely, anger, moderation, and humility or supplication"[30] and music—not theoretically, but practically—has lacked the first. Monteverdi "applied myself with no small diligence and toil to rediscover this genus" (p. 53). His success was to create the *stile concitato,* to set Tasso's combat of Tancred and Clorinda as an "attempt to depict anger," a feat that he considers a "rediscovery" that perfects the range of music (p. 54).

I do not question here the validity of his claims but wish only to stress the line of his thinking.[31] It is a "rediscovery" because the revolution in music at the turn of the sixteenth century, on the part of both amateurs in Florence and thorough professionals like Monteverdi, was seen by its creators not as innovation but as a profoundly conservative act, a reclamation from their Gothic loss of the fabled affective powers of the classical modes and, ultimately, of classical drama. For Giovanni de'Bardi, the ethea were the marvels of music, a good musician being one who can dispose another's mind "to any moral quality," the feat Dryden rhapsodized in "Alexanders Feast."

Bardi argues, out of Aristotle, that "just as the soul is nobler than the body, so the words are nobler than the counterpoint" and must rule. In practice, according to Pietro de'Bardi's letter to Doni, this led to Galilei's experiments in *stile rappresentativo,* from the first, representations of high passion (Dante's lament of Count Ugolino, followed by the Lamentations and Responds of Holy Week), "sweetened" and thus made "capable of moving the passions in a rare manner" by Peri, who went on to set the first opera, *Dafne,* elaborating the lyrical core to a full *dramma per musica.*[32] Galilei himself leveled the same attack against contemporary contrapuntists that Artusi was to make twenty years later against Monteverdi: they "aim at nothing but the delight of the ear, if it can truly be called delight. They have not a book among them . . . that speaks of how to express the conceptions of the mind and of how to impress them with the greatest possible effectiveness on the minds of the listeners." (2:122)

Like many of the literary theoreticians—Minturno, for example—Galilei, with his emphasis on the words, his denigration of distracting counterpoint, assumes that the moving of the audience will be achieved through the force of the conceptions imbedded in the monody. In 1701 in a literary context, Dennis expresses the same belief. The conceptions Galilei was concerned with were the emotions; Dennis retains this bias as well.[33] Thus Galilei ridicules the contrapuntal vice of imitating concepts by word painting—making the music rough when the text speaks of roughness, sliding when it says downward, and so on. The sole purpose here is to delight the ear, whereas for the ancients it was "to induce in another the same passion that one feels oneself," which mere graphic detail can never achieve. One must instead grasp the feeling of the passage as a whole and project that (2:125–29). He opposes thereby the musical equivalent of emblematic literalism to passional wholeness, emotional totality. Among English composers of the same time, Morley takes precisely the opposite position, expressing a practical attitude that holds in English composition for the stage into the Restoration, affecting still Blow and Purcell.

Galilei gives advice on accomplishing such projection, advice that perhaps gave Artusi fuel for his criticism of monodic style. It is, at any rate, counsel that sounds odd, unless one remembers the rhetorical basis of his thought; go to the mummers' plays and watch how they do it; derive from them a norm for any conception. That, after all, is how Timotheus worked his great effects. It is, of course, also the advice that Quintilian gave to the orator, and it is on the basis of such affective rhetorical theory that the late Renaissance could justify to itself the elaboration of emotion as a subject in its own right—by its capacity to teach by imitation through the power to move to parallel feelings. We may doubt whether such an idea ever entered the head of a poet or a composer as he worked, but when asked for a conceptual rationalization, that is what he would probably reply, as, for instance, Davenant did through Aristophanes in the *First Days Entertainment.*

Further, and still part of the classical rhetorical tradition, the artist could see in the imitation his own inspiration. "How, my dear Sir," Monteverdi wrote to Striggio in 1616 concerning a projected—but never completed—opera, *Le Nozze di Tetide,*

> can I imitate the language of winds, which do not speak? And how can I, through the winds, affect an audience? Ariadne moves me because she is a woman, and Orpheus because he is a man, not a wind. . . . The whole plot, as far as my ignorance can make it out, does not affect me in the least. I understand it with difficulty and do not feel that it leads me in a natural way toward a goal that moves me. Adriadne inspires me to a just lament and Orpheus a just prayer, but this tale inspires me to nothing.[34]

Little wonder that Monteverdi avoided allegory.

Monteverdi's classical precedent is of course once again the Horatian *si vis me flere* that would eventually become the vehicle of expressive theory when imitation had been demoted from its throne in aesthetics. This could and would happen earlier in music than in literature, especially once music has been divorced from the verbal text.[35] But in opera the marriage of the two—text and music, as quarrelsome a wedding as Solyman's to Roxolana, remained at least theoretically in the control of the words throughout the century, and with that in the control of imitation. Imitation continues to imply verisimilitude, more and more literally here as throughout the arts. Jonson's Eyes and Nose, Middleton's Starches will not appear at all, finally. In France, the Prologues of praise to Louis that Dryden used as a basis for *Albion and Albanius* will give over finally to what their greatest composer did best, not praise at all, but the direct imitation of the passions that made allegorical artifice an outmoded, awkward avoidance of the issue. Lully did that without the help of any more specific theory than the Restoration dramatists had. What a theorist would make of his accomplishment is instructive, though, both in regard to the limitations of the conceptual notions of the time and to the distance from Dryden that the theorist reads in Lully's achievement.

Charles Saint-Evremond was the most musically knowledgeable writer on opera in England after the Restoration. That he disliked it as it existed about 1677, when he wrote his famous letter to the Duke of Buckingham, is all too obvious. That, given his preconceptions, he could like it any better later is improbable. His primary resistance to opera lay in its lack of verisimilitude, in his conviction that without verisimilitude there could be no intellectually convincing and effectively engaging imitation of life. Saint-Evremond begins his attack with a description of his overall response. The marvels and mere sound become boring, as boring as the recitative, "which possesses neither the charm of the song nor the forcefulness of the spoken word." The mind unengaged, the soul cannot be affected and "forms a secret resistance to the impressions it might receive or, at least, fails to give its approval, without which even the most voluptuous objects cannot please me very much."[36] The reason that Saint-Evremond is bored is implicit in his specific complaints: it is unnatural to sing a play from beginning to end: to call a servant, to command in battle, to deliberate in council in song violates "the spirit of drama." Because singing is unnatural, one thinks not of the hero, but of "the one who makes him sing," of Cavalli, of Lully. The intense artificiality of the form leads one to be a connoisseur of artifice rather than a vicarious participant in mimetically convincing life. *Ars celare artium* hasn't a chance.

Yet Saint-Evremond would not bar music from the stage. There are, as he says, things that "can be sung without offense to propriety and reason." He numbers among these things "all that concerns the cult of the Gods," the passions of love and mourning, which "are naturally expressed by a kind of chant," and the "irresolution of a soul torn between two conflicting emotions." These are "subjects suited to measured poetry and hence to singing." He imagines, then, a kind of semi-opera, not necessarily the English kind, but one in which those dramatic events traditionally expressed, as he sees it, in heightened form will be expressed in music. Saint-Evremond does not seem to recognize the extent to which his allowed musical moments are determined by convention, by sheer custom, but moves always to nature and what is "natural" to justify his preferences. They are "natural" because they are lyrical moments of heightened emotionality. Casting them in music simply adds wings to all the flights of poetry. One could expect, then, that in the five-hundred-year-long operatic struggle for supremacy between poet and composer, Saint-Evremond would come down firmly on the side of the poet, and he does: "The poet should be given the principle authority in all matters concerning the work. The music must be there for the sake of the poetry and not the poetry for the sake of the music."

One composer, Lully, is excepted from Saint-Evremond's general pronouncement, not because Lully conducted a musical action without boring recitative or voluptuous, unengaging spectacle, but because he "knows the Passions better, and enters farther into the heart of man, than the authors themselves."[37] Saint-Evremond does not step back from his otherwise universal dictum and consider the implications of his recognition that music may in itself dramatize the emotions beyond the reach of words, quite apart from questions of what is "natural." True to the century's unwillingness to analyze closely the forms of mediation, he rests in the general and its single epicycle, as Hume has warned us the English literary critics do. Imitation, *vraisemblance*, and the "natural" explain opera's lacks for him; the practical question of the means of projecting the Passions is ignored, left in the notion of Lully's better knowledge of them.

Some of these difficulties exist, of course, in Dryden's own criticism. Some of them he averts by contrary assumptions (the problem of artificiality is, as we know, far less a "problem" for Dryden, his acceptance of conscious artifice making his sense of the allegorical use of music, as in *Tyrannick Love* or *The State of Innocence* as well as the operas, unobjectionable). However, because music as a medium of stage representation was never analyzed any more fully during the century than Saint-Evremond does here, objections to its use continue to outweigh what seem virtually pro forma recognitions of its capabilities. Lully can be cast as exception on empirical grounds that do not extend to the form itself, since an extension would have to be won on other than mimetic grounds.

So long as music is approached mimetically, as it was until well into the eighteenth century, its uses are of necessity limited in serious drama to those to which it was put by Dryden, Dennis, Shadwell, and the rest. These tend to be the uses Saint-Evremond's sense of decorum cordoned off for music, separable moments of heightened emotionality, with the proviso that a literal dramatic justification for their taking place musically could be devised. This led to many allegorical intrusions, to many roles for sorcerers and occasions for masques, but no need for Betterton to learn to sing. I shall explore both the exceptions and the effects of the limitations in the final chapter, but here I wish to elaborate in conclusion Dennis's ideas about the relation of music to the passions, ideas that did not free him from the allegorical and mimetic predispositions of his stage but that instead return us by a back door to the intrusion of nationalistic thinking into the issue.

IV

In 1694, when he wrote his own opera, Dennis's appeal to music is for its positive value as a medium for the expression and evocation of the passions. In 1698, his defense of the stage in general is based on a broader version of the same notion: poetry is an appeal to the passions and in so being ought to be recognized, pace Collier, as a primary vehicle of social order and religious instruction through the pleasure and access it provides. Yet music is very soon separated emphatically from poetry in this task. Dennis had elevated the passions to absolute primacy in the appeal of poetry by assuming that the good writer does not raise those passions that are in conflict with the Reason, because to do so would create a civil war in the breast. Music could take part in the endeavor so long as the same responsibility was exercised, given the experience of its power that Dennis asserted: "There is no man living who is more convinc'd than my self of the Power of Harmony, or more penetrated by the Charms of Musick."[38] Yet he gave this testimonial in a condemnatory context, the broad polemic against "the Invasion of Foreign Luxury" that opera constituted in his eyes by 1706.

Perhaps it was because Dennis had experienced the power of harmony and the charms of music that he distrusted it and saw in the

Italian invasion an undermining of the usefulness of the stage at just those points he had urged against Collier in 1698—poetry's capacity to reinforce religion and national (patriotic) interests. Whatever the failure of *Rinaldo and Armida* may have added to Dennis's motives, his position now against the opera is consistent with his particular elevation of the passions all along. Music, like painting, always was a stepchild to poetry in his thinking, lacking poetry's addition of appeals to sense to its appeal to the senses.[39] "It belongs to poetry only to teach publick Virtue and publick Spirit, and a noble Contempt of Death, with an Expression and with an Air becoming its Godlike Notions." Convinced by the Italian and French examples that opera destroys poetry in the cultures it invades, his fears for England in 1706 are intense.

The Horatian dicta are still in force. Dennis's elevation of the passions, whatever his awareness of the power of harmony, excised rather than included music:

> That the Speech, by which Poetry makes its Imitation, must be pathetick, is evident, for Passion is still more necessary to it than Harmony. For Harmony only distinguishes its Instrument from that of Prose but Passion distinguishes its very Nature and Character. For therefore Poetry is Poetry, because it is more Passionate and Sensual than Prose.[40]

The echoes of Milton in his statement are borne out in his practical criticism where Milton reigns supreme, not as a singer of organ tones, but as the finest exemplar of the true source of passion—Enthusiasm for a great idea. If one asked Dennis how the enthusiasm is mediated, the answer would not be number and measure, mere instruments of harmony, and only instrumental, not essential. The answer is the words and the ideas these embody:

> If any one asks, What sort of Passions these are, that thus, unknown to us, flow from these Thoughts? to him I answer, That the same sort of Passions flow from the Thoughts, that would do from the Things of which those thoughts are Ideas. As for example, If the Thing we think of is great, why the Admiration attends the Idea of it; and if it is very great, Amazement . . . [and on through an array of the passions to the final statement that a religious subject supplies us with those thoughts which produce the greatest enthusiasm and hence the greatest poetry].[41]

For all his elevation of pleasure to its proper place in the aesthetic pantheon, Dennis is, if anything, less open to the power of *rhythmus* or harmony, less prone to respond to either the music of poetry or, perhaps by extension, to music itself. Finally ideas alone are the source of pleasure and of the sublime, whose images spring from the vastness of the conception itself. Like Saint-Evremond, he does not question the sources of the "power of harmony" nor its specific workings.[42] Dennis thus, having given the strongest expression of the century to the place of pleasure and the passions in the arts, stops short, poising at the brink of that expressive theory that will make music the speaker of the soul and other such romantic "falderal," but he retreats in the name of reason and the national well-being. His retreat is symptomatic of the times.

—— 7 ——

Magic and Modeling in the Final Quarter-Century

I have drawn a picture of opera's beginnings in England as positively attached to the epideictic tradition, to its allegorical procedures, its sense of communal function, its conciliatory heroic modeling. Though the greater number of musical dramas of the period fall outside the rubric strictly defined, I have wanted to suggest that the bulk of them are indelibly affected by the Davenant/Dryden line in their degree of abstraction, their conceptualized characterization, their dependence on an externally realized depiction of the passions and on heroism, that ubiquitous theme. To conclude this study, I will discuss several of these works in order to specify the connections. Through these brief analyses, the major themes of the book as a whole can be pulled together and illustrations given of how the manipulation of conventions has altered and where it has led. Some of the sites are a bit depressing; yet through this means, conclusions relevant to the whole tradition can be drawn. I have not chosen a work like Crowne's *Calisto,* which was a cause célèbre in its day but seems to me neither illustrative of anything we have not already seen nor intrinsically interesting. I have instead focused on works that are themselves major advances (Blow's *Venus and Adonis*), inherently superb (Purcell's *Dido and Aeneas*), and theoretically or culturally significant (Dennis's *Rinaldo and Armida*).

I want to begin, though, with Thomas Shadwell, because he, like Dryden, worked in musical theatre for a number of years, producing two of its most successful pieces—*Psyche* and the operatic *Tempest,* both with Matthew Locke as composer. They show us the fits and starts, the particular disarray, of the musical stage in 1675 (*Psyche* was staged 27 February 1674/5) and its early efforts to disengage itself from the masque. Taking Shadwell as an example, we can see what the seductions of the stage resources leave to be mastered even in the hands of a thorough professional. Shadwell was that, and one who had the added benefit of far greater musical knowledgeability than Dryden, having been trained by North's teacher, John Jenkins. Yet his products, for which he always and disconcertingly expresses a cavalier disregard, are little improved by that advantage. I have already remarked on his *Tempest* and turn here to his fuller attempt to leave the masque behind.

Psyche is devoted not to royalist apologetics or wedding praises but to an allegorized representation of the mind's experience of Eros, with little enough of that direct relation to courtly epideixis the operatic *Tempest* displayed. Yet Shadwell works up his allegory in such a fashion that his subject, the mind, is lost in a bewildering array of baroque courtly devices that carry with them the scene of their theatrical—and ultimately courtly poetic—source. The old retirement-from-the-court *debat* on court versus country pleasures inconsequentially begins the opera. It is followed, after much music, by the debate of its paired heroes, Polynices and Nicander, with the priests of Apollo; the debate poses in virtually Drydenian terms materialism versus miraculism, opting intellectually for the former, but dramatically for the latter to allow Shadwell to stage a "melancholy region of Despair," reminiscent of "Lovers Made Men."[1] Just so, the act 3 prelude to Psyche's meeting Cupid is the unintegrated song of Vulcan and Cyclops of "Mercury Vindicated" roots, and so on throughout the opera.

Shadwell, of course, needn't have read the Jonson; he had Molière's *Psyche* before him.[2] The interpenetration of courtly stage materials across the two cultures was intense throughout the century, forming a classically based "diplomatic" language that made it easy now (1675) for Shadwell to try, at Betterton's behest, to sophisticate the British stage. But for all Molière's help, he is never able to bring together the dramatic story of Psyche's rapture before Eros with the allegorical renderings he feels called upon to concretize it in. He would better the French version by the addition of "variety" and by scenes of passion "wrought up with more art" he tells us in the Preface. "More art" involves Shadwell in those descriptions of awareness of the experience of passion we know from the heroic play:

What Divine Harmony invades my Ear?
This is a voice I could forever hear.
O speak again, and strike my ravish'd sense
  With thy harmonious excellence!

. . . .
  No object of my sense could e'er
  Transport me till this hour;
I feel a passion mix'd with Joy and Fear
That's caus'd by this unknown invisible Power.

. . . .
Such pain and pleasure I ne'r felt before.

(2 : 308)

He also projects emotional turns by the dozen in the heroic models, a pair duplicating an irrelevancy in order to establish a love and honor conflict, as Psyche explicates it for us at the conclusion ("Such Friends and Rivals ne'r were found. / How much am I by Love and Honor bound?"). Paired envious sisters and a noble father complete the major cast. The form of the piece, like its particular occasions for music, comes from the masque, each act moving out from its emblematic scenic (and musical) opening to the business of the drama with which it sometimes has scenic and allegorical if not dramatic, relevance.[3] By the fourth act, there seems to be none at all, Psyche's experience and her import lost in a sea of dancing statues, changing sets (Hell and a desert versus Cupid's palace and Apollo's temple), and excitable Furies. When Apollo tells us in the coda that Love should ravish everyone with his celestial fire, we may have forgotten that that is what it was all about.

Though Shadwell's musical drama is always heavily endebted to its detriment to the French *tragedie des machines,* it is reasonably clear in the awkward conjuncture of *Psyche* that he did not only create occasions for spectacle but tried to use music for its real power. His treatment of the Psyche myth, incoherent as it is, concentrates on the passions, albeit insufficiently. As Dent remarks, though the lead characters do not sing, there *is* here "a continual effort to bring them into contact with music"[4] and that effort, like Charles Davenant's in *Circe,* frequently involves an externalization of the mind's emotional experience. It is an allegorical rendering that, given the crowded nature of the text, is too easily dissociated from the character himself, existing as spectacle in its own right, though I would certainly not want to claim that the disjunction, so great for a twentieth-century reader, was as extreme for a seventeenth-century spectator, far more accustomed to figural and allegorical modes. The simplification one longs for on reading through *Psyche* is less of idea and action than of style and realization. Allegory has become onerous. Yet one recognizes that it was one of the few routes left to the Restoration by which to dramatize the internal lives of its characters. Having lost to decorum the Elizabethan freedom of modes, to literal verisimilitude the soliloquy and aside, to a changed poetic standard the verbal multivalence, the stage encountered the practical difficulty discussed from the point of view of theory in the last chapter: finding the means to express externally what is, after all, invisible—the inner life.

One of the means open to Restoration dramatists that could have offset poetic losses was, of course, music. The extant work of Locke, of Blow, and ultimately of Purcell proves that it was not for the absence of capable composers that the means was not triumphantly employed. The problem lay with the incapacity of the writers to disengage musical drama from its allegorical roots, from those literalizations of the spirit that, in materializing mental events, burden them with the body they are designed to escape.[5] Such literalizations underlay the equation of music with irrationality, with illusion and magic that accounts for the bulk of the semi-operatic works and operatic episodes of the Restoration. Dismembered Orpheus was not lightly to be resurrected, even in those few situations where music and text effectively come together, despite the pressure toward allegory.

There were, of course, significant successful attempts to make remembered Orpheus work. The most striking are Purcell's *Dido and Aeneas* (1689) and Blow's *Venus and Adonis* (1682) wherein the expressive groundwork of Purcell's masterpiece is generally considered to have been laid. In both works the masque connection announced in Blow's subtitle is clear not only in the occasions—private productions for Josiah Royce's school and for the court respectively—but also in their forms of allegorization and specific theatrical devices. Yet both transcend the limitations of their mode by making of music those "new wings to all / The flights of Poetry" Davenant had tried time and time again to achieve.

What Blow achieves in *Venus and Adonis* is quite different from what Davenant had attempted in *The Siege of Rhodes*. In the first place, there is little interest in heroic modeling of a visibly political cast and none in full-scale drama. Though the court had already taken part in both in the fulsome masque *Calisto* (1675), this is a far more modest affair. The court effects are limited largely to conditions of production that created for the work some of the *à clef* quality one associates with French court productions of the day—Blow nimbly reversing the tenor of Crowne's Princess Mary as the chaste nymph, Calisto, by casting Mary Davies, one of Charles's mistresses, as Venus.[6] Her daughter, the nine-year-old lady Mary Tudor, sang Cupid. The fact, no doubt, added a fillip to Cupid's Prologue invitation to the lovers of the scene setting to go off to the grove and do whatever they like and a more serious and piquant intensity to the sensuous languors of Venus's and Adonis's opening duet; the emotional identification of players and characters perhaps held throughout the masque. But only the emotional.

From the point of view of its musical structure and scoring, *Venus and Adonis*'s form is usually considered heavily influenced by the French—Lully's overture, prologue, and discrete acts within a narrow tonal range;[7] but texturally the work bears little resemblance to Lully's, whose prologues are quite distinct entities and whose main texts straddle *Venus and Adonis,* the fetes and ballets being far more taken up with dance and reviews and the *tragedies lyriques* much more complex in terms of action and range of characters. Blow's simplicity is commensurable with the English masque tradition's discrete discontinuities and emblematic solidity: a brief atmospherically environing prologue whose main character, Cupid, also figures importantly in the main body of the masque; an act for the hunt; an act for beauty; an act for death; each act begins with an act tune that sets the emotional tone of the segment and ends with a dance entry that closes off the whole ironically, until the third act, where the emotional power of the death lament is not dissipated in what would have been an anomalous and contradictory move.

Insofar as this is drama, it is the drama of discretely staged emotions and of the most direct expression possible of passion and its motives. In that direct expression, the work departs the company of the masque, relying not on allegory and our intellectual understanding but on immediate identification and participation in the emotion projected. Its value in comparison with the workings of the heroic play lies in the simple fact that its music is capable of mediating such direct expression. The text is saved the effort of convincing us that Adonis is fired by the hunt or Venus by Adonis—an effort in which precious few dramatic poets were successful after Beaumont and Fletcher's time. Yet the extent to which Blow trails behind Lully dramatically is evident in the lack of interest in recitative in his work. Where Lully could develop from *ballet* to *tragedie lyrique* on the strength of his creation of a recitative capable of the speed and emotional modulation drama requires, Blow is satisfied to remain within the parameters of masque, in blocks of expressive power whose continuity is left to us, and tonality.

The peak of that power is felt in the death lament, which also opposes French practice. Where Lully/Quinault invariably create a positive choral upswing through the gods for a finale, Blow leaves his conclusion on earth in the G minor lament of Venus, taken up by the Chorus *lento sostenuto*, p p, a step in which he is followed by Purcell in the last bars of *Dido and Aeneas.* That is, the emotional states of the principals are the primary focus and informing forces of the work, here and throughout. In act 1, Venus's and Adonis's shared desire and its conflict with the disruptive force of the boar and hunt are the center. Venus embraces the hunt as a kindler "of new desires" and Adonis as a call to fame. It is left to the music to generate the power of the hunt as focus of these feelings, its ability to sweep a once-resisting Adonis out of Venus's arms and into the act that kills him. Purcell follows the same process in the first act of *Dido and Aeneas.*

The second act bears the clearest marks of the earlier masque procedures. Unconcerned with developing a dramatic plot, it remains emblematically within contemporary female stage psychology, moving easily from direct to indirect expression. The workings of Venus's desire here have little literal relevance to the dramatic situation but a great deal to the embodiment of Venus as an unambiguous emblem of Love, for whom, I suppose, Mary Davies is the Truth of the Type. She who had urged Adonis to join the hunt as an aphrodisiac ("absence kindles new desire") passes the time during his absence playing, Cleopatra-like, at the feminine wiles of the love game, engaging with Cupid in a lesson on the treatment of love-scorners (which Adonis has *not* been; this is Blow's version of Ovid, not Shakespeare's) and general advice on how to keep a wandering eye at home (use him ill). That is, the second act presents Venus as the Restoration coquette surrounded by little cupids who learn the lessons of courtship in a spelling game, full of the nice little cynicisms of the genre (M.E.R. C.E.N. . .). They dress Venus while the Graces sing "she will beget desire and yield delight" and dance a gavotte and a saraband. Venus as love in the guise of courtly sophistication comes to its conclusion purely musically on a long ground of simple harmonies, *ben mercato,* as the case demands, the whole act rescued from banality, if at all, by its sprightly rhythms and happy melody. Its irony depends upon our knowledge of the story and of court life, which Blow presupposes.

The third act announces its complete break with the second not musically, but visually: the "Curtain opens and discovers Venus standing in a melancholy posture" and "a mourning Cupid goes across the stage and shakes an arrow at her." Love, thwarted by death, has altered its guise. We neither see nor hear described one of those ubiquitous "turns" the age loved but hear instead her adagio lament for Adonis. He arrives to die on her bosom in a beautiful duet that modulates on his death from the predominant F to the G minor of lamentation. The lascivious flutes of act 1 are only a memory. Retrospectively, the entire masque takes its shape as an embodiment of Venus's experience of human love; as Blow presents it, it is the experience of mortality truncating desire, the haunting, soaring naming of act 1's eros that enclosed the totality of desire in a being now dead on the stage. The piece evinces more clearly than any purely verbal work of the period the power retained by the masque tradition and its capacity to transform often-fatuous court entertainments into art. It does so through its musical capacity to embody and convey psychic experience. The text is itself trite and commonplace, music filling the gap in the ability to portray psychological depth left by the text's poetic flattening.

Blow's librettist is unknown, but Purcell's for *Dido and Aeneas* is identified as one of the foremost flatteners of the time, Nahum Tate. Tate had written the play *Brutus of Alba* in 1678, a typical heroic reworking of the British historical materials around Brute. Tate's Toryism is everywhere apparent in the play, which relates the love story of Dido and Aeneas, with the names changed to protect Tate's humility. Though Tate's version of the story is heavily given over to plot complications typical of the day, closely linked sorcery and treason, the emphasis lies equally on the emotional explosions that the story and its treatment here afford, and they are many. As in the case of the heroic plays, however, the characters announce their emotional turmoil in scene after scene, while the poetry fails to realize that turmoil for us. More often than not we are given only its bald statement, as Tate, like so many of the heroic dramatists, moves to his primary interest without the means to objectify it. When Asaracus, thought dead, unexpectedly appears, Brutus exclaims: "Asaracus—my grief converts to rapture! / Support me or the Ecstasie will kill me." On the whole, one's response is that given the Second Ambassador after the Queen's declamation on the threat of war he has brought: "Your passion has had scope and now we wait / Your more considerate and final answer." All the passion given scope in the course of the play is as easy to disregard as one awaits final answers.[8]

The play bifurcates into two ill-assorted centers—one, the plot involving political materials, explicitly devoted to the machinations of the treasonous and powerful lord, Soziman, and to the imperial charge of Brutus, which aligns with Soziman's plans to subvert the kingdom, and two, the affective emotional material evolved from the

Queen's love for Brutus, Brutus's love for his friend and for the Queen, Soziman's murderous desires, and the Sorceress Ragusa's hatred of the Queen. There is an academic sense in which the affective material is connected to the political plotting, since all the outbursts are occasioned by turns in the plot; but the plot movement is so often merely fortuitous—as when Asaracus enters to everyone's surprise toward the close of act 1, or in act 5, when an elf arrives to tell Ragusa that her power comes to an end tonight, just when the Queen needs a potion to keep Brutus port-bound—that nothing seems connected to character nor can be expressive of character. As a result the emotional moments float free—of their characters and of a context— making the play a gleaming hodgepodge of violent displays not unlike *Circe.* This early in his career Tate has not even the theatrical sense to pull things together for a focusing finale, but splits the effect of the conclusion between the Queen's death of a broken heart and Soziman's monstrous end, which frames her death: hair afire as a result of Ragusa's magic, he leaves the stage ablaze only to return after the Queen's death scene, stabbing himself with daggers in each hand. One has the sense here that poor Tate attempted to acclimate Virgil by conflating the final acts of Cleopatra (the Queen has her Charmion in Amarante) and of Othello and by the addition to guarantee himself a tragedy. It is a piteous and fearsome display, all right, but more for what it tells us about the stage in 1678 than for anything we feel of human nature.

The miracle is, of course, that Purcell found in this text the basis for his *Dido and Aeneas.* He did it in the same way that Blow had, by making music play the role that the poetry was quite incapable of assuming and by cutting the text down to its bare bones to make room for the music. He did not go directly back to Virgil, but worked with Tate's text as it stood, retaining the Sorceress, retaining the Queen's confidant (Virgil's Anna become Belinda by way of Amarante), retaining the sailors who deliver Asaracus, even though Asaracus and Soziman are gone and with them, the rationale for the non-Virgilian retentions. In each case Purcell has kept what is musically expressible and expressive with little apparent concern for what makes analytic sense. Soziman's excision removes as well any logical reason for the Sorceress's appearance, just as the excision of Asaracus destroyed the logic of the Sailor. Rationales are not necessary when a convention is quite firm, and the Sorceress and Sailor are just that, conventional figures from the masque tradition who conventionally represent the disordering forces of the universe—the allowed evils within heroic destiny.

Take, for instance, the sailors. What is left of the crew, whose desire to move on creates so much concern in Virgil or Marlowe's stage redaction, is now one lusty, traditional sea chanty that parodies in light travesty Aeneas's relation to Dido:

> Come away, fellow Saylors, your Anchors be weighing,
> Time and Tide will admit no delaying,
> Take a Bouze short leave of your Nymphs on the Shore,
> And Silence their Mourning
> With Vows of returning,
> But never intending to Visit them more.[9]

Like brindisi, sea chanties are normal intrusive music in masques and the early operas; they need no rationalization. But like the same songs in *King Arthur,* they do have an effect. They carry with them that perspective of common life we have seen throughout the tradition. One can excessively solemnize the point, to be sure, yet at some level, the introduction of uneffected, and unaffected, common life in explicit juxtaposition to the heroic situation opposes the one to the other, suggesting that the commoners cannot begin to compass either the seriousness or the depth of emotion implicit in the principals' situation. Their capacity to dance as usual while the heroic characters burn heightens the force and seriousness of the fate of Dido and Aeneas, but also questions its significance. How seriously the question will be taken depends—as in the case of *Henry V*—as much on what the viewer brings to the opera as on the opera itself. That is, response will here, as anywhere, change with time and the changing impact of the conventions involved. Their assumed meanings will be altered; even their recognition as old conventions increases the likelihood of ironization. We know from Addison's *Rosamund* that it was high already in the first decade of the eighteenth century and, not inconceivably, a part of Purcell's own intention, though hardly probable that the irony we can see here would have been quite his own.

The sailors are measures of what heroes must overcome in themselves; but the weighty oppositional force is the Sorceress's band of witches who return to exult at the success of their ruse, a mock Mercury to order Aeneas's departure, as the sailors depart. The moment that the witches return is announced fiercely by an abrupt shift from the dancing sailors' melody to the Sorceress's ceremonial dotted rhythm. Along with Dido, the Sorceress is a triumph of the work. Where Aeneas never regains the force he had already lost in Tate's play, so the idea of "dull Empire" and imperial destiny has little presence in either work; in Purcell's version that idea is replaced by a significant power, able to create dramatic conflict.

Virgil gave us the gods and their forceful intervention in human

affairs. Tate, nervously aware of the problem of the pagan supernatural for a Christian audience, eliminated the gods altogether and
transferred their power to demented human agency—to Soziman and
Ragusa—whereby Destiny became null and inoperative through that
trivialization that rationalizing magic enacted in so many musical
dramas of the period.[10] Purcell accepts Tate's excision of the gods and
eliminates rationalized human agency as well, having dropped Soziman and explanations of the Sorceress's hatred of Dido, so that now
the only dramatized force separating Dido and Aeneas is the malign
nature that the unmotivated Sorceress comes to figure and that Dido
excoriates in act 3 as Heaven and Earth who "conspire my fall." When
Aeneas tries to placate her with, it is "the god's decree," she analyzes
his rationale as the usual hypocrisy: thus murderers "Make Heav'n
and Gods the Authors of the Fact." Dido understands Aeneas's destiny—go found your empire and leave me here to die—as Aeneas's
desire, and the work, having turned Mercury into a ruse of the Sorceress, agrees with her. Sorcery is not, as in Tate's play, the tool of a
usurper, but an expression of the conflicted will of Aeneas, whose
achievement of empire is less an act of destiny as externally compel-
ling fate than of destiny as character—of heroic masculine activity
opposed to Dido's feminine passivity.

The Sorceress, as embodiment of a malign delusive power, enters
the scene immediately after the Triumphing Dance of the cupids that
celebrates Dido's impersonally expressed love for Aeneas (never a
word from the principals but a chaconne, the chorus's song and the
dance). Virgil's great cave episode, wherein heaven and earth *do* conspire against Dido, becomes here love, with the guitar chaconne as its
external expression and with the Sorceress allegorically expressing its
internal workings. She calls her wayward sisters to appear, appear,
appear—the word reechoes three times, climbing chromatically—as
the figures appear to unseat "all in prosp'rous state." As purveyors of
destructive illusion, the witches are quite conventional figures, employing echo song, thunder and lighting, and "horrid" music to depict
this Fall. But they are quite unconventionally successful in making this
antimasque speak to us directly, the unsettling power of the emotions,
their capability as destroyers, as energy gone awry, carrying the
psyche before it. No English poetry short of Miltonic power could
muster the demonic force that Purcell's music gives the scene. No
English drama short of Shakespeare's has better realized the destructive power of the passions.

But this opera is not drama in the conventional sense at all. Rather
it suits Dryden's definition and Davenant's affective emphasis. Plot

has been reduced to reference to the Virgilian tale and character, through its allegorical displacement, to an unchanging state. There is to all effect no enacted conflict, no peripety, no reversal. Dido, defeated from her first note, moves like a figure in Dante, her fate, her destiny, decided and complete with her entrance onto the stage, the tale of its enactment told, as it were, retrospectively. One experiences not so much her story as her deepening response to it. The emphasis on the affect of experience is nowhere stronger and more direct in a theatre that devoted its primary concern to just that aspect of the dramatic event. The participatory quality of masque has become purely vicarious as Lully's painting of the passions has replaced chess moves, and one participates in the emotional life of Dido as immediately as it is possible to imagine.

Music, which as vehicle of the dance had been the source of the definitive audience relation to the masque, became through its capacity to recreate the inner life in Blow, and now consummately in Purcell, the strongest resource of the seventeenth-century stage for vicarious dramatic experience. One participates here not in the celebration of power or community but only the life of the ultimate scorned woman, who has nothing to do with the gods or empire either: Soziman and the Ambassadors are gone; there is no Iarbas figure. Perhaps more important, there are no ghosts of Creusa/ Eudemia or Sychaeus/Argaces—an opportunity for a much-loved seventeenth-century form of spectacle wrung by Tate, but by-passed by Purcell—and there are no sons.[12]

The elision of the family isolates Dido and Aeneas in that nondynastic individuality that makes empire building the thoughtlessly self-aggrandizing act Dido makes of it when she harmonizes Aeneas's final turn into essential pettiness, vain and ridiculous. Once the turmoil of the self has become paramount, empire is no longer an excuse for anything, nor of much interest to anyone by comparison to Dido's being.

It is not particularly likely that Purcell intended this to be the case; far more likely that in choosing as his subject the eternally favorite episode from the story of the currently favorite hero, he had something like the opposite in mind. But when he chose to leave the *telos* of Aeneas up to the memory of his audience and to lavish the expressive music on Dido, he opted out of imperial praise.[12] As Dryden tried to broaden the base of national self-congratulation in order to save heroic figures, so Purcell tried to maintain heroic figures by moving their base inward. Yet in the process the hero of empire himself becomes a straw man, an appeal to our memory. The emptying of the hero, his reduction to Mellers's "un-hero," is an effect of the loss of meaning in conventions of the epideictic mode, which had accepted the undramatized evidence of history as proof of its heroic values since at least *Henry VIII* and had depended on the audience's filling in the blanks of destiny again and again, relying on a cultural memory that, once it is gone, takes the hero with it. Aeneas's dramatic minimization, as well as King Arthur's subjection to second causes, results from their authors' certainty that they could count on sheer reference to cultural memory and were free therefore to elaborate their subjects as they wished with little need to underscore the substantiality of Arthur or Aeneas in redundant proofs of their heroism.

Empire has its demise on the public stage in far more intentional and far more fiery forms than Dido's pyre, its ghost laid again and again in the musical drama of the last quarter of the century.[13] In the Jacobean years the event had an ironic practical facticity it never achieved in the Restoration, the stage actually burning down for *Henry VIII.* The Restoration had to be satisfied with mere representation as over and over the baroque *Götterdämmerung* was restaged—in *The Siege of Rhodes,* in *Circe,* in *Masaniello.* The ostensible moral was always the same as Tate's in *Brutus of Alba:* an ambitious character, a usurping figure (compare Davenant's adaptation of *Macbeth*), brings the world down around him, destroying himself in the process. The less overt message—that the pursuit of power is itself totally destructive—is equally emphatic. The mass of clashing passions that eventuate in final cataclysm is illogical and muddy in more of these plays than *Circe,* so that causes become lost amidst the general sense of life become a field of forces, uncontrollable and senseless. That music was thought an appropriate adjunct to such affairs bespeaks the extent to which the dramatists relied upon its power of passional expression and were willing, in effect, to cut it loose, without much regard for its particular affect. The distance between William Davenant's chastely reflective initial debacle of Rhodes and his son's destruction of Sythia measures the depths of a theatrical abyss.

The later works have so regularly been taken as symptomatic of the state of politics in the last quarter of the century that I will only add one point. Illusion, always a part of the psychology of magic, became a primary theme in the reflexive comedy of the masques of the thirties. It was used on through the early musical dramas as a rationalization for the introduction of scenic effects and musical episodes. At the first, William Davenant avoided the bifurcation of the work into music and drama by composing his opera for recitative. Having done that, he avoided the temptation to rationalize musical events. There was no need for a sorcerer of sufficient power to create the illusions that justified the introduction of musical, magical scenes.

But the success of *The Tempest* taught Davenant's peers that magic, quite contrary to the advice of all the critics, was perfectly acceptable to the audience—in fact, welcome. Practically speaking, the discovery was a godsend. One need not hire, as Davenant had for *The Siege of Rhodes,* two casts, actors and singers. One need not forgo the box office appeal of the great nonsinging actors, like Betterton. One could still capitalize on the growing taste for music as a spectator sport (Banister's concerts were doing splendidly) by acquiring scripts that managed to work in a magician to raise illusions that could be musically staged. It was a handy way to update the inherited Jacobean repertoire as well.[14] It little mattered to Charles Davenant that Circe didn't suit very well his Euripidean retelling of the Orestes myth. He wanted a magician. It probably mattered just as little that displacing political motives into illusionary episodes had an effect on meaning. All Charles perhaps wanted to do was write an opera that was also a tragedy. That he ended up with a portrait of a cultural twilight on far more levels than he probably intended is a gift of generic history, of the transition from masque to heroic drama. It took a Dryden to understand the pitfalls and try to work around them.

But *Circe* was at the time a success, even given the record of such productions for costing more than could be cleared on them, satisfying the public's desire for music, for magic's release from literalism, and for the exorcism of the ghosts of absolutism.[15] And thus the rule became not the fully composed *Siege of Rhodes* model (except in private, in *Venus and Adonis* and *Dido and Aeneas*) but the musical event rationalized through the magician or imbedded masque. The practical cause, that is to say, financial and casting considerations, was met by developing a political myth that involves the destruction of the tyrant and the replacement of his power by the illusions of magic and its easy providentialism. The development begins innocuously enough in the Dryden/Davenant *Tempest.* Innocuous, because Shakespeare's Prospero could hardly become a tyrant, but he could, and did, become powerless. I spoke earlier of Ariel's usurpation of Prospero's capability, the replacement of human agency by reified divinity. The power of such magic is underscored in this version by the episode of sympathetic magic in the sword anointing necessary to the unraveling of the plot. When Shadwell had his turn, reworking the Dryden/Davenant version into "opera," he carefully revised the presentation of the *means* of magic here, naturalizing and demystifying them, but left untouched the distribution of power, as also the sword-anointing sequence. This is consonant with his treatment of magic in *Psyche* and *The Lancashire Witches,* self-conscious in its care to approach the device rationally, yet altogether unwilling to forgo its charm. Successors were even less willing and often less careful.

In both what we can see as its successes—*Venus and Adonis, Dido and Aeneas,* successes because they perhaps shortsightedly enter the canon of music as the expression of personality—and its failures, the seventeenth-century stage offers appeals constantly to the suprarational world, to the noumenal either psychological or magical. The musical drama rationalizes the latter directly or allegorically, justifying its genii as vapors, its witches as mere fantasy (though they have real power in the play), its scenes of magic as illusion, the work of evil sorcerers always finally dispelled.[16] It made that place for the suprarational we have seen in *King Arthur,* satisfying the desire for the gods without offending Christian theology and doctrinal rationality, enacting on stage the interconnection of human life and the invisible world that it had to refuse to believe was in any literal sense supportable, making excuses always for its delight in fairies and witches. Opera's machines were a convention with which the noumenal could be staged, moving one back to the unreality of romance that the stage otherwise enjoined. The reification of the noumenal world is the only trait that the widely disparate works of musical drama share: the two essential roles of music on the seventeenth-century stage were to portray the inner life in its emotional affects and to introduce the workings of the divine in their physical manifestations. The second was by far the more important, if one is speaking of sheer bulk. Yet the association of music with emotional realization is often effectual even in the works that use music primarily for the second purpose.

Of the cases in point, I shall speak only of the one that is of interest because of the theoretical position of its author, Dennis. I shall argue that it is precisely his theory that is responsible for his trying to connect the two roles. *Rinaldo and Armida* has the advantage of following *King Arthur,* and owes a good deal to that, the best of the ambigues. Indeed Dennis defended the work against too close a connection by insisting that Eccles had not stolen the fourth act chorus from Purcell's *King Arthur* Frost Scene.[17]

Significantly, he rather ungraciously dissociates his work from Tasso, too. He is as adamant that he has improved on his source, though he is less ingenuous in doing so. The preface printed with the text concentrates on his efforts to regularize Rinaldo, by turning Tasso's hero (like King Arthur, he might have said) into an avatar of

Virgil's hero, correcting Rinaldo's irregularities to make him "very human without weakness."[18] His Rinaldo vows to leave Armida out of the strength of his reason "and not the weakness of his Passion." In this model of explicitness, Dennis explains to the reader how so perfect a character could love Armida, even though she is mad throughout the play (they had spent three months on the island before the play begins, he tells us, and she has only now heard about his intent to leave).

If Dennis is so concerned for rationalizable character, for believable human motive and action, one might ask why he dramatized the Tasso sequence at all. His characters are Restoration Virgil, Armida its Dido as Rinaldo its Aeneas; his verse is replete with Miltonic echoes in image and rhythm. Yet Tasso and opera gave him scope for what was already Dennis's primary concern—the passions. Throughout both the musical and printed prefaces, Dennis speaks consistently of his desire to create affective drama. His acknowledged model is neither Tasso, nor Dryden, nor Milton (though later it would have been, had he ever written another opera), but Sophocles, whose "Sublime and at once Pathetick Air" he hopes to have achieved by making Terror his prevailing passion, as it is Sophocles', and by making the greatness of the sentiments and images answer to the height of the subject.[19]

In the musical preface Dennis expands on this point by adding consideration of the means, not the images, but the music, whose "Design" like that of Poetry and Painting is always "to entertain the Imagination." He elaborates briefly here the applicability to his opera of the notion developed fully at about the same time in *The Usefulness of the Stage*—that the excitation of passion is the soul of aesthetic experience. In the elaboration, Sophocles' prevailing Passion takes a secondary position to the arousal of multiple passions. His reasoning is simple and clear: since nothing entertains the imagination but what moves the passions, the more one moves the passions, the better the art, and since it is the nature of passion to be brief in its response, it follows that only successive extremes will maintain affect (be "Pathetick") over the course of the work. Thus he will arouse "as many Passions as I could successively without doing violence to my subject, as Admiration, Love and Joy, Anger, Compassion, Terror, Grief, Horror, Astonishment, and Despair." Sophocles' prevailing passion has become one in a list of the most extraordinary Motions the spirit undergoes out of the conviction that his full-scale musical entertainment *must* evoke a variety of emotions to maintain its hold on the Imagination. Even the entr'acte music here is to be part of the tragedy and is therefore "always Pathetick," not simply painting the passions imitated in the subject, but affecting the audience almost as continuously as Wagner would attempt at Bayreuth.

But Dennis does not leave it to music to call up the pathetic, nor does he expect a plot to do that unassisted by deeply integrated vehicles of Astonishment, Admiration, and Terror, et al. Let Rymer insist upon the plot as image of the action, Dennis, like most writers of his age, had far greater interest in what the plot allowed one to embed in it, to explicitly and successively arouse those disparate emotions that assured affect. He also knew that you cannot, in 1698, simply restage Greek tragedy to achieve Sophocles' ends.[20] Cultural relativism requires that we reconceptualize Greek tragedy to make it speak to a new set of suppositions, a new religion, different customs. As for Dryden, so for Dennis the Tassonic furniture was the key. It allowed one to arouse Sophoclean emotion by allowing into the play the varying emotions without insulting the cultural presuppositions of the audience. Thus he could say, in the midst of all his rationalizations, that he has kept his machines down to a minimum, though that minimum turns out to be rather large, as necessary to the conduct of the plot as it is effectual in conveying the intentional thematic materials the plot encodes. If we read *Rinaldo and Armida* today, I doubt very much that we are reminded of Sophocles, but this too is perhaps an effect of cultural relativism.

We may, though, not even think of Tasso, who was willing to allow romance character to retain something of its Ariostan inconsequentiality, the inconsequentiality that allowed Dryden to give up Arthur's power to a magus. Dennis, though, wants it consistent and consistently meaningful. He uses machine allegory to make it so. That Armida is a witch seems irrelevant to the "greatness of soul" attributed to her again and again (naturally enough, in her own self-analyses) until the fifth act reveals her henchman, Phaenissa, to be her evil genius, "the source of all her woes" (p. 52). When Armida stabs Phaenissa, she frees herself of an evil intrinsic to but separable from her being. This allegorized and compartmentalized evil both allows Dennis a stellification finale, wherein Armida is invited to reign over the assembled Heroes and Heroines in the clouds, and explains her turn from the Dido-inspired actions of the fourth act. There, encountering Rinaldo's announcement that not his lack of love, but the call to duty and Fame requires his departure, she had first flown into the rage of the scorned woman and then stabbed herself, but she went on to prevent his following her example, out of love. Her greatness of soul had, it seems, been invaded by a foreign substance but remains at root the sort of Greatness that can have attracted Rinaldo, without undermining that rationality that is marked by good judgment.

We are guided through Armida's ups and downs as through Rinaldo's successful resistance to her temptations by an integrated framing action that allows good spirits to compete with Armida's evil illusions before the audience. As in *King Arthur*, the good spirits "have the Conduct and Care of the Action, and the Guardianship of the Persons concern'd in it" (musical Preface, 107). They are led by Urania, who raises no false illusions but leads Carlo, our intermediary, through musical sequences and Rinaldo's experience. With her guidance Carlo learns, and we through him, that the illusions with which they must struggle are heavenly tests, allowed evils that create the possibility of "a glorious Conquest o'er your selves" (p. 8). Rinaldo himself must deal with the masques' old question "Was it illusion or was it real?" after the terrific raising of his parents at Armida's hand in act 2, and he does so in traditional fashion: "Heav'n gave thee Reason for that guide of action" (p. 19). The recognition here leads Rinaldo to a long sequence of self-excoriation on his three-month abandonment of Heaven's guide. The sequence is probably the best thing in the opera, beginning from the strong entrance of the illusory spirits, making its point that a higher power controls Armida's by forcing her illusions to disappear, awakening him, and conducting his self-examination, unaware, before her and Phaenissa, so that we have her recognition of his peripety at the same time that we see the turn enacted. The chorus's redoubling in music the horrors of Hell in act 4's opening is the only musical competitor, and it is not so well integrated dramatically.

It is difficult to know now from the printed page what sort of effect a text like Dennis's could have produced. While it has not the wildness and chaotic disarray of some of its brethren, it seems rather routine in its verse and conception and terribly conventional in its ideas. Certainly the need to spell everything out, rationalize all the magic, justify all the decisions of the characters is destructive of the romance mode it is cast in. And yet Dennis, like so many other writers of the time—like Granville, like Motteux, like even Dryden—wanted romance and its allowed magic to serve serious functions, moral and political as well as psychological.[21] They inveterately staged it allegorically, which allowed them to create those thrills and chills that presumably delighted the audience and at the same time, in the careful moralizations, to placate their own or the management's consciences with a fully worked out didactic point. There seems to me little question, given the evidence of the work itself and of his prose surrounding it, that

Dennis was quite serious in his undertaking and that, slim as the achievement may seem now, he intended its conventional moralism to play that nationally salutary role that justified poetry and the stage for him. Yet there seems as little question that anyone after Dryden was capable of turning these materials into dramatically effective works or extending the tradition of courtly praise out into the world.

That seems to have been Dryden's own final conviction as well. Like Jonson, who began the line of seventeenth-century theatrical epideixis, Dryden too wrote a palinode, affording us an epilogue to the entire tradition. Jonson excoriated the show of the masques ("Court Hieroglyphicks," "Spectacles of State") and the stage itself (in "Come leave the loathed stage," of an "Ode to Himself"), but never his service to the king:

> But when they hear thee sing
> The glories of thy king,
> His zeal to God, and his just awe o'er men:
> They may, blood-shaken then,
> Feel such a flesh-quake to possess their powers
> As they shall cry, "Like ours,
> In sound of peace or wars,
> No harp e'er hit the stars,
> In tuning forth the acts of his sweet reign;
> And raising Charles his chariot 'bove his Wain.

Dryden questions deeply the very service, defending the stage to attack the court, and implicitly the king, suggesting that it was all a lovely fiction, blinding and delusory. He does so in the form of a secular masque (the adjective is significant) embedded in *The Pilgrim*, another of the Jacobean plays updated by this addition of musical allegory. "The Secular Masque" rings out the old, rings in the new century in a minor key, parading the presiding dieties of the Stuarts before us in succession, Diana, Mars, and Venus, that we with Momus may see "What Changes in this Age have been." While Dryden treats the century kindly, resurrecting the vigorous hunt's merry, laughing, "unthinking time," the arms and honour of martial maturity, the reparations of peace and calm, ultimately he puts it all away, denying any change at all but in the clothes:

> All, all of a piece throughout:
> Thy Chase had a Beast in View;
> Thy Wars brought nothing about;
> Thy Lovers were all untrue.
> 'Tis well an Old Age is out,
> And time to begin a New.[22]

Carew's Momus was more hopeful but no less anti-Platonic. Yet this masque concludes as conventionally as Carew's, with a dance of Huntsmen, Nymphs, Warriors, and Lovers.

But the pastoral world innocently, if illogically, implied by the harmonious conclusion is itself eyed askant when, with a Swiftian stroke, Dryden supplies a dialogue between a scholar and his mistress, two lovers, who as Phyllis and Amyntas are the living repudiation of all pastoral. Mad for one another, they now "first meet in Bedlam," held by their keepers. When the joining of body to body and heart to heart apparently cures them, they run out together hand in hand to "call the Man in Black, to mumble o'er his part." The literalization of metaphor rarely produces more acerbic grotesquery.

If it seems too much to suggest that here Dryden is washing his hands of the whole enterprise—of translating reality into courtly language, into fictive romance and allegorical self-affirmation—as an evasion of reality, we have the epilogue he appended to the whole production to state cleanly precisely that. The context, reversing Jonson's position at the beginning of the century, is a defense of the stage, an attack on the court, the interrelation of the two explaining the immorality of the theatre:

> The poets, who must live by Courts, or starve,
> Were proud, so good a Government to serve.

The irony of that "good" is clarified immediately:

> For they, like Harlots, under Bawds professed,
> Took all the ungodly pains, and got the least.
> Thus did the thriving malady prevail;
> The Court its Head, the Poets but the Tail.
> (2.11–12; 15–18)

The poet as harlot, his work "ungodly pains" expressing the bawd of court, was the creator of, among other things, images of the Stuarts in Mars, Venus, Diana, images that covered over the "thriving malady" and allowed it to prevail.

An old man decides to say from the same stage that often bore Mars, Venus, and Diana that that was all lies and that he is implicated in those lies. He will receive the rewards of the benefit performance, a third night designed to relieve his penury. But he dies two days after the revival of *The Pilgrim* opens. It is the stuff of the kind of melodrama sweeping his drama off the stage, and with it, courtly praise.

Appendix
Chronological List of Works in the Epideictic Tradition

Because so many of the works in the epideictic tradition are not well known, the following chronological list is appended, offered as a map of the territory. Not an inclusive catalogue, it is intended to indicate readily some significant works, creators, and trends. All the works mentioned in the text are included, though no effort has been made to list all annual (Lord Mayor's Day pageants) or virtually biannual (court masques) pieces. Of the works included that the text does not consider, some are here to place the tradition in the reader's sense of literary time ("Comus," *Don Sebastian*) and some because they have been considered by many significant for musical or theatrical reasons that I have left unexplored. *Cupid and Death* and *Acis and Galatea* are good examples of the second category.

The map is both temporal, dated by first performance if known, and broadly spatial, distinguishing public from private performance. All dates are new style. A preceding * indicates performance at a public theatre, a succeeding * a civic pageant, a double succeeding ** a private masque. Composers are specified where they seem useful and relevant to my emphases; it is through them rather than through the writers that some continuities exist.

"Dryden's" *Henry VIII* does not appear on the list because, though an acting version, the text is Dryden's on no authority other than that of a publisher who doubtless wanted to sell his books. When I first read the Dublin edition I thought I might be encountering Downes's great hit of 1663, a Davenant *Henry VIII* that ran fifteen days. That adaptation has never been found, though as Mongi Raddadi (*Davenant's Adaptations of Shakespeare* [Uppsala: Studia Anglistica 36, 1979], 157) suggests, the likelihood is that the lost text was for a reduced cast, to suit the Duke's Company, and that it stressed the theatrical pageantry of the play. The Dublin duodecimo does both and, like Davenant's early adaptations, retains Shakespeare's text verbatim insofar as its structural changes allows. A cooler head convinced me that the virtual unintelligibility of Buckingham's death sentence argued for a less theatrically acute author. In addition, there is little of the bold thematic stress Davenant always insists on, and, unfortunately for my hopes, Dryden as well—at least in his later, thoroughly reimagined Shakespearean adaptations. The Dublin edition remains for me, though, an excellent example of Restoration practice whose relevance to my historical argument will have been obvious to anyone who followed me. While the Dublin version is in all probability apocryphal, the point I introduced it for does, I believe, stand. I spoke there of the rationalization of multilevel texts, subject to quite different criteria of dramatic excellence for the Restoration dramatist than for today's lover of ironic reflexivity. The Dublin duodecimo illustrates perfectly, with a text we had already looked at carefully, the critical shift. Whoever wrote the adaptation followed closely the cuts and changes of the only pre-1750 acting version, that of S. Powell, Dublin, 1732. The likelihood that Davenant's hit looked very much like the Dublin "Dryden" seems to me entirely plausible.

First Production or Publication Date	Playwright or Librettist	Title	(Composer)
1591	G. Peele	*Descensus Astraea**	
1595	Shakespeare	**Midsummer Night's Dream*	
1599	"	**Henry V*	
1605	B. Jonson	*Masque of Blackness***	
1607	T. Campion	*Masque in Honor Of Lord Hay***	
1609	B. Jonson	*Masque of Queens***	
	A. Munday	*Camp-bell:or the Ironmongers Faire Field**	
1612	B. Jonson	*Love Restored***	
	T. Dekker	*Troia-Nova Triumphans**	
1613	Shakespeare	**Henry VIII*	
	G. Chapman	*The Memorable Masque***	
1616	B. Jonson	*Mercury Vindicated***	
	"	*Christmas his Masque***	
	A. Munday	*Chrysanaleia:the Golden Fishing**	

1617	B. Jonson	Lovers Made Men**(Lanier)
	T. Middleton	Triumphs of Honour and Industry*
1619	T. Dekker	London's Tempe*
	T. Middleton	*A World Tost at Tennis
1621	B. Jonson	The Gipsies Metamorphosed**
	T. Middleton	The Sunne in Aries*
1622	"	*A Game at Chess
1623	B. Jonson	Time Vindicated**
	A. Munday	Triumphs of the Golden Fleece*
1624	B. Jonson	Neptune's Triumph**
	J. Webster	Monuments of Honour*
1631	B. Jonson	Love's Triumph through Callipolis**
1632	A. Townshend	Tempe Restord**
	"	Albions Triumph**
	J. Tatham	Love Crowns the End (acted by "schollars" at Bingham)
	T. Heywood	Londini Artium et Scientiarum Scaturigo*
1633	"	Londini Emporia*
1634	J. Shirley	Triumph of Peace** (W. Lawes, Ives)
	T. Carew	Coelum Britannicum** (H. Lawes)
	J. Milton	A Masque at Ludlows** (H. Lawes)
	W. Davenant	*Love and Honor
1635	"	Temple of Love** (W. Lawes)
1636	"	Triumphs of the Prince D'Amour**
1637	"	Britannia Triumphans** (W. Lawes)
1638	" (?)	Luminalia**
1639	"	Salmacida Spolia** (L. Richard)
	T. Heywood	Londini Status Pacatus*
1651pbl.	J. Tatham	The Distracted State
1652pbl.	"	The Scotch Figgaries
1653	J. Shirley	Cupid and Death** (Locke, Gibbon)
1654pbl.	R. Fleckno	Ariadne Deserted by Theseus and Bacchus
1656	W. Davenant	The First Days Entertainment at Rutland House (Coleman, Cook et al.)
	"	*The Siege of Rhodes (Locke, Cook et al.)
1658	"	*The History of Sir Francis Drake
1659	"	*The Cruelty of the Spaniards in Peru
pbl.	R. Fleckno	The Marriage of Oceanus and Britannia
1660	J. Tatham	London's Glory*
pbl.	"	The Rump (acted at "private House in Dorset Court" previously)
	"	The Royal Oak*
1663	W. Davenant	A Playhouse to be Let
1664	J. Tatham	Londons Triumphs*
	W. Davenant	*Macbeth

1667	Dryden/Davenant	*Tempest
1669	J. Dryden	*Tyrannick Love
1672	T. Jordan	The City in Jollity and Splendour*
1673	E. Settle	*The Empress of Morocco (Locke)
	Evelyn records attendance at London production of an Italian opera.	
1674pbl	J. Dryden	State of Innocence (never acted)
	Grabu-Perrin	Ariadne played at Drury Lane
	T. Jordan	Goldsmiths' Jubilee*
	T. Shadwell	*Tempest (Locke)
1675	"	*Psyche (Locke)
	T. Crowne	Calisto** (Staggins)
1677	C. Davenant	*Circe (Banister)
1678	T. Jordan	Triumphs of London*
	N. Tate	*Brutus of Alba
1679	T. Jordan	London in Lustre*
1680	N. Lee	*Theodosius (Purcell)
1681	T. Shadwell	*The Lancashire Witches
1682?	J. Blow	Venus and Adonis** (Blow)
1685	J. Dryden	*Albion and Albanius (Grabu)
1689	"	*Don Sebastian
	Purcell	Dido and Aeneas, at Josias Priest's boarding-school in Chelsea, adapts Tate's Brutus of Alba
1690	Betterton	*The Prophetess (Purcell), Fletcher adapt.
1691	J. Dryden	*King Arthur (Purcell)
1692	E. Settle	*The Fairy Queen (Purcell)
1696	P. Motteux	*Loves of Mars and Venus (Eccles)
1698	J. Dennis	*Rinaldo and Armida (Eccles)
	E. Settle	Glory's Resurrection*
1700	J. Dryden	*The Secular Masque (D. Purcell?), in Fletcher adapt., The Pilgrim)
	P. Motteux	*Acis and Galatea (Eccles)
	W. Congreve	*Judgement of Paris, masque opened to composing competition, won by Weldon
1701	E. Settle	*The Virgin Prophetess (Finger)
1705	Motteux	*Arsinoe, Queen of Cyprus (Clayton, Haym)
	Italian co. stages The Loves of Ergasto at Queen's Theatre, Haymarket	
1706	G. Granville	*The British Enchanters (Eccles)
	T. D'Urfey	*Wonders in the Sun
1707	J. Addison	*Rosamund (Eccles)
1710pbl	W. Congreve	Semele (Eccles's score not ready till 1707, the opera was never produced. Handel's oratorio decades later.

Notes

Preface

1. Joseph Kerman, *Opera as Drama* (New York: Vintage Books, 1956), 5, 56.

Chapter 1. Introductory: Models and Their Representation

1. *Dryden: The Dramatic Works,* ed. Montague Summers (London: Nonesuch, 1932), 6, 485.

2. I have adopted the adjective *epideictic* advisedly, in preference to the looser *panegyric* or *encomiastic,* for its pointedly rhetorical connotations. The works I am concerned with are by and large consciously demonstrative in the Aristotelian sense. See *The Rhetoric,* I, 9, particularly the difference between *praise* and *encomium.* James A. Garrison, *Dryden and the Tradition of Panegyric* (Berkeley and Los Angeles: University of California Press, 1975), outlines the evolution of the panegyric ode and its conventions from its Greek and Roman roots. That has, of course, no theatrical provenance. At the other extreme, O. B. Hardison, *The Enduring Monument* (Chapel Hill: University of North Carolina Press, 1962) developed the thesis that virtually all Renaissance literature is the literature of praise.

3. This is an essential concern of Curtis A. Price's *Music in the Restoration Theatre* ([n.p.]: UMI Research Press, 1979), an excellent source of information on musicians and the orchestra as well as the use of dramatic music in general.

4. All of the varied objections will be discussed in their appropriate places, but I should make clear here that my characterization of Addison refers to his parodic opera, *Rosamund,* and not to his *Spectator* essays, which concentrate on the influx of the Italian operas and the anomaly of an audience sitting through an entire production of which it understands not a word. Number 29 of 3 April 1710, is particularly thoughtful and measured, looking forward to an English opera (that, of course, never came). Of Pope, little more will be said, so I shall remind the reader that the Scriblerians to a man detested opera, Pope recognizing its close connection to public epideixis, so that the early *Dunciad* had the "last" City poet, Settle and his pageants, stand for the sins of the

hack. So also Swift staged Lagado (bk. 3, *Gulliver's Travels*) as an operatic set as foolish as the musical arguments that state encouraged. And so Gay wrote *The Beggar's Opera* and buried the genre.

5. I have overstated the case here, limiting myself to major voices. There are other positive positions, which we shall very briefly encounter later. Fleckno's concern for bringing music to the stage is both interesting and maddeningly difficult to interpret. And there are also Ferrand Spence and George Granville, both heartily partisan, if less than convincing in their conceptions.

6. E. M. Dent, *Foundations of English Opera: a Study of Musical Drama in England During the Seventeenth Century* (Cambridge: Cambridge University Press, 1928). Donald Jay Grout, *A Short History of Opera*, 2d ed. (New York: Columbia University Press, 1965) is also a standard and useful, though brief, review of the English materials. It is particularly helpful in placing England in the Continental context.

7. The reader conversant with the work on masque of Enid Welsford (*The Court Masque* [Cambridge, 1927]) and Orgel and Gordon will recognize my debt to them. It is so pervasive that accurate acknowledgment would be constant. I have tried to specify carefully my most significant departures and debts. On the point raised here, see especially Orgel's *The Illusion of Power* (Berkeley and Los Angeles: University of California Press, 1975) but also *The Jonsonian Masque* (Cambridge: Harvard University Press, 1965) and particularly vol. 1 of *Inigo Jones*, with Roy Strong (London: Sotheby Parke Bernet; Berkeley and Los Angeles: University of California Press, 1973).

8. Garrison treats these classical roots in some detail (*Dryden*, p. 7ff.), and analyzes their interpretation by Cowley interestingly on 100–1.

9. "Roles and Mysteries," in *The Renaissance Imagination*, ed. Stephen Orgel (Berkeley and Los Angeles: University of California Press, 1975), 14.

10. As a partner in creating the masque's symbology, according to Mary Chan, who exemplifies and elaborates the point throughout *Music in the Theatre of Ben Jonson* (Oxford: Clarendon Press, 1980). Dent includes *The Vision of Delight*, definitely, and *The Golden Age Restored*, probably, among the fully composed masques.

11. Calvin's fear of music expresses and underlies puritanical attacks on its use and abuse, as his prevailingly sexual imagery makes patent. These attitudes did not, of course, extend to the ruling forces of the Interregnum, as Cromwell and Milton make plain.

12. Cited by John Stevens, *Music and Poetry in the Early Tudor Court* (London: Methuen, 1961), 89.

13. Stevens, *Music and Poetry*, 91; cf. also 64–65.

14. Monteverdi's statement is the best example. It is cited in full below in chapter 6's fuller discussion of the idea of musical affect.

15. See especially 264–69. John Steadman's *The Lamb and the Elephant* (San Marino, Calif.: Huntington, 1974) is the most thorough discussion I know of the literary shift, allegoresis to mimesis, handling tactfully the impossibility of either dating it or ignoring it.

16. By the fourteenth century, tonality had given music a firm and normative base that replaced Pythagorean notions; but the quarrel that ensued in the seventeenth, over the *seconda pratica*, a quarrel about harmonics, was waged in the name of emotional mimesis and affect, not mathematics. Words, the basis of the gamut all the way back to Guido d'Arezzo, reasserted their supremacy over mathematics once again in Monteverdi's pronouncement that the words are "mistress of the harmony." The eternally problematic relation of words and music is hardly settled here, but the direction of

seventeenth-century thinking on the issue clearly indicated. Unfortunately, in England, the poets on the whole took it too literally, the nonreferentiality of music rendering its potential for signification nugatory. See also Brewster Royerson, "The Art of Painting the Passions," *Journal of the History of Ideas* 14 (1953): 68–94.

17. William Davenant, "Preface to *Gondibert*," *Critical Essays of the Seventeenth Century*, ed. J. E. Spingarn (Oxford: Clarendon Press, 1908–9; reprint, Bloomington: Indiana University Press, 1957), 2:6.

18. Eugene Waith, *Ideas of Greatness* (New York: Barnes & Noble, 1971), 194, pointed out that Davenant's conception of epic is formally dramatic to begin with, countering the prevalent notion that Davenant—and Dryden—conceive drama epically.

19. Thomas Rymer, "Preface to Rapin" (1674), in Springarn, *Critical Essays* 2:169. Rymer repeats the same charge against the *Davideis*, where Cowley's failure to show us the man rather than tell us the Idea of him is a sin against Homeric reticence and its artful illusion (p. 172).

20. Cf. his remarks against the lyrical in the *Davideis;* Rymer, "Preface to Rapin," 168.

21. Davenant, "Preface to *Gondibert*," 3.

22. The strongest interpretation of that emphasis is in D. T. Mace, "Dryden's Dialogue on Drama," *Journal of the Warburg & Courtauld Institute* 25 (1962): 87–112, among his several Dryden essays. It is challenged effectively at its root by Edward Pechter, *Dryden's Classical Theory of Literature* (Cambridge: Cambridge University Press, 1975), 55.

23. John Dryden, *Works*, vol. 17, ed. Samuel Holt Monk (Berkeley and Los Angeles: University of California Press, 1971), 76 and in the later citation, 77.

24. Ben Janson *Timber or Discoveries*, ed. G. B. Harrison (London: Bodley Head, 1922), 60.

25. By, for instance, Curtis A. Price, "Music as Drama," *The London Theatre World, 1660–1800*, ed. Robert D. Hume (Carbondale: Southern Illinois University Press, 1980), 210–35, and Phillip Parsons, "Restoration Tragedy as Total Theatre," *Restoration Literature*, ed. Harold Love (London: Methuen, 1972), 27–68, two of the best recent essays on the subject of Restoration musical theatre, disparate in their postulates, but equally responsive to the *Empress*.

26. Dale B. J. Randall, *Jonson's Gypsies Unmasked* (Durham: Duke University Press, 1975), 39–42, also stresses the "counsel" justification in Jonson. He cites as his primary predecessors Ernest W. Talbert, "The Interpretation of Jonson's Courtly Spectacles," *PMLA* 61 (1946): 454–73, and Allan H. Gilbert, "The Function of the Masques in *Cynthia's Revels*," *Philological Quarterly* 22 (1943): 211–30. The Talbert essay is the finest analysis of the classical sources and Jonson's use of them. "The voice of Jonson's courtly spectacle," he concludes (p. 473), "is that of the panegyric *laudando praecipere*," a conclusion Orgel finds troublingly narrow.

27. The iconography so basic to the allegory of court masque has received more attention than any other aspect of the form. Graham Parry summarizes much of it in the first chapter of *The Golden Age Restor'd* (New York: St. Martin's, 1981). The primary iconographic studies come from the Warburg: Frances Yates's numerous essays referred to in the following chapter, D. J. Gordon's essays, collected by Orgel in *The Renaissance Imagination* (Berkeley and Los Angeles: University of California Press, 1975), whose footnotes chronicle the industry fully.

28. The work cited in note 26 examines very closely the first production (of an unusual three) in terms of place, cast, and intellectual milieu. It is particularly rich on Buckingham.

29. Orgel, who thinks *Neptune's Triumph* does fail, uses this phrase first of *Oberon* (in *The Jonsonian Masque,* [Cambridge: Harvard University Press, 1965], 84). Randall's argument about *The Gipsies Metamorphosed* is in a sense an intensive study of exactly how ambiguously multiple meaning and multiple style can cohere toward quasi-covert satire. His interpretation accepted, that masque may be the cleverest subterfuge in Jacobean court theatricals.

30. Orgel, *Jonsonian Masque*, 109.

31. Herbert Lindenberger, *Historical Drama* (Chicago: University of Chicago Press, 1975), 78–80; Eugene Waith, "Spectacles of State," *Studies in English Literature* 13 (1973): 317–30.

32. Orgel, *Jonsonian Masque*, 107.

33. A full discussion of this aspect of both the Tate and the Purcell is given in chapter 7, below.

34. The words are Brooks Otis's in *Virgil: A Study in Civilized Poetry* (Oxford: Clarendon Press, 1964), 330, the best discussion of Aeneas that I know.

35. This is the message of *The Illusion of Power* generally, but it will be found most consistently explicated in the first chapter.

36. Orgel, *Jonsonian Masque*, 48.

37. Cited by Randall, *Jonson's Gypsies Unmasked*, 37, who is as dubious as possible about the ingenuousness of the masque.

38. *Notes of Conversations with Ben Jonson made by William Drummond of Harthornden*, ed. G. B. Harrison (London: Bodley Head Quartos; reprint, New York: Barnes & Noble, 1966), 14.

39. The best recent anthropological study dealing directly with the Elizabethan and Jacobean masque is Clifford Geertz, "Centers, Kings and Charisma," in *Culture and Its Creators*, ed. J. Ben-David and T. Clark (Chicago: University of Chicago Press, 1977), 150–71. One can, of course, avoid symbolic reading altogether, as the Marxists have most successfully done. Yet a version that does for English what Erica Harth has attempted for the French (*Ideology and Culture in Seventeenth-Century France* [Ithaca: Cornell University Press, 1983]) has yet to appear.

40. Though Orgel hedges on the point, *The Illusion of Power* moves in and out of intrinsic reading, suggesting, at times strongly, that Jonson's didacticism had effect. Indeed, finally he must, if his two audiences have any status beyond visions in Jonson's mind, as on revels they surely do for Orgel.

41. "Social Dramas and Stories about Them," *Critical Inquiry* 7 (1980): 141–68.

42. Turner's source for the distinction between "model for" and "model of" is Clifford Geertz who amplifies it in several works, the most immediately relevant his study of the Bali, *Negara: The Theatre State in Nineteenth-Century Bali* (Princeton: Princeton University Press, 1980). Gordon's view is clear in "Chapman's *Hero and Leander*," and "Roles and Mysteries," 113–14 and 20 respectively in *The Renaissance Imagination;* Orgel's, in *Illusion of Power*, 55–57.

43. For Turner, the nature of the model is in question, a ritual model embodying not that determinate nature that the ceremonial model does and being therefore capable of generative reordering. The forms of art become here virtual displacements of absent ritual, functional substitutions, a concept that I recognize is precariously loose unless it is given some firm anchors.

44. Gordon, "Roles and Mysteries," *Renaissance Imagination*, 23.

45. Gordon, "Rubens and the Whitehall Ceiling," *Renaissance Imagination*, 50.

46. The parody of courtly masque went unnoticed, but the direct satire of a specific

political act caused Middleton significant trouble. See Margot Heinemann, *Puritanism and Theatre: Thomas Middleton and opposition drama under the early Stuarts* (Cambridge and New York: Cambridge University Press, 1980).

Chapter 2. Shakespeare and the Imperial Myth

1. In "Queen Elizabeth as Astraea," *Journal of the Warburg & Courtauld Institute* 10 (1947): 27–82; now reprinted in *Astraea* (London and Boston: Routledge & Kegan Paul, 1975), 29–87, Yates outlined the history of the Astraea configuration that lies at the heart of the embedded compliment to Elizabeth in Oberon's lines and specified Shakespeare's use of the myth generally. Gary Schmidgall has a good caveat on the shortcomings of Yates in general in *Shakespeare and the Courtly Aesthetic* (Berkeley and Los Angeles: University of California Press, 1981), 5–7.

2. All my Shakespearean citations, given in the text, and referring to act, scene, and line are to *The Riverside Shakespeare*, ed. G. Blakemore Evans et al. (Boston: Houghton Mifflin, 1974).

3. Louis Adrian Montrose has a fine reading of part of this passage in "'Shaping Fantasies': Figurations of Gender and Power in Elizabethan Culture," *Representations* 1 (1983): 61–84. He would probably disagree with my "stabler key" as a sign of my acceptance of patriarchal presuppositions.

4. Roy Strong, *Splendor at Court: Renaissance Spectacle and the Theater of Power* (Boston: Houghton Mifflin, 1973), 84.

5. The interpretive notion underlying Richard's problem here is classically elaborated in Ernst Kantorowicz, *The King's Two Bodies* (Princeton: Princeton University Press, 1957), a study that gives a firm historical base to the many explications of the ideas of language in the play and of Richard's identity in relation to it.

6. Yates has discussed the Tudor ideological resurrection of chivalric devices in "Elizabethan Chivalry: the Romance of the Accession Day Tilts," *Journal of the Warburg & Courtauld Institute* 20 (1957): 4–25; reprinted in *Astraea*, 88–111. Roy Strong pursues the subject in "The Popular Celebration of the Accession Day of Queen Elizabeth I," *Journal of the Warburg & Courtauld Institute* 21 (1958): 86–103.

7. Gordon traces the classical sources and applies them to *Coriolanus* in "Name and Fame: Shakespeare's *Coriolanus*," *Renaissance Imagination*, 203–19. Having appeared first in 1964, this is one of the earliest of many essays on naming and the power of words in Shakespeare's political texts. On *Coriolanus* Stanley Fish extended the question to speech acts more generally in "How to Do Things with Austin and Searle," *Modern Language Notes* 91 (1976): 983–1035.

8. If legend is true, the desire to see Falstaff again goes back to the revival of the *Merry Wives* in 1600 that reassured an audience that his death is not final. Regarding those who recite the act 3 speeches tongue-in-cheek, Brian Vickers reported unhappily one such production in reviewing *Shakespeare: Pattern of Excelling Nature*, ed. David Bevington and Jay Halio in *Shakespeare Quarterly* 32 (1981): 406. Such shifts as *Henry V* has undergone in production of course follow with critical shifts, which authoritatively substantiate cultural biases, always in process. The quote by Stephen Booth is from *Shakespeare Quarterly* 29 (1978): 268. Lawrence Danson, "*Henry V*: King, Chorus, and Critics," *Shakespeare Quarterly* 34 (1983): 27–43, has developed fully in theatrical terms an account of the play that elaborates what I take to be Booth's more cryptic position. They would differ, though, on the use of the Chorus.

9. Joanne Altieri, "Romance in *Henry V,*" *Studies in English Literature* 21 (1981): 223–240.

10. The most widely influential version is Norman Rabkin's "Rabbits, Ducks, and *Henry V,*" *Shakespeare Quarterly* 28 (1977): 279–96, revised in *Shakespeare and the Problem of Meaning* (Chicago: University of Chicago Press, 1981), chap. 2. My citations are to the original. Mine is, in essence, Danson's resistance, too, to the Rabkin and Barton essays I will deal with shortly. See his *"Henry V,"* pp. 28–29.

11. The first quotation is from Booth, *Review,* 268; Anne Barton has exemplified the last point in her discussion of the disguised king convention in the non-Shakespearean drama as background to his manipulation of it in act 5, scene 2: "The King Disguised: Shakespeare's *Henry V* and the Comical History," in *The Triple Bond,* ed. Joseph G. Price (University Park and London: Penn State University Press, 1975), 92–117.

12. I use Goddard because he is still Rabkin's point of reference in 1981. There are, of course, much more recent examples, e.g., Gordon Ross Smith, "Shakespeare's *Henry V:* Another Part of the Critical Forest," *Journal of the History of Ideas* 37 (1976): 3–26. An example of the earlier histories retained by Holinshed is the early biography of the translator of the authorized Henrican biography of Livio, *Vita Henrici Quinti,* a far earlier piece of Tudor historiography than could have been influenced by Machiavellian notions, a point whose relevance will become clear in moments.

13. Holinshed, *The Third Volume of Chronicles* (1587 ed.) in *Narrative and Dramatic Sources of Shakespeare,* ed. Geoffrey Bullough (London: Routledge & Kegan Paul), 4:394, 397. The reversion to throat-slitting Gary Taylor so much admired in the 1966 RSC production ("Three Studies on the Text of *Henry V,*" in Stanley Wells, *Modernizing Shakespeare's Spelling* [Oxford: Clarendon, 1979], 151) was thus a reversion to Holinshed, not to Shakespeare, but compatible certainly with Q's more ironic text. I will return to the point much later.

14. I recognize that the relation of Folio to quarto may be reversed in time and deal with the issue below. My essential point about the value of Fluellen as Boar's Head displacer stands, in any case.

15. Holinshed, *Third volume of chronicles,* ed. Bullough 4:388, cuts off the passage at "Great gaine of the Englishman." Holinshed continues, as quoted.

16. While I agree with Barton's sense of the real questions raised in the scene, I think her description of the scene loads the dice against the heroic Henry, creating, or accepting, the false dichotomy against which I am arguing, but perhaps this is merely to take too literally the bluntness of analytic tools applied to an infinitely flexible text.

17. Strong, *Splendor at Court,* ch. 3.

18. Dr. Johnson singled both out as faulty drama, Dr. Johnson having here, as elsewhere, little truck with pastoral notions.

19. Rabkin, "Rabbits, Ducks," 296.

20. See Barton, "The King Disguised," p. 100, on the king's prose in this regard.

21. Louis Adrian Montrose, "Gifts and Reasons: The Contexts of Peel's *Araygnement of Paris,*" *English Literary History* 47 (1980): 457–69.

22. The Prologue and Epilogue significantly direct us not to Henry, but to the fates and emotional affects of the tragic characters, especially Katherine, as well as to the affective weight of the action. While I follow R. A. Foakes in taking *Henry VIII* as an essentially Shakespearean text, treating the whole text as the work of one hand, I am aware that Foakes cannot answer the attacks on his assumptions made by Cyrus Hoy in the generally accepted "The Shares of Fletcher and his Collaborators in the Beaumont and Fletcher Canon (7)," *Studies in Bibliography,* ed. Fredson Bowers (Charlottesville:

Bibliographical Society of University of Virginia, 1962), 71–90. Critics usually now bypass, perhaps ungraciously, the statistical linguistic evidence Hoy assembled, but I shall, too, convinced that the text as a whole follows out many of the implications of *Henry V.*

23. As in the case of *Henry V,* modern interpretation bifurcates along the line of idealistic versus realistic political representation and here, because *Henry VIII* emerges from the theatrical context of the masque, the bifurcation is absolute—Machiavelli versus Plotinus. An ironic sense of Henry as a Machiavellian figure governs Tom McBride in *"Henry VIII* as Machiavellian Romance," *Journal of English and Germanic Philology* 76 (1977): 26–40; as a Platonic/courtly heroic king John Cox in *"Henry VIII* and the Masque," *English Literary History* 54 (1978): 390–409. Like every modern commentator, Cox tries to bring the two poles together, in his case wisely, I think, by invoking the popular tradition. Yet his weighting of the play is all to the courtly side, failing to allow the substantive force of the popular tradition that he acknowledges only in the *de casibus* falls. Orgel's influence is also paramount in Edward Berry's *"Henry VIII* and the Dynamics of Spectacle," *Shakespeare Studies* 12 (1979): 229–46, wherein the transition from Wolsey's theatre to the final pageant is seen as an education in revels. Henry himself plays little part in this reading.

Yates' interpretation of the play is central to the thesis of her *Shakespeare's Last Plays: A New Approach* (London: Routledge & Kegan Paul, 1975): the last plays are best understood as parts of the Elizabethan revival of 1610 to 1612 that accompanies new cultural hopes in Prince Arthur and Princess Elizabeth as focuses of the Protestant Imperial myth. Foakes's essay is the introduction of his edition of *Henry VIII* in the Arden Shakespeare (London: Methuen and Cambridge: Harvard University Press, 1957).

24. In the following discussion I reiterate a number of the points made by Lee Bliss in "The Wheel of Fortune and the Maiden Phoenix of Shakespeare's *Henry VIII,"* *English Literary History* 42 (1975): 1–25, which I think the best contemporary essay on the play. My sense of the play is essentially the same as Bliss's, but my idea of how the play's meanings are dramatized is substantially different.

25. I should note that Stone, remarking on history and not literature, calls our attention to the fact that "although there were several aristocratic rebellions against the sovereign throughout the sixteenth century, not a single one of the defeated conspirators maintained the justice of his cause on the scaffold. Without exception they acknowledged themselves justly condemned to death for an offense against God and the King" (Lawrence Stone, *The Crisis of the Aristocracy 1558–1641,* abridged ed. [London: Oxford University Press, 1967], 132. As in the parallel scene in *Henry V* (2, 2), the King and not the man is at issue and another of the modern world's ironies Shakespeare's realism.

26. William R. Elton, *King Lear and the Gods* (San Marino, Calif.: Huntington, 1966) developed the relevance of the *deus absconditus* to *Lear* and in the process gives a useful history of the concept and its ramifications. See esp. pp. 30–37, 59ff. On Lutheranism in this regard see Quentin Skinner, *The Foundations of Modern Political Thought* (Cambridge: Cambridge University Press, 1978), 2:3–19.

27. Gordon, "Roles and Mysteries," 18.

28. Gordon cites Chapman in explicating the iconography of the *Memorable Masque,* performed for Princess Elizabeth's wedding; "Chapman's *Memorable Masque,"* *Renaissance Imagination,* 194.

29. I part company finally from Bliss here who sees the implementing of the masque allowing Shakespeare, as Berry agrees (p. 243), to "remain true to the ideals potential within reality without sacrificing reality itself." This view of the masque effects ignores,

I think, the far greater limits on idealization that are placed on Henry VIII as compared with the active, self-projecting Henry V. The quote on literary meaning is from Jerome J. McGann, "The Meaning of the Ancient Mariner," *Critical Inquiry* 8 (1981): 38.

30. McGann, "Meaning of the Ancient Mariner," 54.

31. I obviously have no quarrel at all with the reduced-cast hypothesis, though it seems to me here an infinitely malleable proposition. When Taylor notes that critical and aesthetic criteria must finally determine our judgments (*Three Studies*, p. 152), he has my complete agreement. I think that my critical and aesthetic sense of the play does call some of his numerically derived conclusions into question. Chief among them is the temporal priority, of course, though not the final authority of Folio.

Chapter 3. Reception and Dissemination

1. Angus Fletcher's review of Stephen Orgel's *Illusion of Power, Georgia Review* 29 (1975): 969.

2. Stone has stressed the number of Puritan connections—and opinions—at Court in *Crisis*. See pp. 338ff. and passim in the abridged edition (London: Oxford University Press, 1967). Though it remains prevalent, the notion of the court as a monolithic entity that supported a single identifiable style has been vigorously attacked by Philip J. Finkelpearl in "The Role of the Court in the Development of Jacobean Drama," *Criticism* 24 (1982): 138–58.

3. In *The Renaissance Imagination*, p. 155. Cited internally henceforth.

4. Francis Bacon, "Of Masques and Triumphs," *Works*, ed. Spedding, Ellis, and Heath (London: Longmans, 1870), 6:467–68. The essay does not appear in the two earlier editions, a fact perhaps reflecting its topicality for Bacon in 1625. That costs had become ridiculous in the Caroline years is a regular generalization given specificity in the records of costs incurred in *The Middle Temple Documents relating to George Chapman's The Memorable Masque and . . . to James Shirley's The Triumph of Peace*, ed. Tucker Orbison (London: Malone Society, 1983).

5. Cited from Herford and Simpson by Orgel, *Complete Masques*, p. 30.

6. See esp. the "Expostulation with Inigo Jones," ll. 46–48, 54–55. Orgel nods at the problem in his defence of the allegorical figures' self-explication, *Illusion of Power*, pp. 24–26. John Steadman, in *The Lamb and the Elephant*, p. 104, cites Anthony Blunt: the "themes of most Mannerist fresco cycles are so obscure that they can only have been chosen by a trained theologian." Blunt goes on to describe the Council of Trent's desire for clarity and accuracy, ignored according to his critics by Michelangelo in the "last Judgment" in favor of mystical allegory that obscured the literal meaning so important to the Counter-Reformation program. Michelangelo's concern for the critics was probably no greater than Jonson's for Dekker.

7. Jonson, too, used Bruno, whose *Eroici furori*, more lightly held than the Bruno in Carew, served as a basis for the late *Love's Triumph through Callipolis*.

8. In Louis L. Martz, *The Wit of Love* (Notre Dame and London: University of Notre Dame Press, 1969), 73.

9. Stephen Orgel and Roy Strong, *Inigo Jones: The Theatre of the Stuart Court* (London and Berkeley: Sotheby Parke-Bennett and the University of California Press, 1973), 1:50–51.

10. Lines 61–64 of "In answer of an Elegiacall Letter upon the death of the King of *Sweden* from Aurelian Townsend, inviting me to write on that subject," *The Poems of Thomas Carew with his Masque Coelum Britannicum*, ed. Rhodes Dunlap (Oxford: Claren-

don Press, 1949), 74–77. All citations to Carew in my text are to this edition.

11. Orgel discusses the prerogative "argument" between the two masques in *The Illusion of Power,* pp. 73ff. Leah Marcus has effectively stressed the importance of topicality in "'Present Occasions' and the Shaping of Ben Jonson's Masques," *English Literary History* 45 (1978): 201–25.

12. Bruno himself is more explicit: "It seems to me to be fitting (since the river Eridanus has the property of being at the same time suppositiously and personally in various parts) that we let it be whatever it will be imagined to be, named, called upon, and revered." Giordano Bruno, *The Expulsion of the Triumphant Beast,* trans. and ed. Arthur D. Imerti (New Brunswick: Rutgers University Press, 1964), 258.

13. David Bergeron, *English Civic Pageantry, 1558–1642* (Columbia: University of South Carolina Press, 1971), 70–78, specifies the debt in its physical particulars to James's 1603 London entry.

14. The best recent study of the pageants, and one that shares my cultural emphasis, is Theodore B. Leinward, "London Triumphing: The Jacobean Lord Mayor's Show," *Clio* 11 (1982): 137–53. He also reviews the bibliography concisely. See also Susan Wells, "Jacobean City Comedy and the Ideology of the City," *English Literary History* 48 (1981): 37–60, which touches on the pageants.

15. *Londini Emporia,* reprinted in "Two Pageants by Thomas Heywood," in *Theatre Miscellany,* ed. A. M. Clark (Oxford: Blackwell, 1953), 1–47. I cite *Londini Emporia* and *Londini Artium et Scientarum Scaturigo* from this as the most accessible source.

16. Regarding Jordan, the 1672 show for Robert Hanson is probably the best example. For Middleton, see *The Sunne in Aries* (London, 1621) where Fame speaks slightingly of the conversion of "Granaries for the Poore, / Though now converted to some Rich mens Store / (The more the Ages misery)" sig. B2^r. Middleton is also the most internationalist of the earlier pageant writers, see, for example, 1617's *Triumphs of Honor and Industry.*

17. William Davenant, *Salmacida Spolia* (London: Thomas Walkley, 1639), sig. B.

18. Thomas Heywood, *Londini Status Pacatus* (London, 1639), sig. B2^r. Heywood is using here the same rhetorical strategy that Carew employed in the response to Aurelian Townshend on Gustavus Adolphus. For Carew, the "throwes" of Germany call into remarkably delicate question the value of martial heroism, setting up his claims for the masquing world of Charles.

19. Regarding the first point, Bergeron, (*English Civic Pageantry,* passim) attributes the changes in content as well as structuring to the skills of the particular writers responsible for the shows. While this of course has importance, the genre overall exerts developmentally different pressure on the writers, deriving from changes in the theatre and from political concerns. A comparison of the writers' Lord Mayor's Day productions with their other plays tends to confirm my point. The general structure of the show is fairly constant through the century, answering to the procession's physical route; the means of realizing the praise through drama, through music, through spectacle alters quite as Bergeron has described.

Both Tatham and Jordan explain the process of their allegorizing within the text, reminding an audience in the sixties or seventies that it is seeing figural allegory. So Justice in the first pageant of Jordan's 1674 show tells the mayor, "You are the Truth, my Lord, I'm but the Type," as Orpheus tells the mayor-elect in Tatham's show that "the Type must vanish when the truth appears." Much earlier Munday had explained "our morall methode" in detail by simply explicating the meaning of the devices, for example the 1609 and 1616 pageants.

20. Heywood, who was particularly taken with numerology and encyclopedic knowl-

edge—disquisitions on six and twelve, bestiary information—frequently excuses his printed interpolations. The poetry itself will sometimes be extended with the explanation that it was too long for the barge, or the crowd.

21. Heywood is not alone in remarking interpolations in the printed text, which does not suffer the constraints of pageant performance. Webster, too, elaborated excuses. See note 26, below.

The pageant equivalents of the antimasque are there from the beginning in Peele's *Descensus Astraea* (1591) with its figures of Superstition, a Friar and Ignorance, a priest, and a pair of "Malecontents." Since antimasque in the proper sense cannot exist in the City pageants, that one should exclude Dekker's Envy pageant in the 1612 *Troia-Nova Triumphans* is questionable. Here Envy even returns after the Guildhall dinner in a bit of unexpected drama wherein Virtue defeats him. Yet Heywood's textless cutups are more obviously drawn to the court pattern for an antimasque. So I would not dispute Bergeron's assertion (p. 218) that Heywood introduced the antimasque: he is the first who gives drolls and figures of dissension their own pageants, separating them from ordered hierarchy as absolutely as the masque itself does. As in his desire to include courtly arts in the body of the show, Heywood's self-consciousness about the textless antimasque ("more Mimicall than Materiall inserted for the Vulgar, who rather love to feast their eyes," etc.) marks him parvenu, consonant with his shift toward the courtly from Dekker's and Middleton's more mundane and common stances.

22. Heywood, *Londini Scaturigo*, p. 33.

23. John Tatham, *Londons Triumphs* (London, 1664), 7.

24. The address to the monarch, which in Peele makes up the body of the text, becomes less and less sizable as time goes on, leaving one with the impression that James stopped attending altogether and that monarchy is present solely in figural representations and historical reference. With Charles II, the person returns, emphatically.

25. To Stone's *(Crisis of the Aristocracy)* attention to this social phenomenon (see esp. pp. 25–32, 89, 161–62) one may also add Peter Laslett, *The World we have lost*, 2d ed. (New York: Scribner's, 1973), 34ff., 195ff., whose more general treatment of social mobility at the time situates the merchants in their broader context.

26. Webster's 1624 show is clearest on this, taking as its theme "Monuments of Honor" and running through the company worthies of the past, then their regal connections. Pride of place, though, goes to the poets, who preserve the heroes' names, creating the monuments. Webster's show, despite its bow to Chaucer, Gower, Lidgate, More, and Sidney, is no richer in its poetry than the shows usually are, and he is aware of this, appending a paragraph to the text that claims he could have worked his theme up "more curious and elaborate," but he didn't want to bore the mayor or puzzle the understanding of the common people.

27. Not precisely. Tatham had planned on Fame's speaking at Foote Lane, but something interfered, so she spoke at the Great Conduit in Cheapside. My text for *London's Glory* is *The Dramatic Works of John Tatham* edited by James Maidment and W. H. Logan (Edinburgh: Paterson, 1879). All my citations to Tatham are to this edition and are included in my text.

28. John Evelyn, *The Diary*, ed. E. S. de Beer (London: Oxford, 1959), 408.

29. *The Diary of Samuel Pepys*, ed. R. Latham and W. Matthews (Berkeley and Los Angeles: University of California Press, 1970), 1:277.

30. Concerning who rode where in the procession, D. J. Gordon interestingly analyzes a letter of Lotti in this regard: "The Florentine Agent Goes to a Masque," in the Clark, *Theatre Miscellany*, 123–29. The concern of the agent for the seating plan and the diplomatic problems of attendance illustrates my point.

Dustin Griffin explores the theatricality in "Dryden's Charles: the Ending of *"Absalom and Achitophel," Philological Quarterly* 57 (1978): 359–82.

31. Tatham's nineteenth-century editors make the points about both Pepys and Mrs. Behn.

32. Of the three, Tatham has most regard for Harrington, whom he still hopes may reform and return to the king, a hope not based on Harrington's works, which he condemns as "a demy-semy in the Rump's musick" occasioning innumerable poor puns on music, wheels, and oceans. The likelihood that his hope is based instead on Harrington's past life, on his friendship with Charles I, and his presence on the scaffold at the beheading, is suggested by his editors and suits Tatham's habits of mind, which run continually to the *ad hominem* (Milton is an "old heretick" "that by his will would shake off his governours, as he doth his wives, four in a fourtnight.") Of Needham, "one of the spokes of Harrington's Rota, till he was turned out for cracking," he has little enough to say beyond a cruel succession of such puns, and of Milton he shows us the kind of unsubstantive fear and derision that the pamphlets met: *Eikonoklastes* is those "scandalous papers against the late King's book"; the *Ready and Easy Way* is condemned for fanciful novelty.

Chapter 4. Conversion: Davenant

1. Dennis' remarks on Davenant and the Interregnum poets are in *The Usefulness of the Stage*, pt. 1, chap. 4, in *The Critical Works of John Dennis*, ed. Edward Niles Hooker (Baltimore: Johns Hopkins Press, 1939), 1 : 160–63.

Even in Venice, the most broadly based of the early operatic theatres, the houses were owned and financially supported by noble families.

2. *Luminalia*'s authorship is not perfectly clear, but it is generally attributed to Davenant. *The Triumphs* was not precisely a *court* masque, as shall be explained shortly.

3. The major Davenant scholars, still Alfred Harbage (*Sir William Davenant* [Philadelphia: University of Pennsylvania Press, 1935]) and Arthur H. Nethercot (*Sir William Davenant* [Chicago: University of Chicago Press, 1938]), particularly the latter, fall under the second category, suspicious of all Davenant's activities and hating the epideictic enterprise. Their attitude survives in the bulk of Davenant commentary, even when it is far more measured. Laura S. Brown, for instance, in *English Dramatic Form, 1660–1760* (New Haven: Yale University Press, 1981) uses *The Siege of Rhodes* to illustrate that heroic forms cannot serve demotic purposes, thereby condemning the work for achieving what it attempted. She could do so primarily because she looked forward to the novel rather than around at the work's context. Rather than enumerate the dozens of critics who have pilloried Davenent, I refer the reader to an important positive voice, Philip Parsons, "Restoration Tragedy as Total Theatre," in *Restoration Literature*, ed. Harold Love (London: Methuen, 1972), 27–68. His essay can be illuminatingly positive because he is one of the few who has carefully considered Davenant's masque beginnings.

4. Walter Benjamin, *The Origins of German Tragic Drama*, trans. John Osborne (London: New Left Books, 1977), 62. See also 120ff.

5. Henry Herbert's report, cited in Murray Lefkowitz, ed., *Trois Masques a la Cour de Charles Ier D'Angleterre* (Paris: Centre National de la Recherche Scientifigue, 1970), 113–14. I follow his text of *The Triumphs* and cite it internally.

6. In a sense, this is a variation on Carew's Gustavus Adolphus poem, the works together indicating that the primary defense a poet could find for Charles's avoidance

of the continental wars was an effort to undercut martial exploits. Carew naturally elaborates a far more fully thought-out alternative.

7. I assume, possibly oversimply, that this stands behind the frequent sense of a lack of continuity in pieces of this sort. It is the case in Welsford *The Court Masque* and Lefkowitz, *Trois Masques,* 116.

8. Though the text is not definitive on this point, it appears to be the case and would, I suppose, support the argument for a decrease in participation in these later masques.

9. Lefkowitz, *Trois Masques,* 117, attributes these qualities to the unusual fact of amateur performance in the antimasque. That seems unlikely, since wordless, pantomimic antimasques were as common to the court masque as to the City pageant, and antic dancing probably required as much skill as reciting lines. It is true, though, that amateur performance in the antimasque was rare.

10. Andrew J. Sabol, *Songs and Dances for the Stuart Masque* (Providence: Brown University Press, 1958), 1–3.

11. Mary Chan, *Music in the Theatre of Ben Jonson* (Oxford: Clarendon Press, 1980), 184. She suggests the possibility of irregular orchestration as well. Sabol, (*Songs and Dances,* 3) though, finds less emblematic musical contention in, for instance, *The Masque of Queens'* double rhythms (duple in the treble, triple in the bass).

12. Chan, *Music in the Theatre of Ben Jonson,* 272, raises the possibility of a serious contention between Jonson and Ferrabosco not unlike his difficulties with Jones. Perhaps he was as unwilling to give to music as to stage properties a share in the poet's authority. At any rate, the comedy grows without it. I should apologize to the reader unacquainted with the bulk of Jonson's masques for the appearance in my text now of what will have to seem a plethora of mere titles. Should the points be of interest, the masques can be referred to easily, once cited (see Jonson, *Complete Masques*). To have omitted them would have left me with no substantiation beyond the few masques I can deal with in detail.

13. That order was poet, designer, infrequently choreographer, and even less so musician. Of the eleven known Caroline masques, music survives for only three; complete music is not had till the 1653 Locke and Gibbons' score of *Cupid and Death.* Lefkowitz, *Trois Masques,* contains detailed information on the scores and the attributions.

14. Welsford's resistance to the comedy in later Jonsonian masques is based on that recognition—that the development of comedy within the masque perverts the masque as a form. Orgel's reply—that it is the comedy itself that is Jonson's primary area of concern, becoming the seat of revels as education—does not so much answer her objection as shift the question from one about form to one about function. It is obvious that I feel Orgel minimizes the tensions that the works formally contain, smooths them out, as it were, into something less (perhaps raggedly) dynamic than they are.

15. Lefkowitz, *Trois Masques,* 73, discusses the point in some detail.

16. Pp. 190–91 in Lefkowitz, *Trois Masques,* whose text of *Britannia Triumphans* I use throughout.

17. Carew is the most successful in this as in all things in these thirties masques: the dramatic comic encounter between Momus and Mercury rivals Jonson in its verbal energy, giving their debate a dramatic convincingness lacking in the Davenant.

18. In the *Advancement of Learning* he had said. "The use of Feigned History hath been to give some shadow of satisfaction to the mind of man in those points wherein the nature of things doth deny it . . . [poesy] doth raise and erect the mind, by submitting the shew of things to the desires of the mind; whereas reason doth buckle and bow the

mind unto the nature of things." But in *The Great Instauration* he warns more simply, "God forbid that we should give out a dream of our own imagination for a pattern of the world." Perhaps that explains his attitude toward the masque.

19. Anne Barton, *Shakespeare and the Idea of the Play* (London: Chatto & Windus, 1962); Jackson Cope, *The Theater and the Dream* (Baltimore: Johns Hopkins University Press, 1973).

20. It does, of course, complexify the dramatic situation. Both Parsons and Curtis Price comment on this function, Parsons the more elaborately and energetically, in "Restoration Tragedy," 49–52. Price's more sober elucidation is in *Music in the Restoration Theatre*, ([n.p.] UMI Research Press, 1979), 30–31, as a brief example of the use of masques within Restoration plays. He developed the implications more fully in "Music as Drama," *The London Theatre World, 1660–1800*, ed. Robert D. Hume (Carbondale: Southern Illinois University Press, 1980), 210–35.

21. Cited from *The Works of Sir William Davenant*, the London 1673 edition reissued New York: Benjamin Blom, 1968, p. 72. The musician's definition came as a defense of the imitative validity of musical declamation against the icastic attack of the player, who thinks it unnatural for actors to sing "unless you would Metamorphise men into Birds," an event that occurs later in the play in the eyes of the even more unsophisticated housekeeper, who thinks the Priest of the Sun in his Papageno costume is a "humane Bird": one thinks of M. Jourdan. Reflexive theatre loves a rube.

22. Edward Dent, *The Foundations of English Opera: A Study of Musical Drama in England During the Seventeenth Century* (Cambridge: Cambridge University Press, 1928), 66–68.

These attitudes towards the music remain the received idea. Michael Robinson, *Opera Before Mozart* (New York: William Morrow, 1966), 81, still follows Dent, as do Sophia Blaydes and Philip Bordinat in *William Davenant* (Boston: Twayne, 1981) despite Ann Mari Hedbäck's strong counter-argument in her critical edition of *The Siege of Rhodes* (Uppsala: Studia Anglistica, no. 14, 1973), lxviii–lxxv. My citations to the play in what follows are to her text.

23. See John Freehafer, "Brome, Suckling, and Davenant's Theatre Project of 1639," *Texas Studies in Language and Literature* 10 (1968): 367–83 and "The Formation of the London Patent Companies in 1660," *Theatre Notebook* 20 (1965): 6–30. Dennis Arundell had earlier made the same assertion regarding 1639, but Freehafer's reading of the 1660 patent has been challenged by Gunnar Sorelius, "The Early History of the Restoration Theatre: Some Problems Reconsidered," *Theatre Notebook* 33 (1979). Mongi Raddadi, *Davenant's Adaptations of Shakespeare* (Uppsala: Studia Linguistica, no. 36, 1979), 21, follows Sorelius and argues that the adaptations were not formally required but depend from Davenant's "awareness of the function of the drama's reflecting the age, as well as being pleasing and instructive" (154).

24. Parsons ("Restoration tragedy") compared Davenant's sense of opera far too closely to Gordon Craig's much later, and I believe, much different "total theatre." He cites Davenant in *The First Day's Entertainment* and comments " 'Vertue, in those Images of the *Heroes*, adorn'd with that Musick, and these Scenes, is to be enliven'd with Poetry. Poetry is the subtle Engine by which the wonderful Body of the *Opera* must move.' It is a striking analysis. Davenant's operatic conception of drama posits an art of the *ensemble*, a total 'Poetry (whose several beauties make up the shape of the *Opera*)' " (p. 37). If we grant that Davenant's metaphor has taken on the mechanistic language of the Hobbist, there is little to separate the embedded notion here not so much from Craig as from Jonson, for whom soul and body are always the metaphoric basis of the union of poetry and spectacle in the masque, though engines may make no appearance. The complete disappearance of the opera's music also casts some suspicion on the extent to which

Davenant, Pepys, or Mrs. Pepys viewed the work as a media totality in anything like Craig's sense.

25. The emblem points back, for the OED, to the entry of the king, or the mayor, or the emperor on his progress—that is, to epideictic occasions. Regarding the second part, there was at least one performance of it as a sung work, though no record of its music survives at all. Evelyn saw it on 1 September 1662, in "recitative music."

26. 1656 Preface, p. 3.

27. Victor Turner, "Social Dramas and Stories About Them," *Critical Inquiry* 7 (1980): 149.

28. Michael Walzer, in *Regicide and Revolution* (London: Cambridge University Press, 1974), 42–46, 86–89, made the case that Geertz repudiates in "Centers, Kings and Charisma."

29. Though even that was a late addition, its first, and more appropriate, having been *The Courage of Love*, its second, *The Nonpareils, or The Matchless Maids.*

30. John Downes, *Roscius Anglicanus,* introduced by John Loftis (Los Angeles: Augustan Reprint Society #134, 1969), 10.

31. Cited by Turner, "Social Dramas," p. 163.

Chapter 5. Dryden's Recapitulation

1. One of the best sources for the *ballet de cour* is James R. Anthony, *French Baroque Music* (New York: W. W. Norton, 1974). He is equally helpful on most matters of French musical theatre in the period. Regarding Fleckno, had he had court connections perhaps the claims advanced by Eugene Haun (*But Hark! More Harmony* [Ypsilanti: Eastern Michigan University Press, 1971], 35) might have been true—that is, Fleckno might then have antedated Davenant in bringing opera to England. As it is, since neither the work on which Haun bases the claim, *Ariadne Deserted by Theseus* (1654), nor the later *Marriage of Oceanus and Britannia* was apparently ever staged, the claims are academic, though they do call our attention to broader early musical efforts than we at times remember. Fleckno's first piece is virtually pure masque, though his preface, which Haun prints in toto, intelligently discusses the problem that will remain central in these experiments: how to create a recitative adequate to English and to the unification of "the scattered limbs of *Orpheus (Musick* and *Poetry)."* Fleckno claims to have found the solution in Italy, particularly in the work of Claudio Montanendo [*sic*], yet his score, if he ever did write one, is lost. The works do seem to be masques, though the second is so brokenly conceived that saying that much is perhaps saying too much. It even adds rope dancers to *Ariadne's* emphasis on English panegyric.

2. See *Roger North on Music,* ed. John Wilson (London: Novello, 1959), 307. Granville's remarks preface *The British Enchanters,* in *Poems on Several Occasions* 1706; (reprinted, Dublin, 1732). The essay is of interest in showing the thinking of a writer of a very successful, according to Downes, British opera at the time of the Italian onslaught. For Granville the nature of the entertainment commits one to a magician plot, to characters who illustrate love and honor, and to minimizing the ridiculousness of singing Catos and Alexanders. Granville sporadically echoes both Dryden and St. Evremond, but with no attention to first principles. He is laudably concerned for the integration of lyric and dramatic, though the work itself does not show much achievement in that regard. The serviceable Eccles wrote the music.

3. Three, if we assume the early court production of *The Empress,* as some do, six if we count from its public debut on 3 July 1673.

4. *The Dramatic Works of Sir William Davenant* (Edinburgh: Paterson, 1873), 4:6.

5. Dent, *Foundations of English Opera*, 52–53, 74–75. His description is quite accurate to *First Day*, though it does *not* extend to *Cruelty*. Like *The Siege of Rhodes*, *The First Day's Entertainment* was a privately staged musical, scored primarily by the same composers who did *The Siege* (Cook, Colemen, Henry Lawes, and George Hudson are cited in the London, 1657 text.) Unlike the *Siege*—or *Cruelty*—this work makes no gesture at plot, narrative, or character; it is a debate pro and contra "Publique Entertainment by Moral Representations," with Diogenes first presenting the negative (oddly enough, the source of Parsons's "total theatre" opera definition) and Aristophanes responding in the affirmative. Their declamations are followed by a typological pair, a Parisian and a Londoner, each presenting the case for their city's preeminence. Appropriate music is interspersed (for example, "of French composition" for the Parisian, doleful for Diogenes, imitation of the waites for the Londoner).

What is of interest in the piece is its notes on staging practices (for example, curtains drawn at all scenic breaks, music to establish moods and a character's principal psychological affect) and its clear recitation of theoretical maxims that will be reiterated through the next half-century—on moral modeling, on musical affect, on illusion and deception, on the value of "active" [that is, dramatic] over merely written moral precepts.

6. All citations to Davenant, excluding *The Siege of Rhodes*, hereafter continue to be to the 1968 Blom reissue of the 1673 edition.

7. By his own count Dryden wrote three operas. I exclude *The State of Innocence*, despite its telling use of conventions, for two reasons: it was never set or staged (except as a puppet play after Dryden's death), and it does not answer to any of Dryden's mature ideas of what makes an opera. In general, Dryden's operas have been a source of embarrassment to his commentators, in part because of a steady insistence on seeing them in the context of later notions of dramatic opera. Thus Parsons considers them poems rather than plays, too verbal to have taken advantage of the full range of theatrical resources that characterize "total theatre." Similarly, Curtis Price, in "Music as Drama," *The London Theatre World, 1660–1800*, ed. Robert D. Hume (Carbondale: Southern Illinois University Press), 210–35, sharing Parsons' conviction of Dryden's limited dramatic sense, argues that the music drama of the period is more truly operatic than the operas; and of course, they are, in Price's sense. Yet I find highly questionable the idea that the masterwork of Price and Parsons, *The Empress of Morocco*, is a better play than *King Arthur* and wonder about the applicability to seventeenth-century theatre of a definition of drama or opera posited on personality and its display, commensurately negligent of systematic appeals to the mind, however lightly enacted.

8. All citations to *Albion and Albanius* are to Dryden's *Works*, vol. 15, ed. Earl Miner et al. (Berkeley and Los Angeles: University of California Press, 1976) and are given within the text.

9. Zimmerman's remark is in the musical commentary to Dryden's *Works*, 15:351.

10. Miner's commentary points out much of the nautical symbology to better effect than the Jonson comparison; *Works*, 15:528.

11. The capacity of recitative to erase that tendency altogether is experienced in all good opera, but for the model well known to the Restoration one goes naturally to Lully. His dramatic skill with recitative is examined in detail by Joyce Newman in *Jean-Baptiste de Lully and his Tragedies Lyriques* ([n.p.]: UMI Research Press, 1979). Fleckno's recognition of the problem of recitative for English indicates a willingness to attack a difficulty that the ambigue tried to ignore, but Dryden certainly knew that the results existed.

12. Quite why my spokesman for the average, Granville, declared both of these not

opera at all, but masques, I do not pretend to know. It may have had to do with the kind of humor their integration of the media promotes: Granville clearly wanted drama to be thoroughly serious. Perhaps he would have changed his mind about *Semele* if he had heard Handel's much later setting. More likely, at any rate, their lack of magicians to rationalize their magic barred them from his canon; but then one wonders what his criteria for masque were. Terms, at the time, were hardly settled.

13. From the first edition of Addison's *Rosamund* (London: Tonson, 1707), 11. Anyone who has enjoyed the comic operas of the later eighteenth century (for instance the Arne/Bickerstaff *Thomas and Sally* [1760] so successfully staged in Regent's Park rain in June 1983) will recognize both the longevity and parodic perfection of Addison's fully theatrical techniques.

14. Dryden's *Works,* vol. 17, ed. Samuel Holt Monk et al. (Berkeley and Los Angeles: University of California Press, 1971).

15. John Downes calls *The Lancashire Witches* opera, though not the Lee/Purcell *Theodosius.* For him, "machines for flying" were more definitive than music (*Roscius Anglicanus* [1708; reprinted, Augustan Reprint Society, 1969], 38). Evelyn's diary entry of June 1645 highlights perspective scenery, machines, cost, but also the singing.

16. "A Discourse Concerning the Original and Progress of Satire," in *John Dryden: Of Dramatic Poesy and Other Critical Essays,* ed. George Watson (London: Dent, 1962), 2:88.

17. Dryden, "Life of Plutarch," *Works,* 17:252–53. The succeeding page continues the discussion of beneficient versus malevolent spirits' development in a description that is duplicated in Philidel's changes under Merlin's tutelage: he "refines" himself and whitens just as Grimbald, moving in the opposite direction, complains of having grown hoarse since his fall and not having much voice any longer.

18. Calling Daniel a "source" for this prophecy is perhaps disingenuous of me since the apocalyptic books and their tradition go well beyond Daniel. Yet the "Discourse's" outlining the full latter part of Daniel makes obvious its being one of the apocalyptic prophecies in Dryden's mind. Merlin as the dispenser of national prophecies was common in romance, though. Indeed in *Orlando furioso,* another exemplary text in the "Discourse," Merlin's primary identification is as prophet, and Arthur appears in Ariosto all but once in connection with Merlin's prophecies.

19. Graham Parry, *Golden Age Restor'd* (New York: St. Martin's, 1981), 60, 70–75, is very useful on this point. An older book, dealing exclusively with the myth in literature, but more partisanly than is perhaps warranted is Roberta Florence Brinkley, *Arthurian Legend in the Seventeenth Century* (Baltimore: Johns Hopkins University Press, [1932]).

20. In *Harmonious Meeting* (London: Dobson, 1965), 204–14, Mellers sought to except *Dido and Aeneas* from what he conceived the prevailing materialism of the baroque by discerning in that opera his sense of the tragic as the ritual of Becoming, the recognition of mortality turning man to the transcendent. Lacking any evidence of movement upward, transcendence seeking must go inward, and Dido's lament provides the means; the heroine's passivity is what is interesting and musically expressible.

21. Dedication "to the Marquis of Halifax," *King Arthur, The Works of John Dryden,* ed. Walter Scott and George Saintsbury (Edinburgh: Wm. Patterson, 1884), 8:135–36. All succeeding references to *King Arthur* are to this text and are parenthetically cited by act, scene, and page number.

22. Dedication of *The Spanish Friar,* in *Essays of John Dryden,* ed. W. P. Ker (1900; reprint, Russell & Russell, 1961), 1:245.

23. D. T. Mace, "Musical Humanism, the Doctrine of Rhythmus, and the St. Cecilia Odes of Dryden," *Journal of the Warburg and Courtauld Institute* 27 (1964): 251–92.

24. See "Defense of an Essay," Watson, *Of Dramatic Poesy,* 1:114, and Epistle Dedica-

tory for the "Vocal and Instrumental Musick of *The Prophetess*," Dryden's *Works*, 17 : 325.

The status of the expressive in seventeenth-century music is not self-evident nor the distinction between musical effects and emotional expression. Dryden's own treatment of the two in "A Song for St. Cecilia's Day, 1687" is witness. The same melding of objective and subjective perspectives seems to me to undercut the meaningfulness of calling Dryden an affective dramatist (in the sense in which Eric Rothstein developed the designation, in *Restoration Tragedy* [Madison: University of Wisconsin Press, 1967], but now broadly adopted). One of the clearest and most interesting discussions in regard to music, but relevant generally, is John Stevens' in *Music and Poetry in the Early Tudor Court* (London: Methuen, 1961), 63ff. and 88ff., cited in the Introduction.

25. "The Author's Apology for Heroic Poetry," Ker, *Essays of John Dryden*, 1 : 185.

26. "A Parallel Betwixt Poetry and Painting," Watson, *Of Dramatic Poesy*, 2 : 186.

I do not mean to suggest here that Dryden's attitude toward music per se can be equated with, for instance, that of North, who rejected Vossius's idea that measure alone excites the passions. North on music, though, *is* equivalent to Dryden on fiction: harmony is necessary to appeals to the intellect, which are necessary to passionate responses. There is no "pleasing sense" in North without thinking. Memory is the key here in a line of thought similar to music in Hobbes (*The Elements of Law*, 1.8.2) and it seems to me, to Dryden on fiction, though there is no reason to think Dryden knew music well enough to follow North there. See North, *Roger North on Music*, 291, for North's argument.

27. Clarence DeWitt Thrope, *The Aesthetic Theory of Thomas Hobbes* (Ann Arbor: University of Michigan Press, 1940), chap. 4 and esp. 123–33.

28. Michael Alssid, in the fullest literary study of the opera ("The Impossible Form of Art: Dryden, Purcell, and *King Arthur*," *Studies in the Literary Imagination* 10 [1977]: 125–44) is essentially interested in the work's theme of theatrical ambiguity and discusses fully its various reflexive maneuvers. He takes Dryden's and Purcell's attitude toward mental "dominion" to be far more ambivalent than I have here.

29. J. A. Westrup's description of the music in *Purcell*, rev. ed. (London: Dent, 1960), 133, would underscore this. He speaks of the "contrapuntal stodginess" of the Saxon ode suggesting conventional oratorio rather than opera and contrasts it to the "four-square English folk song" of the Britons.

30. Irving Lowen, "St. Evremond, Dryden, and the Theory of Opera," *Criticism* 1 (1959): 243–44, argues that Dryden's definition of opera implies a far more Italianate notion than Saint Evremond's ideal, derived from Lully/Quinault. Corneille's remark is in the preface to *Andromede* and St. Evremond's in the letter to the Duke of Buckingham. Both excerpted in Ulrich Weisstein, *The Essence of Opera* (1964; reprint, New York: W. W. Norton, 1969).

31. Dryden, To John, Lord Marquess of Normanby, Watson, *Of Dramatic Poesy*, 2 : 228.

32. "The Character [of Saint Evremond]," Watson, *Of Dramatic Poesy*, 2 : 58. We know Dryden's similar efforts for Charles. Dustin Griffin, "Dryden's Charles: The Ending of *Absalom and Achitophel*," *Philological Quarterly* 57 (1978): 359–82, argues that his means were far more flexible than current typological criticism allows. I follow his sense of Dryden's aesthetic pragmatism.

33. I refer the reader back to the Introduction's comment on Eugene Waith's "Spectacles of State." When Waith interprets *KA* as a transforming compliment to William, an effort to draw the royal dedicatee into the heroic world of the play (328–30), he is following Orgel's paradigm past the now-changed status of the king. While Arthur is a

fine model for William, his relation to the other characters suggests that he is conceived as a wider model and the compliment a wider one as well, as befits a play publicly produced in 1691. The economic symbiosis adumbrated in Davenant, fully understood in Dryden, seems to me completely consonant with the movement toward "interest" as the cement of society posited by historians like J. R. Jones (*Country and Court: England 1658–1714* [Cambridge: Harvard University Press, 1979], 80–81). He takes "interest" as central to the ideology that emerged after the mid-century, replacing hierarchic sacramentalism. On "interest" Albert O. Hirschman's *The Passions and the Interests* (Princeton: Princeton University Press, 1977) should be of great interest to students of literature because of its concern for the intensive concatenation of ideas masquerading over time under unchanging words for changing concepts.

34. Indications of the wealth that proves the worth of Arthur and his future consort include the extended byplay between Emmeline and Matilda in act 2, scene 1, where blind Emmeline's education in what Arthur must look like is carried out in terms of gold value, but also the occasional remarks and metaphors throughout, especially from Albanact, the most gruff and ready of the Englishmen. Regarding Arthur's impersonality, attempts to decipher topical allusions presumably lost in revisions of the text stretch at least from Scott's first edition to Franklin Zimmermann, fueled by Dryden's statements in the dedication about politically necessary changes in a text conceived seven years before its production. While such attempts seem doomed to failure, Zimmermann's suggestion—that William's Irish campaign is celebrated here—seems to me particularly far afield, misleading about both the opera's mode and its politics. The evidence John Loftis adduces (in "Political and Social Thought in the Drama," in Robert D. Hume, *The Development of English Drama in the Late Seventeenth Century* [Oxford: Clarendon Press, 1976], 265–67) for the political consistency of Dryden's plays after the Revolution supports my sense that William as specific figure plays little part here.

35. In *The Lamb and the Elephant*, John Steadman examines the interactions of mimesis and allegoresis over the fifteenth through seventeenth centuries and warns one powerfully against absolute generalization, insisting upon the universal existence of both modes during the time. But he too ultimately accepts the modal shift.

36. George Winchester Stone, Jr. gives the relevant figures in "The Making of the Repertory," in Hume, *Development of English Drama*, 198. *King Arthur*, while it in no sense competes with those stellar lights, did have a long and interesting stage history. It remained viable, with the addition of new music by Arne, until the early nineteenth century, and was repeated several times thereafter, finally and predictably at a university, as satire, satire of precisely what Dryden's economics and politics led him to praise: the set for the 1928 Cambridge production was a bright penny backdrop for the once and future king.

37. Thomas Shadwell, *The Tempest*, in *The Complete Works of Thomas Shadwell*, ed. Montague Summers (London: Fortune Press, 1927), 2:265.

Chapter 6. Representation in Contemporary Theory

1. Robert D. Hume, *The Development of English Drama in the Late Seventeenth Century* (Oxford: Clarendon, 1976), 150–58, and 173–85.

2. Brewster Rogerson, "The Art of Painting the Passions," *Journal of History of Ideas* 14 (1953): 72. Hirsch, Mace, Kirsch et al. are also seeking evidence of an understanding

of the "contagion," though precisely what is gained by assigning that designation to an avowedly rhetorical writer is not always apparent. D. T. Mace gives the fullest explication of it, in "Dryden's Dialogue on Drama;" *Journal of the Warburg & Courtauld Institute* 25 (1962): 87–112; see esp. pp. 96–99. His essay gives Descartes his proper weight, yet undervalues the rhetorical tradition. It is arguable that Jonson or Sidney were as affective in their intentions as Davenant and Dryden, that only the sense of means had altered. Pechter's reservations about Mace, cited above, are connected to this point.

3. René Descartes *The Passions of the Soul*, in *The Philosophical Works of Descartes*, trans. Elizabeth S. Haldane and G. R. T. Ross (Cambridge: Cambridge University Press, 1911), 1: 172. Cited by part and article number within the text henceforth.

4. In Earl Wasserman, "The Pleasures of Tragedy," *English Literary History* 14 (1947): 287ff. Wasserman coupled Descartes and Hobbes more closely on the sources of pleasure than is warranted, I believe, by minimizing the role of consciousness in Descartes. Nevertheless, his remains the classic statement on the subject.

5. Desire in Descartes, an analyzed passion in its own right (2:57, 86–90), is also treated as a faculty in mind that is instrumental over the range of passions other than admiration, the first and only purely unself-interested passion; admiration is beyond desire (2:53, 70–78) and therefore of primary effect in acting out passion's role, "perpetuating in the soul thoughts which it is good it should preserve" (2:74).

6. The "full implications" could not be elaborated until some positive sense of the imagination as a creative faculty had been postulated. James Engell, *The Creative Imagination: Enlightenment to Romantic* (Cambridge: Harvard University Press, 1982) has lately pushed the date of that achievement well back into the eighteenth century.

7. John Dennis, *The Advancement and Reformation of Poetry*, in *Critical Works*, ed. Hooker 1:217.

8. John Dryden, *Dryden: The Dramatic Works*, ed. Montague Summers (London: Nonesuch Press, 1932), 3:i.

9. Specifically Meditation III in Descartes, *Meditations on First Philosophy*.

10. By the "Preface" to *Troilus and Cressida* Dryden consciously separates the two, but goes on immediately to conflate them: "Under this general head of manners, the passions are naturally included as belonging to the characters. I speak not of pity and of terror, which are to be moved in the audience by the plot; but of anger, hatred, love, ambition, jealousy, revenge, etc., as they are shown in this or that person in the play. To describe these naturally, and to move them artfully, is one of the greatest commendations which can be given to a poet: to write pathetically says Longinus, cannot proceed but from a lofty genius." The influence of Rapin probably accounts, as Rothstein suggests, for the second sentence, Dryden's own habitual thinking for the succeeding one.

11. Roger Boyle, *Mustapha* 2, p. 29 in Bonamy Dobree, ed., *Five Heroic Plays* (London: Oxford University Press, 1960).

12. John Dennis, *Rinaldo and Armida* (London, 1699), 2.1, p. 24.

13. Settle, *The Empress of Morocco* 4. 3, p. 150, in Dobree, *Five Heroic Plays*.

14. The conventions of representation are not confined to the heroic play, of course; that is only their freest ground. In the Dryden/Davenant *Tempest*, Ariel's description of Hippolito's soul's activity when he encounters death is a physiological explanation that, robbed of its delightful childhood metaphors, would read as a parody of Descartes's—even down to the pineal gland: Hippolito tells Dorinda the soul is "A small blew thing that runs about within us," a conscious vulgarization of Descartes's description of the animal spirits (*Passions* 1. 6–10). One of the serious appeals of Descartes for Dryden

would of course have been his maintenance of an intimate relation of body and soul (see esp. 1. 34) without sacrificing materiality, as stressed in the passage L.A. Beaurline reprints from the dedicatory of Q1 of *Aureng-Zebe, Four Tragedies* (Chicago: University of Chicago Press, 1967), 108: "Our minds are perpetually wrought on by the temperament of our Bodies: which makes me suspect they are nearer alli'd, than either our Philosophers or School-Divines will allow them to be."

15. Dryden, *Works* 17:32. Dryden is of course echoing Davenant in the thought and image.

16. This passage, p. 15, has been often analyzed, most relevantly for me by Mace, "Dryden's Dialogue," pp. 89–90, 97–99, and Robert D. Hume, *Dryden's Criticism* (Ithaca: Cornell University Press, 1970), 187–206. It should be obvious that I differ with Hume radically on the notion that Dryden's antirealism is a new direction in theory and also on his interpretation of Dryden's sense of the passions, but not on the effect, for which I am endebted to Hume.

17. The cited sentence is from Dennis, the Preface to *Rinaldo and Armida* and will be discussed in detail in the final chapter.

18. *Poetics,* 50a15. In 50b8 Aristotle is explicit about the moral quality of character. See pp. 78–79 in Allan H. Gilbert's edition, *Literary Criticism: Plato to Dryden* (1940; reprinted, Detroit: Wayne State University Press, 1962).

19. The point perhaps requires no documentation any longer. The opinion is stated from the "Essay on Dramatic Poetry" through the Preface to *Troilus and Cressida.*

20. Beaurline outlines succinctly the sort of mood shifts I mean in relation to *All For Love* in his introduction to *Four Tragedies,* pp. 18–19.

21. As, for instance, Eric Rothstein has insisted in both "English Tragic Theory in the Late Seventeenth Century," *English Literary History* 29 (1962): 306–23, and his later *Restoration Tragedy* (Madison: University of Wisconsin Press, 1967), chap. 1.

22. See still Rosemund Tuve's *Elizabethan and Metaphysical Poetry* (Chicago: University of Chicago Press, 1947), especially chapter 7, "The Criterion of Rhetorical Efficacy."

23. Like my citations to *The State of Innocence,* the play to which it is attached, "The Author's Apology for Heroic Poetry" is cited from John Dryden, *Dramatic Works,* ed. Montague Summers (London: Nonesuch Press, 1932), 3:419–20.

24. Citation and discussion in Meyer Abrams, *The Mirror and the Lamp,* (London and New York: Oxford, University Press, 1953), 72.

25. Dryden, "Notes and Observations on The Empress of Morocco," London, 1674; facsimile in Maximilian E. Novak, ed., *The Empress of Morocco and Its Critics* (Los Angeles: University of California, Clark Memorial Library, 1968), 7.

26. Parsons, "Restoration Tragedy," pp. 49–52; Price in Hume, ed., *London Theatre World,* 230.

27. The full subtitle description stresses the tragedy, much as the retention of all the fall speeches and scenes does: the Dublin 1752 duodecimo makes the point: "Containing the following historical relations: I. The Execution of the Duke of Buckingham II. The Tryal and Divorce of Queen Catherine III. The Fall of Cardinal Wolsey IV. The Marriage and Coronation of Anne Bullen V. The Christening of Queen Elizabeth." The clarity of design stressed here is also apparent. See Appendix for authorial discussion.

28. Caccini, *Le Nuove Musiche,* in Oliver Strunk, ed., *The Baroque Era: Source Readings in Music History* (New York: W. W. Norton, 1965), 22.

29. *Delle imperfezioni della moderna musica,* Strunk, *The Baroque Era,* 34. Cited within the text by page number hereafter.

30. Forward to *Madrigali guerrieri ed amorosi*, Strunk, *The Baroque Era*, 53.

31. For a question about his position see Gary Tomlinson, "Music and the Claims of the Text: Monteverdi, Rinuccini, and Marino," *Critical Inquiry* 8 (1982): 565–89.

32. Oliver Strunk, ed., *The Renaissance: Source Readings in Music History* (New York: W. W. Norton, 1965), 105; and Strunk, *The Baroque Era*, 4. Hereafter *The Baroque Era* is referred to as 3, *The Renaissance* as 2 in the text.

33. The same belief is expressed in John Dennis, *The Advancement and Reformation of Modern Poetry*, in Hooker *The Critical Works*, 1:198ff.; the bias is devoted most fully in *The Usefulness of the Stage*, Ibid., 148ff.

34. In Weisstein, *The Essence of Opera*, p. 24.

35. The literature on this point is extensive. As regards music in relation to poetry see Gunther Schueller, "'Imitation' and 'Expression' in British Music Criticism in the Eighteenth Century," *Musical Quarterly* 34 (1948): 544–68 and Alan P. Lessem, "Imitation and Expression: Opposing French and British Views in the 18th Century," *Journal of the American Musicological Society* 27 (1974): 325.

36. Gloria Flaherty, *Opera in the Development of German Critical Thought* (Princeton: Princeton University Press, 1978) has stressed Saint-Evremond's influence in German operatic thought through the late seventeenth and early eighteenth centuries. She opposes that rationalizing line to the practical experience of music in the theatre, concluding that the Saint-Evremond influence was in essence detrimental but reflects the weight of neoclassical thinking, which she represents with his essay. The last quotation is from "Letter to the Duke of Buckingham," in *The Essence of Opera*, trans. and ed. Ulrich Weisstein, p. 32. Cited internally henceforth.

37. This extension beyond what Weisstein translates is the basis of Irving Lowens' claim that Saint-Evremond understood the potential of opera far better than Dryden. it will be clear in what follows that I think Lowens's contention must be taken within a very limited interpretation, circumscribed by suppositions and a vocabulary that make the comparison close to meaningless, though the initial distinction is just. Irving Lowens, "Saint-Evremond, Dryden, and the Theory of Opera," *Criticism* 1 (1959): 226–48.

38. Dennis, *The Usefulness of the Stage*, in *Critical Works*, ed., Hooker, 1:150; and "Essay on the Operas," Ibid., 385.

39. Dennis's argument in *Usefulness* is too long to be redacted usefully for my point. Part 2. 1–3 develops the usefulness of the stage to governance, Part 3. 1–2 contains the center of the case for its service to religion. It is a perfect example of the 1700 state of the Horatian rationale of the arts. Regarding my last point, Dennis, *The Advancement and Reformation of Poetry* makes its case here by denying poetic efficacy to Syphace and Corelli (*Critical Works* 1:264) The citation that follows, however comes from pp. 201–2.

40. Dennis, *Advancement, Critical Works* 1:215. While it is true that Dryden displays in his own poetry a far stronger sense of the value of rhythm for the depiction of the passions than Dennis ever shows, I do not believe he differs in essence from this position, phrased in terms of harmony, but a harmony that includes *rhythmus*, both instrumental qualities, thoroughly subservient because inarticulate.

41. Ibid., 217. I differ with Abrams, *The Mirror and the Lamp*, 75, on this point, though I concur in his sense of Dennis more generally and in the important point that the expressive enters in Dennis here, the quality of the poetry revealing something of the greatness of soul of the writer. This is, of course, in no way inconsistent with neoclassical theory.

42. I am perhaps somewhat unfair to Dennis, who does seek out particularities of Milton's sublimity in the 1721–22 *Proposals for Printing by Subscription . . . Miscellaneous Tracts* in *Critical Works*, ed. Hooker, 2:221–30. Yet his discussion here is limited really to

pointing out "beauties"—images of sublimity—and rationalizing the visible presentation of the incorporeal spirits.

Chapter 7. Magic and Modeling in the Final Quarter-Century

1. Montague Summers remarks with scorn on Shadwell's use of the witches in *The Lancashire Witches and Tegue O Divelly, the Irish Priest,* in large part because in his notes Shadwell has made clear his sense of the irrationality of witchhunting and the unreality of witches and yet in the play given the witches power anyway. While the fact does make nonsense of the play's man of sense, Sir Edward, Shadwell's point is well taken—that had he not given the witches real power, he would—like Sir Edward by Smerk—have been accused of atheism. The supernatural is hugely problematic for Restoration dramatists, however serious the play. Summers's remarks are in the notes to his edition of the play, vol. 4 of *The Complete Works of Thomas Shadwell* (London: Fortune Press, 1927). All my citations for Shadwell are to this edition.

2. Shadwell well may have read Jonson. Such masques were certainly printed throughout the period, whether or not they were staged; one can find Jonson's and Carew's in advertising lists frequently. Jonson's were still well enough known as productions for Tatham to have made his previously cited remark, assuming recognition.

3. This is an advance over the operatic *Tempest* where the musical material remains remarkably excrescent, most particularly the closing masque.

4. Dent, *Foundations of English Opera*, p. 120. Dent is making the case that Shadwell has a far more unified sense of the operatic enterprise than Molière had evidenced and conceives the various parts—machines, music, and play—much more organically. This may be true and bode well for a potential future for opera, but it seems to me to do little enough for the opera in hand.

5. Walter Benjamin, in *The Origins of German Tragic Drama* cited above, would of course deny that there is any such design, instead seeing allegory as the truth of the baroque style. But by 1675 we have entered on a high enough degree of rationalization, connected to the self-consciousness concerning spirituality on the stage, to make my formulation reasonably accurate to the Restoration.

6. One of John Crowne's primary concerns in writing *Calisto* (London, 1675) was to match the moral significance of the real Princess Mary to the figure she would play. See his preface. I doubt his concern was singular.

7. See Anthony Lewis's commentary in his edition of John Blow, *Venus and Adonis* (Paris: L'Oiseau Lyre, [n.d.]). All my references are to this edition. More contextual particulars are available in James R. Anthony, *French Baroque Music* (New York: W. W. Norton, 1974), 70 ff. and 96–97.

8. Tate states in the Preface that, on the advice of friends, he has decided not to compete with Virgil. "Rather than be guilty of a breach of Modesty" he altered the "Dido and Aeneas" he had written. The primary alterations appear to have been the creation of a long narrative for Brutus in act 1, scene 1, giving his biography and stressing its difference from Aeneas's: he is to found Albion, not Rome, and its formation will require the loss of his friend Asaracus: "Thus Niggard Destiny by halves oblig'd me, / Gave me dull Empire while it snatcht my friend." The loss of Asaracus adds a turn and a theme. Citations from *Brutus of Alba* are to the edition published by Tonson, London, 1678.

9. My text for Henry Purcell's *Dido and Aeneas* is edited by William Cummings (New York: Broude Bros., [n.d.]), cited by act and page number, here 3, 7.

10. In the Prologue to *Brutus of Alba,* Tate discusses his use of magic, explaining that our sophisticated age of course does not believe in it, yet you will be delighted by its beauty and exercise of fancy.

11. Anchises is mentioned early on in the narration that is relied on to call Virgil's story back into our minds, but the past and the future of both of the characters is left to a very few such references.

12. In *Sex and Sensibility* (Chicago: University of Chicago Press, 1980), 106–12, Jean Hagstrum has discussed Dido as the primary example of those women who "carry the sensuality of the earlier period [the Restoration] when it was fully acknowledged, into the Augustan age, when it was not" (p. 100). He justly makes her part of the shift into profound subjectivity that accompanies the family emotions' displacement of the religious during the period.

13. Both Parson's ("Restoration Tragedy") and Price ("Music as Drama"), among many others, remark on the phenomenon.

14. This was a standard means, ranging in its amounts from the mere witchery in Davenant's *Macbeth* to the intense and dramatically telling additions to Fletcher in *The Prophetess* that brought Purcell to Dryden's attention.

15. Downes *(Roscius Anglicanus),* who is always interested in the box office and in the financial difficulties created by the expense of operatic staging, records its success, p. 36.

16. Discussing the shift toward "the reduction of the poetic principle to pure effect," Ernest Tuveson instances Dryden's concern for the decorum of the supernatural, what I have called its rationalization, as a prime example of Neo-Aristotelian imitation, opposed to Addison's subjective emphasis where vivid impressions on the imagination supersede the imitation of nature. Given the amount of supernatural action on the stage, Addison's perception probably reflects widespread responses, though its theoretical statement is as singular as Ernest Tuveson states in *The Imagination as a Means of Grace* (1960; reprinted, New York, Gordian Press, 1974), 124–26.

17. Not particularly effectively, either: Eccles's music is better than Purcell's, he tells us, and that chorus is not the best music in the opera; "If therefore he has borrow'd the Worst from Mr. Henry Purcell, I would ask his Accusers from whom he has borrow'd the Best?" "Musical Entertainments in *Rinaldo and Armida,*" ed. Herbert Davis, 106.

18. I have used the awkward and somewhat inaccurate designations "printed Preface" and "musical Preface" to distinguish between the essay Dennis published with the text of the opera and the essay, essentially on the music and the play as musical entertainment, which Davis published in 1953 in the *Theatre Miscellany* volume edited by A. M. Clark (Oxford: Blackwell, 1953). My references to the printed preface, like my references to the text, are to the Huntington Library copy of the 1699 London edition. Hooker does not print the Davis text.

19. Printed Preface, A2v.

20. He had explained why in "The Impartial Critick" (1693) when he took Rymer to task for the latter's attack on opera: "And I wonder that Mr. *Rymer* should cry up a Chorus, in the very same Book in which he cries down Opera; for no Man can give any Reason, why an Opera is an extravagant thing; but I will, by retorting the same Reason, prove a Chorus extravagant too." This is part of a lengthy argument for accepting cultural relativism, in Dennis, *Critical Works* 1 : 11.

21. The awkwardness that we may feel in the discrete compartmentalizations in psychological projection was not a threat to that seriousness, probably not awkwardness for the audience at all, but a chance to savor the actor's capacity to realize each particular. That seems to me, at least, to be one of the points behind Titon de Tillet's praise of

Marie Rochaes in the French *Armide:*"When she began to move and sing, she alone dominated the stage. This struck me above all in the opera *Armide*, in which she played the greatest, the most powerful role in our opera. . . . What raptures to see her . . . sword in hand, ready to pierce the breast of Renaud. . . . Rage animated her features, love took possession of her heart; first one, then the other acted upoon her in turn. . . . What true and beautiful poses! How many different movements and expressions in her eyes and on her face during the monologue of twenty-nine lines." (*Le Parnasse francois,* as translated in Anthony, *French Baroque Music,* 81.)

22. Text from *Dryden: The Dramatic Works,* 9.

Bibliography of Works Cited

I. Primary

The bibliography does not repeat all the masques and City pageants mentioned in the text. Unless another source is listed here, they were read in the first (and frequently only) London edition.

Addison, Joseph. *Rosamund.* London: Tonson, 1707.

Bacon, Francis. *Works.* Edited by James Spedding, R. L. Ellis and D. D. Heath. London: Longmans, 1870.

Blow, John. *Venus and Adonis.* Edited by Anthony Lewis. Paris: L'Oiseau Lyre, n.d.

Bruno, Giordano. *The Expulsion of The Triumphant Beast.* Translated and edited by Arthur D. Imerti. New Brunswick: Rutgers University Press, 1964.

Carew, Thomas. *The Poems . . . with his Masque Coelum Britannicum.* Edited by Rhodes Dunlap. Oxford: Clarendon Press, 1949.

Congreve, William. *Semele.* In *Works,* vol. 2. London, 1710.

Crowne, John. *Calisto.* London, 1675.

Davenant, Charles. *Circe.* 2d ed. London: Tonson, 1685.

Davenant, William. Preface to *Gondibert. In Critical Essays of The Seventeenth Century,* edited by Joel E. Spingarn. Oxford: Clarendon Press, 1908–9.

———. *Salmacida Spolia.* London: Thomas Walkley, 1639.

———. *The Siege of Rhodes.* Edited by Ann-Mari Hedbäck. Uppsala: Studia Anglistica, no. 14, 1973.

———. *The Works.* London, 1673. Reissue New York: Benjamin Blom, 1968.

———. *Works.* Edited by James Maidment and W. H. Logan. Edinburgh: Paterson, 1873.

Dennis, John. *The Critical Works of John Dennis.* Edited by Edward Niles Hooker. 2 vols. Baltimore: Johns Hopkins University Press, 1939.

———. "Musical Entertainments in *Rinaldo and Armida.*" Edited by Herbert Davis. In *Theatre Miscellany,* edited by A. M. Clark, Oxford: Blackwell's, 1953.

———. *Rinaldo and Armida.* London, 1699.

Descartes, René. *The Passions of the Soul. Meditations on First Philosophy.* In *The*

Philosophical Works of Descartes, translated by Elizabeth S. Haldane and G. R. T. Ross. Cambridge: Cambridge University Press, 1911.

Dobree, Bonamy, ed. *Five Heroic Plays.* London: Oxford University Press, 1960.

Downes, John. *Roscius Anglicanus.* 1708. Reprint. Los Angeles: Augustan Reprint Society, 1969.

Dryden, John. *Dryden; The Dramatic Works.* Edited by Montague Summers. London: Nonesuch Press, 1932.

———. *Essays of John Dryden.* Edited by W. P. Ker. 2 vols. 1900. Reprint. New York: Russell & Russell, 1961.

———. *Of Dramatic Poesy and Other Critical Essays.* Edited by George Watson. 2 vols. London: Dent, 1962.

———. *Works.* Edited by Walter Scott and George Saintsbury. Vol. 8. Edinburgh: Wm. Patterson, 1884.

———. *Works.* Vol. 15. Edited by Earl Miner et al. Berkeley and Los Angeles: University of California Press, 1976. Vol. 17. Edited by Samuel Holt Monk et al. Berkeley and Los Angeles: University of California Press, 1971.

Evelyn, John. *The Diary.* Edited by E. S. de Beer. London: Oxford University Press, 1959.

Fleckno, Richard. *Ariadne Deserted by Theseus and Found and Courted by Bacchus.* London, 1654.

———. *The Marriage of Oceanus and Brittania.* London, 1659.

Granville, George. *Poems on Several Occasions with The British Enchanters.* 1706. Reprint. Dublin, 1732.

Heywood, Thomas. *Londini Artium et Scientarum Scaturigo and Londini Emporia Theatre Miscellany.* Edited by A. M. Clark. Oxford: Blackwell, 1953.

———. *Londini Status Pacatus.* London, 1639.

Hobbes, Thomas. *The Elements of Law.* Edited by F. Tonnies. Cambridge: Cambridge University Press, 1889.

Jonson, Ben. *Complete Masques.* Edited by Stephen Orgel. New Haven: Yale University Press, 1969.

———. *Notes of Conversations with Ben Jonson made by William Drummond of Hawthornden.* Edited by G. B. Harrison. London: Bodley Head, n.d.

———. *Timber or Discoveries.* Edited by G. B. Harrison. London: Bodley Head, 1922. Reprint. New York: Barnes & Noble, 1966.

Middleton, Thomas. *The Sunne in Aries.* London, 1621.

———. *Triumphs of Honor and Industry.* 1617.

Pepys, Samuel. *The Diary of Samuel Pepys.* Edited by R. Latham and W. Matthews. Berkeley and Los Angeles: University of California Press, 1970.

Purcell, Henry. *Dido and Aeneas.* Edited by William Cummings. New York: Broude Brothers, n.d.

Rymer, Thomas. "Preface to Rapin." In *Critical Essays of The Seventeenth Century,* edited by Joel Spingarn. Vol. 2. Oxford: Clarendon Press, 1908–9.

Shadwell, Thomas. *The Complete Works.* Edited by Montague Summers. London: Fortune Press, 1927.

Shakespeare, William. *The Riverside Shakespeare.* Edited by G. Blakemore Evans et al. Boston: Houghton Mifflin Company, 1974.

Tate, Nahum. *Brutus of Alba.* London: Tonson, 1678.

Tatham, John. *London's Triumphs.* London, 1664.

———. *The Dramatic Works of John Tatham.* Edited by James Maidment and H. Logan. Edinburgh: Paterson, 1879.

II. Secondary

Abrams, Meyer. *The Mirror and The Lamp.* London, New York: Oxford University Press, 1953.

Alssid, Michael. "The Impossible Form of Art: Dryden, Purcell, and *King Arthur.*" *Studies in The Literary Imagination* 10 (1977): 125–44.

Altieri, Joanne. "Romance in *Henry V.*" *Studies in English Literature* 21 (1981); 223–40.

Anthony, James R. *French Baroque Music.* New York: W. W. Norton, 1974.

Barton, Anne. "The King Disguised: Shakespeare's *Henry V* and the Comical History." In *The Triple Bond,* edited by Joseph G. Price, 92–117. University Park: Pennsylvania State University Press, 1975.

———. *Shakespeare and the Idea of the Play.* London: Chatto & Windus, 1962.

Beaurline, L. A. *Four Tragedies.* Chicago: University of Chicago Press, 1967.

Benjamin, Walter. *The Origins of German Tragic Drama.* Translated by John Osborne. London: New Left Books, 1977.

Bergeron, David. *English Civic Pageantry, 1558–1642.* Columbia, S.C.: University of South Carolina Press, 1971.

Berry, Edward. "*Henry VIII* and the Dynamics of Spectacle." *Shakespeare Studies* 12 (1979): 229–46.

Blaydes, Sophia, and Philip Bordinet. *William Davenant.* Boston: Twayne, 1981.

Bliss, Lee. "The Wheel of Fortune and The Maiden Phoenix of Shakespeare's *Henry VIII.*" *English Literary History* 42 (1975): 1–25.

Booth, Stephen. "Shakespeare in San Francisco." *Shakespeare Quarterly* 29 (1978): 268–69.

Brinkley, Roberta Florence. *Arthurian Legend in the Seventeenth Century.* Baltimore: Johns Hopkins University Press, [1932].

Brown, Laura S. *English Dramatic Form, 1660–1760.* New Haven: Yale University Press, 1981.

Bullough, Geoffrey, ed. *Narrative and Dramatic Sources of Shakespeare.* Vol. 4. London: Routledge & Kegan Paul, 1961.

Chan, Mary. *Music in The Theatre of Ben Jonson.* Oxford: Clarendon Press, 1980.

Cope, Jackson. *The Theatre and the Dream.* Baltimore: Johns Hopkins University Press, 1973.

Cox, John. "*Henry VIII* and the Masque." *English Literary History* 45 (1978): 390–409.

Danson, Lawrence. "*Henry V:* King, Chorus, and Critics." *Shakespeare Quarterly* 34 (1983): 27–43.

Dent, Edward J. *Foundations of English Opera: a Study of Musical Drama in England During the Seventeenth Century.* Cambridge: Cambridge University Press: 1928.

Elton, William R. *King Lear and The Gods.* San Marino: Huntington Library Press, 1966.

Engell, James. *The Creative Imagination: Enlightenment to Romantic.* Cambridge: Harvard University Press, 1982.

Finkelpearl, Philip J. "The Role of the Court in the Development of Jacobean Drama." *Criticism* 24 (1982): 138–58.

Fish, Stanley. "How to do things with Austin and Searle." *Modern Language Notes* 91 (1976): 983–1035.

Flaherty, Gloria. *Opera in the Development of German Critical Thought.* Princeton: Princeton University Press, 1978.

Fletcher, Angus. Review of *The Illusion of Power,* by Stephen Orgel. *Georgia Review* 29 (1975): 367–70.

Foakes, R. A., ed. Introduction to *Henry VIII,* by William Shakespeare. London: Methuen; Cambridge: Harvard University Press, 1957.

Freehafer, John. "Brome, Suckling, and Davenant's Theatre Project of 1639." *Texas Studies in Language and Literature* 10 (1968): 367–83.

———. "The Formation of the London Patent Companies in 1660." *Theatre Notebook* 20 (1965): 6–30.

Garrison, James A. *Dryden and The Tradition of Panegyric.* Berkeley and Los Angeles: University of California Press, 1975.

Geertz, Clifford. "Centers, Kings and Charisma." In *Culture and Its Creators,* edited by J. Ben-David and T. Clark, 150–71. Chicago: University of Chicago Press, 1977.

———. *Negara: The Theatre State in Nineteenth-Century Bali.* Princeton: Princeton University Press, 1980.

Gilbert, Allan H. "The Function of the Masques in *Cynthia's Revels.*" *Philological Quarterly* 22 (1943): 211–30.

———. *Literary Criticism: Plato to Dryden.* 1940. Reprint. Detroit: Wayne State University Press, 1962.

Gordon, D. J. "The Florentine Agent Goes to a Masque." In *Theatre Miscellany,* edited by A. M. Clark, 123–29. Oxford: Blackwell, 1953.

———. *The Renaissance Imagination.* Edited by Stephen Orgel. Berkeley and Los Angeles: University of California Press, 1975.

Griffin, Dustin. "Dryden's Charles: The Ending of *Absalom and Achitophel.*" *Philological Quarterly* 57 (1978): 359–82.

Grout, Donald Jay. *A Short History of Opera.* 2d ed. New York: Columbia University Press, 1965.

Hagstrum, Jean. *Sex and Sensibility.* Chicago: University of Chicago Press, 1980.

Harbage, Alfred. *Sir William Davenant.* Philadelphia: University of Pennsylvania Press, 1935.

Hardison, O. B. *The Enduring Monument.* Chapel Hill: University of North Carolina Press, 1962.

Haun, Eugene. *But Hark! More Harmony.* Ypsilanti: Eastern Michigan University Press, 1971.

Hirschman, Albert O. *The Passions and the Interests.* Princeton: Princeton University Press, 1977.

Hoy, Cyrus. "The Shares of Fletcher and his Collaborators in the Beaumont and Fletcher Canon (VII)." *Studies in Bibliography,* 1962, pp. 71–90.

Hume, Robert D. *The Development of English Drama in The Late Seventeenth Century.* Oxford: Clarendon Press, 1976.

———. *Dryden's Criticism.* Ithaca: Cornell University Press, 1970.

Jones, J. R. *Country and Court: England 1658–1714.* Cambridge: Harvard University Press, 1979.

Kantorowicz, Ernst. *The King's Two Bodies.* Princeton: Princeton University Press, 1957.

Kerman, Joseph. *Opera as Drama.* New York: Vintage Books, 1956.

Laslett, Peter. *The World We Have Lost.* 2d ed. New York: Scribners, 1973.

Lefkowitz, Murray, ed. *Trois Masques a la Cour de Charles I er D'Angleterre.* Paris: Centre National de la Recherche Scientifique, 1970.

Leinwand, Theodore B. "London Triumphing: The Jacobean Lord Mayor's Show." *Clio* 11 (1982): 137–53.

Lessem, Allan P. "Imitation and Expression: Opposing French and British Views in The Eighteenth Century." *Journal of the American Musicological Society* 27 (1974).

Loftis, John. "Political and Social Thought In the Drama." In *The London Theatre World, 1660–1800,* edited by Robert D. Hume. Carbondale: Southern Illinois University Press, 1980.

Lindenberger, Herbert. *Historical Drama.* Chicago: University of Chicago Press, 1975.

Lowen, Irving. "Saint-Evremond, Dryden, and the Theory of Opera." *Criticism* 1 (1959): 226–48.

McBride, Tom. "*Henry VIII* as Machiavellian Romance." *Journal of English and Germanic Philology* 76 (1977): 26–40.

Mace, D. T. "Dryden's Dialogue on Drama." *Journal of the Warburg & Courtauld Institute* 25 (1962): 87–1122.

———, "Musical Humanism, the Doctrine of Rhythms, and the St. Cecilia Odes of Dryden." *Journal of the Warburg & Courtauld Institute* 27 (1964): 251–92.

McGann, Jerome J. "The Meaning of the Ancient Mariner." *Critical Inquiry* 8 (1981).

Marcus, Leah. "'Present Occasions' and the Shaping of Ben Jonson's Masques," *English Literary History* 45 (1978): 201–25.

Martz, Louis L. *The Wit of Love.* Notre Dame and London: University of Notre Dame Press, 1969.

Mellers, Wilfrid. *Harmonious Meeting.* London: Dobson, 1965.

Montrose, Louis Adrian. "'Shaping Fantasies': Figurations of Gender and Power in Elizabethan Culture." *Representations* 1 (1983): 61–84.

———. "Gifts and Reasons: The Contexts of Peele's *Araygnement of Paris.*" *English Literary History* 47 (1980): 433–61.

Nethercot, Arthur H. *Sir William Davenant.* Chicago: University of Chicago Press, 1938.

Newman, Joyce. *Jean-Baptiste de Lully and his Tragedies Lyriques.* [n.p.]: UMI Research Press, 1979.

North, Roger. *Roger North on Music.* Edited by John Wilson. London: Novello, 1959.

Novak, Maximilian E., ed. *The Empress of Morocco and Its Critics.* Los Angeles: University of California Press, 1968.

Orgel, Stephen. *The Illusion of Power.* Berkeley and Los Angeles: University of California Press, 1975.

———. *The Jonsonian Masque.* Cambridge: Harvard University Press, 1965.

Orgel, Stephen, and Roy Strong. *Inigo Jones: The Theatre of the Stuart Court.* London and Berkeley: Sotheby Parke Bernet and University of California Press, 1973.

Otis, Brooks. *Virgil: A Study in Civilized Poetry.* Oxford: Clarendon Press, 1964.

Parry, Graham. *The Golden Age Restor'd.* New York: St. Martin's, 1981.

Parsons, Phillip. "Restoration Tragedy as Total Theatre." In *Restoration Literature,* edited by Harold Love, 27–68. London: Methuen, 1972.

Pechter, Edward. *Dryden's Classical Theory of Literature.* Cambridge: Cambridge University Press, 1975.

Price, Curtis A. "Music as Drama." In *The London Theatre World, 1660–1800,* edited by Robert D. Hume, 210–235. Carbondale: Southern Illinois University Press, 1980.

———. *Music in the Restoration Theatre.* [n.p.]: UMI Research Press, 1979.

Rabkin, Norman. "Rabbits, Ducks, and *Henry V.*" *Shakespeare Quarterly* 28 (1977): 279–96.

———. *Shakespeare and the Problem of Meaning.* Chicago: Chicago University Press, 1981.

Raddadi, Mongi. *Davenant's Adaptations of Shakespeare.* Uppsala: Studia Anglistica, no. 36, 1979.

Randall, Dale B. J. *Jonson's Gypsies Unmasked.* Durham: Duke University Press, 1975.

Robinson, Michael. *Opera before Mozart.* New York: William Morrow, 1966.

Rogerson, Brewster. "The Art of Painting the Passions." *Journal of the History of Ideas* 14 (1953): 68–94.

Rothstein, Eric. "English Tragic Theory in The Late Seventeenth Century." *English Literary History* 29 (1962): 306–23.

———. *Restoration Tragedy.* Madison: University of Wisconsin Press, 1967.

Sabol, Andrew J. *Songs and Dances for The Stuart Masque.* Providence: Brown University Press, 1959.

Schmidgall, Gary. *Shakespeare and The Courtly Aesthetic.* Berkeley and Los Angeles: University of California Press, 1981.

Schueller, Gunther. "'Imitation' and 'Expression' in British Music Criticism in The Eighteenth Century." *Musical Quarterly* 34 (1948): 544–68.

Skinner, Quentin. *The Foundations of Modern Political Thought.* Cambridge: Cambridge University Press, 1978.

Smith, Gordon Ross. "Shakespeare's *Henry V:* Another Part of the Critical Forest." *Journal of the History of Ideas* 37 (1976): 3–26.

Sorelius, Gunnar. "The Early History of the Restoration Theatre: Some Problems Reconsidered." *Theatre Notebook* 33 (1979).

Steadman, John. *The Lamb and the Elephant.* San Marino: Huntington Library Press, 1974.

Stevens, John. *Music and Poetry in The Early Tudor Court.* London: Methuen, 1961.

Stone, George Winchester Jr. "The Making of The Repertory." In *The London Theatre World, 1660–1880,* edited by Robert D. Hume. Carbondale: Southern Illinois University Press, 1980.

Stone, Lawrence. *The Crisis of the Aristocracy 1558–1641.* Abridged ed. London: Oxford University Press, 1967.

Strong, Roy. "The Popular Celebration of the Accession Day of Queen Elizabeth I." *Journal of The Warburg & Courtauld Institute* 21 (1958): 86–103.

———. *Splendor at Court: Renaissance Spectacle and the Theater of Power.* Boston: Houghton Mifflin, 1973.

Strunk, Oliver, ed. *The Baroque Era: Source Readings in Music History.* New York: W. W. Norton, 1965.

———. *The Renaissance: Source Readings in Music History.* New York: W. W. Norton, 1965.

Talbert, Ernest W. "The Interpretation of Jonson's Courtly Spectacles." *PMLA* 61 (1946): 454–73.

Taylor, Gary. *Three Studies in the Text of "Henry V,"* with Stanley Wells. *Modernizing Shakespeare's Spelling.* Oxford: Clarendon, 1979.

Thorpe, Clarence deWitt. *The Aesthetic Theory of Thomas Hobbes.* Ann Arbor: University of Michigan Press, 1940.

Tomlinson, Gary. "Music and the Claims of the Text: Monteverdi, Rinuccini, and Marino. *Critical Inquiry* 8 (1982): 565–89.

Turner, Victor. "Social Dramas and Stories about Them." *Critical Inquiry* 7 (1980): 141–68.

Tuve, Rosemund. *Elizabethan and Metaphysical Poetry.* Chicago: University of Chicago Press, 1947.

Tuveson, Ernest. *The Imagination as a Means of Grace.* 1960. Reprint. New York: Gordian Press, 1974.

Vickers, Brian. Review of *Shakespeare: Pattern of Excelling Nature,* edited by David Bevington and Jay Halio. *Shakespeare Quarterly* 34 (1981): 402–7.

Waith, Eugene. *Ideas of Greatness.* New York: Barnes & Noble, 1971.

———. "Spectacles of State." *Studies in English Literature* 13 (1973): 317–30.

Walzer, Michael. *Regicide and Revolution.* London: Cambridge University Press, 1974.

Wasserman, Earl. "The Pleasures of Tragedy." *English Literary History* 14 (1947): 283–307.

Weisstein, Ulrich. *The Essence of Opera.* New York: W. W. Norton, 1969.

Wells, Susan. "Jacobean City Comedy and the Ideology of the City." *English Literary History* 48 (1981): 37–60.

Welsford, Enid. *The Court Masque.* Cambridge: Cambridge University Press, 1927.

Westrup, J. A. *Purcell.* Rev. ed. London: Dent, 1960.

Yates, Frances. "Elizabethan Chivalry: The Romance of the Accession Day Tilts." *Journal of the Warburg & Courtauld Institute* 20 (1957): 4–25. Reprinted in *Astraea,* 88–111. London: Routledge & Kegan Paul, 1975.

———. "Queen Elizabeth as Astraea." *Journal of the Warburg & Courtauld Institute* 10 (1947): 27–82. Reprinted in *Astraea,* 29–87. London: Routledge & Kegan Paul, 1975.

———. *Shakespeare's Last Plays: A New Approach.* London: Routledge & Kegan Paul, 1975.

Index